Teacher's Reso

# HOUSING DECISIONS

by
**Evelyn L. Lewis**
Professor Emeritus, Home Economics
Northern Arizona University
Flagstaff, Arizona

Publisher
**The Goodheart-Willcox Company, Inc.**
Tinley Park, Illinois

**Copyright © 2006**

by

**The Goodheart-Willcox Company, Inc.**

Previous editions copyright 2004, 2000, 1994, 1987, 1984

All rights reserved. No part of this work may be reproduced, stored, or transmitted for resale.
Manufactured in the United States of America.

Teacher's Resource Guide
ISBN-13: 978-1-59070-536-0
ISBN-10: 1-59070-536-X

Teacher's Resource Portfolio
ISBN-13: 978-1-59070-537-7
ISBN-10: 1-59070-537-8

Teacher's Resource CD
ISBN-13: 978-1-59070-538-4
ISBN-10: 1-59070-538-6

2 3 4 5 6 7 8 9 10 – 06 – 11 10 09 08 07 06 05

# Table of Contents

**Introduction**
Using the Text . . . . . . . . . . . . . . . . . . . . . . . .5
Using the *Student Activity Guide* . . . . . . . . .6
Using the *Teacher's Annotated Edition* . . . . .6
Using the *Teacher's Resource Guide* . . . . . . .7
Using the *Teacher's Resource Portfolio* . . . . .8
Using the *Teacher's Resource CD with*
  **Exam***View*® *Test Generator Software* . . . . . .8
Strategies for Successful Teaching . . . . . . . .9

Assessment Techniques . . . . . . . . . . . . . . .11
Using Other Resources . . . . . . . . . . . . . . . .12
Evaluating Individual Participation . . . . . . .25
Evaluating Individual Reports . . . . . . . . . . .26
Evaluating Group Participation . . . . . . . . . .27
Correlation of National Standards for
  Housing, Interiors, and Furnishings
  with *Housing Decisions* . . . . . . . . . . . . . . .29
Scope and Sequence . . . . . . . . . . . . . . . . . .35
Basic Skills Chart . . . . . . . . . . . . . . . . . . . .40

**Part One: Housing for You** . . . . . . . . . . . . . . . . . . . . . . . . . . . . . . . . . . . . . . . . . . . . . . **43**
  Chapter 1: Housing and Human Needs . . . . . . . . . . . . . . . . . . . . . . . . . . . . . . . . . . . . . . 49
  Chapter 2: Influences on Housing . . . . . . . . . . . . . . . . . . . . . . . . . . . . . . . . . . . . . . . . . 65

**Part Two: Making Housing Choices.** . . . . . . . . . . . . . . . . . . . . . . . . . . . . . . . . . . . . . . . **79**
  Chapter 3: Using Decision-Making Skills . . . . . . . . . . . . . . . . . . . . . . . . . . . . . . . . . . . . 85
  Chapter 4: Choosing a Place to Live . . . . . . . . . . . . . . . . . . . . . . . . . . . . . . . . . . . . . . . 95
  Chapter 5: Acquiring Housing . . . . . . . . . . . . . . . . . . . . . . . . . . . . . . . . . . . . . . . . . . . 107

**Part Three: From the Ground Up** . . . . . . . . . . . . . . . . . . . . . . . . . . . . . . . . . . . . . . . . **121**
  Chapter 6: The Evolution of Exteriors. . . . . . . . . . . . . . . . . . . . . . . . . . . . . . . . . . . . . . 127
  Chapter 7: Understanding House Plans. . . . . . . . . . . . . . . . . . . . . . . . . . . . . . . . . . . . 137
  Chapter 8: House Construction . . . . . . . . . . . . . . . . . . . . . . . . . . . . . . . . . . . . . . . . . . 153
  Chapter 9: The Systems Within . . . . . . . . . . . . . . . . . . . . . . . . . . . . . . . . . . . . . . . . . . 163

**Part Four: The Inside Story** . . . . . . . . . . . . . . . . . . . . . . . . . . . . . . . . . . . . . . . . . . . . . **175**
  Chapter 10: Elements of Design. . . . . . . . . . . . . . . . . . . . . . . . . . . . . . . . . . . . . . . . . . 181
  Chapter 11: Using Color Effectively . . . . . . . . . . . . . . . . . . . . . . . . . . . . . . . . . . . . . . . 191
  Chapter 12: Using the Principles of Design . . . . . . . . . . . . . . . . . . . . . . . . . . . . . . . . . 201
  Chapter 13: Textiles in Today's Homes. . . . . . . . . . . . . . . . . . . . . . . . . . . . . . . . . . . . . 209
  Chapter 14: Creating Interior Backgrounds . . . . . . . . . . . . . . . . . . . . . . . . . . . . . . . . . 219
  Chapter 15: Furniture Styles and Construction . . . . . . . . . . . . . . . . . . . . . . . . . . . . . . 227
  Chapter 16: Arranging and Selecting Furniture . . . . . . . . . . . . . . . . . . . . . . . . . . . . . . 237
  Chapter 17: Addressing Windows, Lighting, and Accessories. . . . . . . . . . . . . . . . . . . . 249
  Chapter 18: Selecting Household Appliances . . . . . . . . . . . . . . . . . . . . . . . . . . . . . . . 257

**Part Five: A Safe and Attractive Environment** . . . . . . . . . . . . . . . . . . . . . . . . . . . . . . **265**
    Chapter 19: The Outdoor Living Space and Environment . . . . . . . . . . . . . . . . . . . . . . . . 271
    Chapter 20: Keeping Your Home Safe and Secure . . . . . . . . . . . . . . . . . . . . . . . . . . . 279
    Chapter 21: Maintaining Your Home . . . . . . . . . . . . . . . . . . . . . . . . . . . . . . . . . . . 289

**Part Six: Progress in Housing** . . . . . . . . . . . . . . . . . . . . . . . . . . . . . . . . . . . . . . . . . . . . **301**
    Chapter 22: Housing for Today and Tomorrow. . . . . . . . . . . . . . . . . . . . . . . . . . . . . 307
    Chapter 23: Careers in Housing. . . . . . . . . . . . . . . . . . . . . . . . . . . . . . . . . . . . . . . 317
    Chapter 24: Preparing for Career Success . . . . . . . . . . . . . . . . . . . . . . . . . . . . . . . 327

# Introduction

*Housing Decisions* is designed to help students make important decisions about their housing with assurance and competence. Students will learn about homes as an environment for human growth and development, the selection of a house, the components and systems within a house, the process of furnishing and maintaining a house, trends in housing, and an overview of related careers.

The book is directed primarily to students, but it is also suitable for use as a reference for anyone interested in acquiring and furnishing a home. The goal is to help readers learn to apply the decision-making process to the various aspects of housing.

In addition to the text, the *Housing Decisions* learning package includes the *Student Activity Guide, Teacher's Resource Guide, Teacher's Resource Portfolio,* and the *Teacher's Resource CD with G-W Test Creation Software*. Using these components can help you develop an effective housing program tailored to your students' unique needs.

## Using the Text

From cover to cover, *Housing Decisions* contains important features designed to support your curriculum and to help meet the needs of your students. The text is written in a concise, easy-to-read style that your students will understand. Logically organized into six parts, the text contains 24 chapters.

Hundreds of color photographs, drawings, and charts are used throughout the text to illustrate key concepts and add visual appeal. References to all illustrations are included in the lesson to reinforce learning by helping students associate the visual images with the written material.

The text also includes an expanded table of contents to give students an overview of the wide variety of topics they will be studying. The glossary helps students learn the key terms found in each topic of the text. The appendices include an overview of housing legislation and suggested energy-saving tips. An extensive index is provided to help students find the information they want quickly and easily. Each of the chapters in the text includes the following features:

**To Know.** These are key terms students will encounter as they read the chapter. You may want to introduce students to these terms before they begin reading. Encourage students to watch for these terms, which first appear in bold italic type, as they read the material. The terms are defined in the body of the text as well as in the glossary. Less important terms appear in italic type.

**Objectives.** These are performance goals that students will be expected to achieve after studying the chapter. Review the objectives in each chapter with students so they are aware of the skills they will build as they read the chapter material.

**Summary.** This section is a review of the major concepts covered in the chapter.

**To Review.** This section poses questions to help students evaluate their knowledge of the chapter's content. A combination of true/false, short answer, multiple choice, and fill-in-the-blank questions are provided. Review questions are designed to help students recall, organize, and use the information presented in the text. Answers to the review questions are in the *Teacher's Annotated Edition* as well as the *Teacher's Resources*.

**In Your Community.** These activities encourage students to seek answers from area resources or apply concepts to situations in their own communities.

**To Think About.** The activities encourage students to apply many of the concepts learned in the chapter to real-life situations. You can adapt the activities to meet the needs of the particular students in your classroom. Activities are suggested for both individual and group work.

**Using Technology.** A camera, video recorder, or computer is needed to accomplish the activities in this section. Projects requiring a computer involve researching information on the Internet or using the computer's formatting capabilities to create surveys, charts, graphs, other specialized document layouts, or PowerPoint® presentations.

## Using the *Student Activity Guide*

The *Student Activity Guide* for use with *Housing Decisions* helps students recall and review concepts presented in the text. It also helps students apply what they have learned to realistic housing decisions.

The activities in the *Guide* are divided into chapters that correspond to the chapters in the text. By reading the text first, students will have the information they need to complete the activities. Students should try to do the activities without looking in the text. Then they can use the text to check their answers and answer the questions they could not complete.

The pages of the *Student Activity Guide* are perforated for easy removal. Students can remove completed activity pages for your evaluation, and they can also store the pages in a three-ring notebook.

The *Student Activity Guide* includes various types of activities. Some, such as crossword puzzles and short-answer questions, have "right" answers. Students can use these activities to review as they study for tests and quizzes. Answers to these activities are in the *Teacher's Resources*.

Other activities, such as case studies and checklists, ask students for opinions, evaluations, and conclusions that cannot be judged "right" or "wrong." These activities allow students to form their own ideas about information presented in the text by considering alternatives and evaluating situations thoughtfully. The activities can often be used as a basis for classroom discussion by asking students to defend, explain, and justify their answers and conclusions. The use of each activity is described in the *Teacher's Resources* as a student learning experience under the related instructional concept.

## Using the *Teacher's Annotated Edition*

The *Teacher's Annotated Edition* of *Housing Decisions* is a special edition of the student text. It is designed to help you more effectively coordinate materials in the Student Activity Guide and Teacher's Resources. It also provides you with additional suggestions to help you add variety to your classroom teaching.

The introduction of the *Teacher's Annotated Edition* includes an explanation of the various components in the teaching package for *Housing Decisions* and suggestions for teaching learners with special needs. In addition, the following materials are included to assist you in developing lesson plans and evaluating student learning.

### Correlation of National Standards with *Housing Decisions*

The National Standards for Family and Consumer Sciences Education is a comprehensive guide that provides family and consumer sciences educators with a structure for identifying what learners should be able to do. This structure is based on knowledge and skills needed for work life and family life, as well as family and consumer sciences careers.

The National Standards Components include 16 areas of study, each with a comprehensive standard that describes the overall content of the area. Each comprehensive standard is then broken down into content standards that describe what is expected of the learner. Competencies further define the knowledge, skills, and practices of the content standards and provide the basis for measurement criteria.

By studying the *Housing Decisions* text, students will be prepared to master most of the competencies listed for the area of study called "Housing, Interiors, and Furnishings." To help you see how this can be accomplished, a correlation chart is included in the *Teacher's Annotated Edition*. The chart is called the Correlation of National Standards for Housing, Interiors, and Furnishings with *Housing Decisions*. If you want to prepare students to meet the National Standards for Family and Consumer Sciences Education, this chart will interest you.

### Annotations

Annotations are located in the outside margins of the text. The following types of annotations are used in this edition:

- **Activity** suggestions present exercises to promote student retention of chapter concepts. Whenever possible, the specific

nature of the activity is identified in the title, such as *Writing Activity* or *Math Activity*.
- **Answers** appear next to the end-of-chapter *To Review* questions and the *Discuss* annotations for which an answer is identified in the lesson. (Possible answers for brainstorming questions are not included.)
- **Discuss** items reinforce learning through class dialogue.
- **Enrich** activities challenge students to enhance their knowledge through role-playing, researching, debating, surveying, and actively listening to guest presenters.
- **Example** items illustrate important points in the chapter material.
- **Note** items include statistics, facts, or historical references to spark student interest.
- **Reflect** questions pose issues of a more personal nature for students to consider quietly and mentally evaluate for their own lives.
- **Resource** materials for students to use from the *Student Activity Guide* or *Teacher's Resources* are keyed to chapter topics.
- **Vocabulary** activities reinforce key terms through defining, comparing, using in sentences, and using the glossary.

## Answer Keys

Throughout the text wherever students are asked questions that have specific answers identified in the lesson, the answers appear nearby on the same page. Many questions intended to inspire brainstorming or the higher-order thinking skills are also asked, but no answers are shown since these are intended to elicit many answers and no one "right" answer exists.

## Portfolio Project

The last item of each chapter is a recommended portfolio project that encourages students to creatively apply the concepts from the chapter. These activities can become part of a student's portfolio for those teachers who use this method of assessment.

## Using the *Teacher's Resource Guide*

The *Teacher's Resource Guide* for use with *Housing Decisions* provides a variety of materials to assist you in presenting the concepts in the text to students. Like the *Student Activity Guide*, the *Teacher's Resource Guide* follows the chapter format of the text. Each chapter in the *Teacher's Resource Guide* includes the following features:

**Objectives.** These are the behavioral objectives that students will be able to accomplish after studying the chapter.

**Bulletin Boards.** Two or more bulletin board ideas are described for each chapter to stimulate interest in the topics students will be studying. Many of these ideas are illustrated for you.

**Teaching Materials.** A list of all text, *Student Activity Guide*, and *Teacher's Resources* materials available to supplement each chapter is provided. The list includes the names of all activities in the *Student Activity Guide* that relate to the chapter. The list also includes reproducible masters, transparency masters, and chapter test masters.

**Introductory Activities.** These motivational activities are designed to stimulate student interest in the chapter content. These activities encourage a sense of curiosity that students will want to satisfy by reading the chapter.

**Strategies to Reteach, Reinforce, Enrich, and Extend Text Concepts.** A variety of student learning strategies is described for teaching the major concepts discussed in the chapter. Each major concept is listed in the guide in bold type, followed by learning experiences for teaching them. Activities that are found in the accompanying *Student Activity Guide* are also described for your convenience in planning daily lessons. These activities are identified with the letters *SAG* after the title and letter of the activity.

The number of each learning strategy is followed by a code in bold type. These codes will help you identify the teaching goals the various strategies are designed to help you accomplish. The following codes have been used:

- **RT** identifies activities that are designed to help you reteach concepts to students. These strategies provide another presentation of the chapter concepts (beyond reading the chapter) to allow an additional opportunity for students to learn.
- **RF** identifies activities that are designed to help you reinforce concepts. These strategies use different approaches and activities to clarify facts, terms, principles, and concepts, thus making them more understandable for students.

- **ER** identifies activities that are designed to help you enrich learning. These are strategies that help students learn more about the concepts presented by involving them more fully in the lesson. These strategies provide diverse experiences, such as demonstrations, field trips, guest speakers, and surveys.
- **EX** identifies activities that are designed to help you extend learning. These are strategies that promote thinking skills, such as critical thinking, creative thinking, problem solving, and decision making. Students must use higher-order thinking skills of analysis, synthesis, and evaluation to complete these activities. The application of text information to new situations or the students' own lives is often required.

**Chapter Review.** This section lists activities that can be used to review the chapter concepts.

**Answer Key.** Answers are included for the *To Review* questions following the text chapters, worksheets in the *Student Activity Guide*, activities in reproducible masters, and chapter tests.

**Reproducible Masters.** Reproducible masters are included in each chapter to enhance the presentation of concepts. Some of the masters are designated as transparency masters for use with an overhead projector. Often these charts or graphs can be used as a basis for class discussion of important concepts. They can also be used as student handouts. Some masters are designed for use as reproducible masters. Each student or group of students can be given a copy of the activity. These activities encourage creative and critical thinking as well as class discussion.

**Chapter Test Masters.** Individual tests with clear, specific questions that cover all the chapter topics are provided. True/false, multiple choice, and matching questions are used to measure student learning about facts and definitions. Essay questions are also provided in the chapter tests. Some of these require students to list information, while others allow students to express their opinions and creativity. You may wish to modify these tests to meet your evaluation needs.

## Scope and Sequence

A *Scope and Sequence* chart is included to identify the major concepts presented in each chapter of the text. This special resource is provided to help you select for study those concepts that meet your curriculum needs.

## Basic Skills Chart

Students enrolled in your course have the opportunity to develop and use the following basic skills: verbal, reading, writing, mathematical, scientific, and analytical. (Analytical skills involve the higher-order thinking skills of analysis, synthesis, and evaluation in problem-solving situations.)

A *Basic Skills Chart* is included to identify activities that encourage the development of these basic skills. The chart includes activities from the *Student Activity Guide* and the student learning experiences from the *Teacher's Resources*. Incorporating a variety of the activities into your daily lesson plans will assure your students of receiving vital practice in the development of their basic skills. Also, if you find that students in your class are weak in a specific basic skill, more activities can be selected that will develop that particular skill area. This chart can also be used to show those outside the field how basic skills are taught in family and consumer sciences classrooms.

In addition to the items mentioned, the *Teacher's Resource Guide* also includes the Correlation of National Standards for Housing, Interiors, and Furnishings with *Housing Decisions*.

## Using the *Teacher's Resource Portfolio*

The *Teacher's Resource Portfolio* for *Housing Decisions* contains all the materials from the *Teacher's Resource Guide*. In addition, 30 color transparencies are provided, at least one for each chapter. These materials are in a convenient three-ring binder. Reproducible materials can be removed easily. Handy dividers included with the binder help you organize materials so you can quickly find the items you need.

## Using the *Teacher's Resource CD* with ExamView® Test Generator Software

The *Teacher's Resource CD* includes all the contents of the *Teacher's Resource Portfolio* plus Exam*View*® Test Generator Software. The CD format allows you to view and print resource pages exactly as they appear in the *Teacher's Resource Portfolio* from your computer. The color transparencies are in PowerPoint format as well as PDF format. Lesson plans are also included.

To produce overhead transparencies, print transparency master pages onto acetate film designed for your printer. If you are printing a color transparency, you will need a color printer to produce a transparency that appears as it does on your screen. However, you can print color transparencies in gray scale using a black ink printer.

The **Exam**View® *Test Generator Software* database includes all the test master questions from the *Teacher's Resource Portfolio* plus an additional 25 percent new questions prepared just for this product. The new program features guide you step-by-step through the creation of a formatted test! You can choose to have the computer generate a test for you with randomly selected questions. You can also opt to choose specific questions from the database and add your own questions to create customized tests to meet your classroom needs. You may wish to make different versions of the same test to use during different class periods. Answer keys are generated automatically to simplify grading.

## Strategies for Successful Teaching

By using a variety of teaching strategies, you can make *Housing Decisions* exciting and relevant for your students. Many suggestions for planning classroom activities appear in the teaching supplements that accompany this text. As you plan your lessons, you might also want to keep the following points in mind.

### Helping Your Students Develop Critical Thinking Skills

As today's students leave their classrooms behind, they will face a world of complexity and change. They are likely to work in several career areas and hold many different jobs. Providing young people with a base of knowledge consisting only of facts, principles, and procedures is not enough. Students must also be prepared to solve complex problems, make difficult decisions, and assess ethical implications. In other words, students must be able to use critical thinking skills, the higher-order thinking skills that Benjamin Bloom listed as follows:

- analysis—breaking down material into its component parts so that its organizational structure may be understood
- synthesis—putting parts together to form a new whole
- evaluation—judging the value of material for a given purpose

In a broader perspective, students must be able to use reflective thinking to decide what to believe and do. According to Robert Ennis, students should be able to do the following:

- Define and clarify problems, issues, conclusions, reasons, and assumptions.
- Judge the credibility, relevance, and consistency of information.
- Infer or solve problems and draw reasonable conclusions.

To think critically, students must possess knowledge that goes beyond simply memorizing or recalling information. Critical thinking requires individuals to use common sense and experience, apply their knowledge, and recognize the controversies surrounding an issue.

Critical thinking also requires creative thinking to construct all the reasonable alternatives, possible consequences, influencing factors, and supporting arguments. Unusual ideas are valued and perspectives outside the obvious are sought.

The teaching of critical thinking does not require exotic and highly unusual classroom approaches. Complex thought processes can be incorporated in the most ordinary and basic activities, even reading, writing, and listening, if these activities are carefully planned and well executed.

Help your students develop their analytical and judgmental skills by going beyond what they see on the surface. Rather than allowing students to blindly accept what they read or hear, encourage them to examine ideas in ways that show respect for others' opinions and different perspectives. Encourage students to think about points raised by others. Ask them to evaluate how new ideas relate to their attitudes about various subjects.

Debate is an excellent way to thoroughly explore an issue. You may want to divide the class into two groups, each examining an opposing side. You can also have students explore an issue from all sides in small groups. With both methods, representatives can be chosen to summarize the key thoughts expressed within each group.

### Helping Students Develop Decision-Making Skills

An important aspect in the development of critical thinking skills is learning how to solve problems and make decisions. Important decisions lie ahead for your students, particularly related to their future education and career choices. Chapters 23 and 24 of *Housing Decisions* will help students prepare for career success.

Case studies allow students to evaluate situations in which they are not directly involved. These help students recognize the variety of ways certain problems can be solved. Simulation games and role-plays allow students to practice solving problems and making decisions in non-threatening circumstances. Role-playing allows students to examine others' feelings as well as their own. It can help them learn effective ways to react or cope when confronted with similar situations in real life.

## Using Cooperative Learning

The use of cooperative learning groups in your classroom will give students an opportunity to practice teamwork skills, which are highly valued in the community and the workplace. During cooperative learning activities, students learn interpersonal and small-group skills that will help them to function as part of a team. These skills include leadership, decision making, trust building, communication, and conflict management.

When planning for cooperative learning, you will have a particular goal or task in mind. First, specify the objectives for the lesson. Then, match small groups of learners based on the task and assign each person a role. Group members should be selected to include a mix of abilities and talents so opportunities for students to learn from one another exist. As groups work together over time, individuals' roles should rotate so everyone has an opportunity to practice and develop different skills.

The success of the group is measured not only in terms of group outcome, but also in terms of the successful performance of each member in his or her role. Interdependence is a basic component of any cooperative learning group. Students understand that one person cannot succeed unless everyone does. The value of each group member is affirmed as learners work toward the group's goal.

You will also need to monitor the effectiveness of the groups, intervening as necessary to provide task assistance or help with interpersonal or group skills. Finally, evaluate the group's achievement and help members discuss how well they collaborated.

## Helping Students Recognize and Value Diversity

Your students will be entering a rapidly changing workplace—not only in matters pertaining to technology, but also in the diverse nature of its workforce. The majority of the new entrants to the workforce are women, minorities, and immigrants, all representing many different views and experiences. The workforce is aging, too, as over half the people in the workforce are between the ages of 35 and 54. Because of these trends, young workers must learn how to interact effectively with a variety of people who are unlike them.

The appreciation and understanding of diversity is an ongoing process. The earlier and more frequently young people are exposed to diversity, the more quickly they can develop skills to bridge cultural differences. If your students are exposed to various cultures within your classroom, the process of understanding cultural differences can begin. This is the best preparation for success in a diverse society. In addition, teachers find the following strategies for teaching diversity helpful:

- Actively promote a spirit of openness, consideration, respect, and tolerance in the classroom.
- Use a variety of teaching styles and assessment strategies.
- Use cooperative learning activities whenever possible, making sure group roles are rotated so everyone has leadership opportunities.
- When grouping students, have each group's composition as diverse as possible with regard to gender, race, and nationality. If groups present information to the class, make sure all members have a speaking part.
- Make sure one group's opinions are not over-represented during class discussions. Seek opinions of under-represented groups or individuals if necessary.
- If a student makes a sexist, racist, or other comment that is likely to be offensive, ask the student to rephrase the comment in a manner that it will not offend other members of the class. Remind students that offensive statements and behavior are inappropriate in the classroom.

- If a difficult classroom situation arises involving a diversity issue, ask for a time-out and have everyone write down his or her thoughts and opinions about the incident. This helps to calm the class down and allows you time to plan a response.
- Arrange for guest speakers who represent diversity in gender, race, and ethnicity, even though the topic does not relate to diversity.
- Have students change seats occasionally throughout the course and introduce themselves to their new "neighbors" so they become acquainted with all their classmates.
- Several times during the course, ask students to make anonymous, written evaluations of the class. Have them report any problems that may not be obvious.

## Assessment Techniques

Various forms of assessment are used with students to fully evaluate their achievements. Written tests have traditionally been used to evaluate performance. This method of evaluation is good to use when assessing knowledge and comprehension. Other methods of assessment are preferable for measuring the achievement of the higher-level skills of application, analysis, synthesis, and evaluation. The text includes the following:

- A *To Review* section follows each chapter to evaluate students' recall of key concepts.
- Activities listed at the end of each chapter, under headings titled *In Your Community*, *To Think About*, and *Technology Applications*, provide opportunities to assess your students' abilities to use critical thinking, problem solving, and application.
- *Portfolio Project* concludes each chapter, requiring synthesis of the lesson concepts, creativity, and personal interpretation. Many of these provide an informal type of career-connecting activity.

In the *Teacher's Resources*, the following two means of assessing learning are found:

- An objective test for each chapter appears in the *Teacher's Resource Guide/Portfolio/CD*.
- A tool to create customized tests exists in the *Teacher's Resource CD with G-W Test Creation Software*.

## Performance Assessment

When you assign students some of the projects appearing at the end of each chapter, a different form of assessing mastery or achievement is required. One method that teachers successfully use is a rubric. A rubric consists of a set of criteria that includes specific descriptors or standards used for determining performance scores for students. A point value is given for each set of descriptors, leading to a range of possible points to be assigned, usually from 1 to 5. The criteria can also be weighted. This method of assessment reduces the guesswork involved in grading, leading to fair and consistent scoring. The standards clearly indicate to students the various levels of mastery of a task. Students are even able to assess their own achievement based on the criteria.

When using rubrics, students should see the criteria at the beginning of the assignment. Then they can focus their effort on what needs to be done to reach a certain performance or quality level. They have a clear understanding of your expectations of achievement.

Though you will want to design many of your own rubrics, several generic versions are included in the front section of the *Teacher's Resource Guide* and *Teacher's Resource Portfolio*. The rubrics are designed to assess the following:

- *Individual Participation*
- *Individual Reports*
- *Group Participation*

These rubrics allow you to assess a student's performance and arrive at a performance score. Students can see what levels they have surpassed and what levels they can still strive to reach.

## Portfolios

Another type of performance assessment frequently used by teachers is the student portfolio. A portfolio consists of a selection of materials that students assemble to document their performance over a period of time. The purpose of the portfolio determines the type of items it should contain. Portfolios basically serve two purposes—to gauge progress or demonstrate employability.

For portfolios developed to gauge student progress in a course, items should demonstrate problem-solving and critical-thinking skills. A

Introduction 11

self-assessment summary report should be included that explains what has been accomplished, what has been learned, what strengths the student has gained, and which areas need improvement.

Items chosen for the portfolio are discussed with the teacher in light of educational goals and outcomes. When portfolios are evaluated for a grade, students should be given a portfolio rubric to follow and guidance on how creativity will affect their grade. Portfolios should remain the property of students when they leave the course.

For a job portfolio, items should provide evidence of employability and academic skills. These portfolios are appropriate for displaying at job interviews. Students select their best work samples to showcase their achievements. Some items appropriate for job portfolios are as follows:

- work samples (including photographs, assessments, and so forth) that show mastery of specific skills
- writing samples that show communication skills
- resume
- letters of recommendation that document specific career-related skills
- certificates of completion
- awards and recognition

Portfolio assessment is only one of several evaluation methods teachers can use, but it is a powerful tool for both students and teachers. It encourages students to make a thorough self-reflection and self-assessment. Traditional evaluation methods of tests, quizzes, and reports have their place in measuring the achievement of some course objectives, but portfolios and other assessment tools should also be used to fairly gauge the realization of other desired outcomes.

## Using Other Resources

Learning in your class can be reinforced and expanded by exposing your students to a variety of viewpoints. Information may be obtained through various government offices, trade and professional organizations, and consumer publications. Local sources of information might include cooperative extension offices.

The Internet serves as a vast source of information relating to topics students will study in your classroom. You will want to encourage students to utilize this technology, but emphasize that not all information on the Internet is reliable. Coach students to verify information by checking multiple sources.

The following lists include sources of information and materials that may be useful to you and your students. The first half identifies resources relevant to specific chapters, while the last half lists resources for the general study of housing and interiors. Please note that phone numbers and Web site information may have changed since publication.

## Chapter-by-Chapter Resources

### Chapter 1  Housing and Human Needs

**Americans with Disabilities Act (ADA)**
*usdoj.gov/crt/ada/adahom1.htm*
Explains ADA requirements and has a question-and-answer section.

**Center for Universal Design**
*ncsu.edu/ncsu/design/cud*
Contains easy-to-understand visuals and descriptions of principles of universal design.

**Great Buildings Collection**
*greatbuildings.com*
Excellent resource for obtaining a broad perspective of architecture worldwide.

**National Coalition for the Homeless**
*nationalhomeless.org*
Helpful fact sheets, personal experiences, advocacy information, legislation, and other issues related to homelessness.

**F. Schumacher & Co., Waverly Products ON LINE Lifestyle Quiz**
*waverly.com*
Provides a quiz that relates fabric selections to the identified lifestyle. Select *How to Decorate*, then *Lifestyle*.

**Universal Designers and Consultants, Inc.**
*universaldesign.com*
Has newsletter, magazine, and a good list of related sites regarding universal design.

## Chapter 2  Influences on Housing

**Environmental Protection Agency**
*epa.gov*
Resource on environmental issues, laws, consumer tips, and background information.

**Habitat for Humanity**
*habitat.org*
Humanitarian effort to build housing for people who otherwise would not be able to afford it.

**National American Indian Housing Council**
*naihc.indian.com*
Provides information on culturally appropriate housing and related sites.

**Native American Technology and Art**
*nativetech.org*
Describes the cultural differences of various Native American groups.

**U. S. Census Bureau**
*census.gov*
Has Census statistics and discussions of demographic trends.

**U.S. Department of Energy**
*eren.doe.gov*
Covers all aspects of energy conservation.

**U. S. Department of Housing and Urban Development**
*hud.gov*
Reference site for federal housing laws and programs.

**U. S. Government**
*usa.gov*
Reference for federal laws and agencies.

## Chapter 3  Using Decision-Making Skills

**Consumer World**
*consumerworld.org*
Has links to consumer resources in many areas including house and home. Contains information to compare appliances and other consumer products.

**Mind Tools**
*mindtools.com*
Contains decision-making and time-management resources.

## Chapter 4  Choosing a Place to Live

**Apartment Renter's Resource**
*aptrentersresource.com*
Comprehensive source for quick and easy answers about renting.

**Ginnie Mae**
*ginniemae.gov*
Provides data on all aspects of the home-buying process. Also, search *Buy vs. Rent* for information on financial and other factors to consider before buying a home.

**National Council on Economic Education (NCEE)**
*econedlink.org/lessons*
Provides information for teaching various lessons on economics, including buying versus renting a home.

**HomeRoute Online Real Estate Services**
*homes101.net*
Several online tests for understanding the facts in buying and selling a house. Can locate available housing for city, county and state geographic areas according to price ranges.

**Monster.com, TMP Worldwide**
*monstermoving.com*
Information about relocation resources and goods needed to successfully manage all stages of the moving process.

**U.S. Dept. of Housing and Urban Development**
*hud.gov/renting/index.cfm*
Offers the Renter's Kit, a primer for those preparing to rent.

**Texas Apartment Association**
*taa.org*
Tips on renting versus owning.

## Chapter 5 Acquiring Housing

**Apartment Rental Service**
*forrent.com*
National service to locate apartment by geographical location. Can enter city and state.

**Ameriquest Mortgage**
*ameriquestmortgage.com*
Quick and easy tool to calculate monthly mortgage payments. (Enter loan amount, interest rate, and length of mortgage). Good source to have students compare impact of interest rates.

**eHow, Inc.**
*ehow.com*
Site for how to do just about everything. Also, an excellent site for locating an apartment.

**National Association of Home Realtors**
*realtor.com*
Source for locating realtors in various areas as well as single-family houses and apartments by location and price. Has numerous articles about home buying.

## Chapter 6 The Evolution of Exteriors

**American Architectural Foundation**
*archfoundation.org*
Resource for research information and educational materials on the importance of architecture in current designs.

**American Institute of Architects**
*aia.org*
Source for current trends in architecture.

***Architecture Week* Magazine**
*architectureweek.com*
A source for current housing trends and information on design, technical, and cultural issues.

**Benjamin Moore & Co.**
*benjaminmoore.com*
Listing of architectural styles with brief descriptions and sketches. (Go to *homeowner index*.)

**Frank Lloyd Wright Resource Website**
*cypgrp.com/flw*
This site includes extensive photo list of Frank Lloyd Wright houses.

**Great Buildings Collection, Artifice, Inc.**
*greatbuildings.com*
Excellent source for exterior period housing designs.

**The National Park Service Historic American Buildings Survey/Historic American Engineering Record**
*cr.nps.gov/habshaer*
Good reference for historical buildings, criteria for selection, and photos.

## Chapter 7 Understanding House Plans

**Broderbund LLC**
*broderbund.com*
Creator of the popular *3D Home Architect*® software program.

**ePlans.com House Plans Superstore**
*eplans.com*
Extensive site for examining house plans, renderings, and virtual tours of new homes.

**Family Education Network, Inc.**
*teachervision.com*
Easy lesson plans for understanding floor plans. Designed especially for teachers to use in the classroom. (Search *floor plans*.)

**The COOL House Plans Company**
*coolhouseplans.com*
Contains hundreds of house plans, categorized by styles and sizes.

**The House Designers**
*thehousedesigners.com*
Offers floor plans, exterior views from all sides, and some renderings of rooms in various plans.

## Chapter 8 House Construction

**Building Products, A to Z**
*ebuild.com*
Resources for residential building products.

**Cellulose Insulation Manufacturers Association**
*cellulose.org*
Graphic presentation of cellulose information and installation.

**Composting Toilets**
*envirolet.com/enwatsel.html*
Description and photos of self-contained waterless toilets.

**Home Building Industry Reference Information**
*builderonline.com*
Has variety of information pertinent to the home building industry including trends, news, special reports, building products, and house plans. Good place to browse.

**Homeowner Problems**
*lakesidepress.com/dreams*
Actual cases of homeowner problems with builders and defects in new construction.

**House Construction Course**
*howstuffworks.com/house.htm*
Excellent photos and descriptions of how houses are constructed.

## Chapter 9  The Systems Within

**Building Energy Codes, U.S. Dept. of Energy**
*energycodes.gov*
A resource for tools to facilitate energy code training, compliance, development, adoption, implementation, and enforcement.

**Faucet Direct, Inc.**
*faucetdirect.com*
Extensive display of plumbing fixtures.

**Handyman USA LLC—Recommended R Values for the USA and Canada**
*handymanwire.com*
Displays a national map of zones and a chart specifying recommended r values for insulation. (Go to *Attics*, then *R Values*.)

**Honeywell Corporation**
*honeywell.com*
Contains solutions for automation and security systems.

**Kohler Co.**
*kohler.com*
Shows extensive product line for kitchen and bath fixtures.

**Truebro**
*www.truebro.com*
Provides lavatories that satisfy the Americans with Disabilities Act.

## Chapter 10  Elements of Design

**About, Inc., A PRIMEDIA Company**
*interiordec.about.com/cs/designprinciples*
Information about using the principles of design for interior decorating.

**Virtual Library Museums**
*icom.org/vlmp*
Listing of museum sites, many having virtual tours.

## Chapter 11  Using Color Effectively

**Color Matters, J.L. Morton**
*colormatters.com*
Good source for reviewing the importance of color and how people react to different colors.

**Color Theory Online**
*members.cox.net/mrsparker2/intro.htm*
Extensive online interactive activities including puzzles, games, and PowerPoint® presentation that can be downloaded.

**River City Graphics Design**
*home.att.net/~gary-weirich/ioctheory.html*
Interesting site on color theory with a section on the impact of color.

**The Sherwin-Williams Company**
*sherwin.com*
Excellent site for studying color groupings.

## Chapter 12  Using the Principles of Design

**Gefen Productions**
*thehome.com*
Good source for quick and easy reference to new home products and trends.

**HomeDecorating.com**
*decorating-your-home.com*
Source for planning an office and handling many other do-it-yourself projects.

*Note: Phone numbers and Web site addresses may have changed since the publication of this product.

## Chapter 13 Textiles in Today's Homes

**Fibersource: American Fiber Manufacturers Association**
*fibersource.com*
Excellent resource on fabric definitions, statistics, and general industry information.

**Fiber World Classroom, American Fiber Manufacturers Association**
*fiberworld.com*
General reference for fiber products, common uses, care/maintenance, and fiber history.

**Upholstery Fabric Online**
*upholstery-fabric.com*
Shows examples of different types of upholstery materials for home furnishings.

## Chapter 14 Creating Interior Backgrounds

**Armstrong World Industries**
*armstrongfloors.com*
Good visuals of up-to-date flooring materials.

**Ceramic Tile Institute of America**
*thetiledoctor.com*
Has tile glossary and explanation of how tile is made.

**Consentino Group**
*silestone.com*
Explanation and visual display of engineered quartz used in countertops.

**Florida Tile Industries, Inc.**
*floridatile.com*
Good source for ceramic tile product information, installation designs, and visuals.

**Interior Acoustical Products**
*silentsource.com*
Good source to locate acoustical items on the market for interior walls, ceilings, and floors.

**The Home Depot, Inc.**
*homedepot.com*
Source of product and consumer information on home improvement materials and services.

**Wilsonart International**
*wilsonart.com*
Includes a full line of flooring products as well as laminate and solid surface materials for countertops.

## Chapter 15 Furniture Styles and Construction

**American Furniture Manufacturers Association**
*afma4u.org*
Visuals of furniture styles and good glossary of furniture styles and terms.

**Domain**
*domain-home.com*
Simple, quick online quiz for determining decorating style.

**Gefen Productions**
*thehome.com/woodfurn.html*
Lists common furniture construction types on the market and includes a furniture buying guide.

**Iowa State University**
*iastate.edu*
Excellent source for fabric flammability questions. (Search the keyword *flammability*.)

## Chapter 16 Arranging and Selecting Furniture

*Better Homes and Gardens* **Magazine**
*bhg.com*
Provides online software for arranging a room to download.

**Decorating Alternatives**
*decoratingalternatives.com*
Excellent photos on redesign of space achieved partially by rearranging furniture.

**Ethan Allen Furniture**
*ethanallen.com*
Uses good visuals to show an extensive line of furniture and fabrics.

**PowerHomeBiz.com LLC**
*powerhomebiz.com/vol12/furniture.htm*
Includes tips on buying all types of furniture including home office furniture.

## Chapter 17 Addressing Windows, Lighting, and Accessories

**American Lighting Association**
*americanlightingassoc.com*
Information on how to choose lighting for the house.

**Andersen Corporation**
*andersenwindows.com*
Contains product photos of an extensive variety of windows.

**Efficient Windows Collaborative, U.S. Dept. of Energy**
*efficientwindows.org/selection.html*
Excellent guide for selecting energy-efficient windows and learning how they are made.

**International Association of Lighting Designers**
*iald.org*
Consumer information on working with a lighting designer and the importance of doing so.

**Lowe's Home Improvement Warehouse**
*lowes.com*
Has full line of lighting products and helpful consumer information.

**North Carolina State University Cooperative Extension**
*ces.ncsu.edu/depts/fcs*
Offers publications and web links on many housing topics including accessories.

## Chapter 18 Selecting Household Appliances

*Appliance* **Magazine**
*appliance.com*
Up-to-date information from the industry on new product lines and appliance features.

**Association of Home Appliance Manufacturers**
*aham.org*
Statistics on appliances and the appliance industry.

**University of Kentucky Cooperative Extension**
*ca.uky.edu/fcs/homeappliances*
Good source for current issues, new technology, professional organizations, listing of brand names, and related web sites.

**U.S. Environmental Protection Agency**
*energystar.gov*
Description of Energy Star products and the criteria for the designation.

**Websites of Appliance Manufacturers**

Individual companies provide available products as well as helpful information on shopping and selection. A number of these companies are listed below:
Amana: *amana.com*
Frigidaire: *frigidaire.com*
General Electric: *geappliances.com*
Jennair: *jennair.com*
Kenmore: *sears.com*
Kitchen Aid: *kitchenaid.com*
Maytag: *maytag.com*
Sub-Zero: *subzero.com*
Whirlpool: *whirlpool.com*

## Chapter 19 The Outdoor Living Space and Environment

**American Society of Landscape Architects**
*asla.org*
Contains information about working with landscape architects. Also has consumer publications about landscaping.

**iVillage, Inc.**
*ivillage.com/home*
Contains diverse information on gardening topics as well as other home decorating subjects.

*Southern Living* **Magazine**
*southernliving.com*
Many articles on gardening and design of outdoor space.

## Chapter 20 Keeping Your Home Safe and Secure

**Building Science Corporation**
*buildingscience.com*
Articles on preventing and treating mold in housing.

*Note: Phone numbers and Web site addresses may have changed since the publication of this product.

**Gefen Productions**
*thehome.com/wincov.html*
Lists ways to make window treatments safe for children.

**Healthy Home Institute**
*hhinst.com*
Has indoor air quality information including asthma triggers and an audit to analyze home moisture problems.

**National Lead Information Center, U.S. Dept. of Housing and Urban Development**
*hud.gov/offices/lead/outreach/nlic.pdf*
Provides consumer information about existing laws and regulations regarding the prevention of lead poisoning in housing.

**National Safety Council**
*nsc.org*
Contains consumer information on health safety legislation regarding housing, including lead-based paint.

**North Carolina State University Cooperative Extension**
*ces.ncsu.edu/depts/fcs*
Numerous articles, fact sheets, and related resources on health issues in the home. (Go to the *Housing* link.)

**U. S. Environmental Protection Agency**
*epa.gov*
Information on air quality, pollution prevention, and environmental concerns. Students can locate environmental issues by neighborhood. Has section on resources for teachers.

## Chapter 21 Maintaining Your Home

**Bob Vila Show**
*bobvila.com*
Has extensive information on home improvement projects, gardening, energy conservation, and water conservation.

**DoItYourself, Inc.**
*doityourself.com*
Offers helpful information on home repair and many other home-related projects.

**Gefen Productions**
*thehome.com/harfloor.html*
Guide to maintaining hardwood floors.

**North Carolina State University Cooperative Extension**
*ces.ncsu.edu/depts/fcs*
Excellent preventive maintenance guide and general references on home repair.

**This Old House Online**
*thisoldhouse.com*
Excellent source for renovating and remodeling old homes. Covers all aspects of home and garden with excellent visual materials and references.

## Chapter 22 Housing for Today and Tomorrow

**Biosphere 2**
*bio2.edu*
The largest ecosystem on earth, an affiliate of Columbia University, with virtual tours inside the center and many photos.

***Electronic House* Magazine**
*electronichouse.com*
Lists new home automation products.

**Florida Solar Energy Center, University of Central Florida**
*fsec.ucf.edu*
Provides research on solar applications and numerous consumer publications.

**North Carolina State University Solar Center**
*ncsc.ncsu.edu*
Source for information on solar applications in residences. Has solar demonstration house and extensive consumer information sources.

**Southface Energy Institute**
*southface.org*
Source for information on sustainable housing.

**The Massachusetts Institute of Technology Home of the Future**
*architecture.mit.edu/house_n/web*
Research house focused on how the home and its related technologies, products, and services should evolve to meet the challenges of the future.

## Chapter 23  Careers in Housing

**American Institute of Architects**
*aia.org*
Professional organization that offers new information and addresses member needs. Has descriptive ethics section.

**American Society of Interior Designers**
*asid.org*
Has search features to find information about interior design careers and presents guidelines on beginning a business.

**American Society of Landscape Architects**
*asla.org*
Site has information for landscapers and general public. Publications are of particular interest.

**Foundation for Interior Design Education Research**
*fider.org*
Listing of accredited postsecondary and university programs in interior design.

**National Society of Professional Engineers**
*nspe.org*
Professional organization for engineers. Contains requirements for licensure.

## Chapter 24  Preparing for Career Success

**America's Career InfoNet**
*acinet.org*
Excellent source of information on job and wage trends, career preparation, and available jobs. Links to America's Job Bank.

**CareerBuilder LLC**
*careerbuilder.com*
Provides students an opportunity to search for jobs by geographic location. Students can also post their resumes.

**Job Shadowing**
*jobshadow.org*
Helpful guidelines for establishing shadowing arrangements. Sponsored by Monster.com and News Corporation.

**TMP Worldwide**
*monster.com*
Online search tool for jobs around the country and the world. Also offers resume-writing and career-building assistance.

**Southeastern Oklahoma State University Career Office**
*job-interview-questions.com*
Contains a list of actual interview questions, from simple to difficult, with sample answers.

# Additional Resources for Housing and Interiors

## Publications

**Architectural Digest**
*condenet.com/mags/archdigest*

**Better Homes and Gardens**
*bhg.com*

**Consumer Reports**
*consumerreports.org*

**Fine Homebuilding**
*taunton.com/finehomebuilding/index.asp*

**Home Magazine**
*homemag.com*

**House and Garden**
*condenet.com/mags/hg/*

**Interior Design**
*interiordesign.net*

**Journal of Family and Consumer Sciences**
*aafcs.org*

**What's New in Family and Consumer Sciences**
*whats-new-mag.com/*

## Trade and Professional Organizations

**Air-Conditioning and Refrigeration Institute**
(703) 524-8800
*ari.org*

**Aluminum Association**
(202) 862-5100
*aluminum.org*

*Note: Phone numbers and Web site addresses may have changed since the publication of this product.

**American Architectural Manufacturers Association**
(847) 303-5664
*aamanet.org*

**American Association of Family and Consumer Sciences (AAFCS)**
(703) 706-4600
*aafcs.org*

**American Concrete Institute**
(248) 848-3700
*aci-int.org*

**American Design Drafting Association**
(803) 771-0008
*adda.org*

**American Fiber Manufacturers Association, Inc.**
(202) 296-6508
*fibersource.com*

**American Gas Association**
(202) 824-7000
*aga.org*

**American Hardware Manufacturers Association**
(847) 605-1025
*ahma.org*

**American Lighting Association**
(800) 274-4483
*americanlightingassoc.com*

**American Plastics Council**
(800) 2-HELP-90
*plasticsinfo.org*

**American Plywood Association**
(235) 565-6600
*apawood.org*

**American Printed Fabrics Council**
(212) 695-2254

**American Society for Testing and Materials (ASTM)**
(610) 832-9585
*astm.org*

**American Society of Furniture Designers**
(910) 576-1273
*asfd.com*

**American Society of Interior Designers**
(202) 546-3480
*asid.org*

**American Textile Manufacturers Institute, Inc.**
(202) 862-0518
*atmi.org*

**American Wool Council**
(303) 771-3500
*americanwool.org*

**Architectural Woodwork Institute**
(703) 733-0600
*awinet.org*

**Association for Career and Technical Education**
(800) 826-9972
*acteonline.org*

**Association of Home Appliance Manufacturers**
(202) 872-5955
*aham.org*

**Barrier Free Environments Inc.**
(919) 839-6380

**California Redwood Association**
(888) 225-7339
*calredwood.org*

**Craft Yarn Council of America**
(704) 824-7838
*craftyarncouncil.com*

**Crafted with Pride in the USA Council, Inc.**
(202) 775-0658
*craftedwithpride.org*

**Family, Career and Community Leaders of America (FCCLA)**
(703) 475-4900
*fccla.com*

**International Association of Lighting Designers**
(312) 527-3677
*iald.org*

**International Fabricare Institute**
(800) 638-2621
*ifi.org*

**International Technology Education Association**
(703) 860-2100
*iteawww.org*

**Kitchen Cabinet Manufacturers Association**
(703) 264-1690
*kcma.org*

**Manufactured Housing Institute**
(703) 558-0400
*manufacturedhousing.org*

**National Association of Home Builders**
(800) 386-5242
*nahb.com*

**National Association of the Remodeling Industry**
(800) 611-6274
*nari.org*

**National Cotton Council of America**
(901) 274-9030
*cotton.org*

**National Council of Better Business Bureaus, Inc.**
(703) 276-0100
*bbb.org*

**National Foundation for Consumer Credit**
(800) 388-2227
*nfcc.org*

**National Fraud Information Center/Internet Fraud Watch**
(800) 876-7060
*fraud.org*

**National Institute for Consumer Education**
(734) 487-2292
*nice.emich.edu*

**Plumbing, Heating, and Cooling Information Bureau**
(312) 372-7331

**Sustainable Buildings Industries Council**
(202) 628-7400
*sbicouncil.org*

**The Soap and Detergent Association**
(202) 347-2900
*sdahq.org*

## Corporate Resources

**Alcoa Building Products**
(800) 962-6973
*alcoahomes.com*

**Alcoa Vinyl Windows**
(800) 238-1866

**American Olean Tile Co.**
(215) 855-1111
*americanolean.com*

**Andersen Windows**
(651) 264-5150
*andersenwindows.com*

**AristOKraft**
(717) 359-4131
*aristokraft.com*

**Armstrong World Industries Inc.**
(800) 233-3823
*armstrongfloors.com*

**BASF Corp.**
(704) 423-2000
*basf.com*

**Benjamin Moore & Co.**
(800) 344-0400
*benjaminmoore.com*

**Brown Jordan International**
(800) 473-4252
*brownjordan.com*

**Bruce Hardwood Floors**
(214) 887-2000
*bruce.com*

**Burlington Industries Inc.**
(333) 379-2000
*burlington.com*

**Carrier Air Conditioning Co.**
(800) 227-7437
*carrier.utc.com*

**Clorox Co.**
(800) 292-2200
*clorox.com*

**Colgate-Palmolive Co.**
(800) 468-6502
*colgate.com*

*Note: Phone numbers and Web site addresses may have changed since the publication of this product.

**Congoleum Corp.**
(800) 274-3266
*congoleum.com*

**Cotton Inc.**
(212) 413-8300
*cottoninc.com*

**Delta Faucets Co.**
(800) 345-3358
*deltafaucet.com*

**Dow Chemical USA**
(989) 636-5955
*dow.com*

**Dupont Fibers**
(800) 441-7515
*dupont.com*

**Ethan Allen Inc.**
(888) EAHELP1
*ethanallen.com*

**F. Schumacher & Co.**
(800) 988-7775
*fschumacher.com/*

**Faultless Starch/Bon Ami Co.**
(816) 472-4987
*bonami.com*

**Georgia-Pacific Corp.**
(800) 284-5347
*gp.com*

**Hoover Co.**
(800) 944-9200
*hoover.com*

**Hunter Douglas**
(800) 366-4327
*hunterdouglasgroup.com*

**Kirsch**
(800) 817-6344
*kirsch.com*

**Kohler Co.**
(800) 456-4537
*kohler.com*

**KraftMaid Cabinetry**
(888) 562-7744
*kraftmaid.com*

**Lane Furniture**
(804) 369-5641
*lanefurniture.com*

**Laufen International**
(800) 331-3651
*laufen.com*

**Lennox Industries Inc.**
(972) 497-5000
*davelennox.com*

**Levolor Home Fashion**
(800) 538-6567
*lexmark.com*

**Masco Corp.**
(313) 274-7400
*masco.com*

**Mannington Mills, Inc.**
(800) 356-6787
*mannington.com*

**Marvin Windows**
*marvin.com*

**Mills Pride**
(800) 441-0337
*millspride.com*

**Minwax/Sherwin-Williams**
(800) 526-0495
*minwax.com*

**Nu Tone Inc.**
(513) 527-5231
*nutone.com*

**Owens-Corning Fiberglas Corp.**
(800) 438-0465
*owenscorning.com*

**Peachtree Doors**
(888) 888-3814
*peach99.com*

**Peerless**
(800) 438-6673
*peerless-faucet.com*

**Pella Windows and Doors**
(641) 628-6376
*pella.com*

**Pendleton Woolen Mills**
(800) 760-4844
*pendleton-usa.com*

**Pfaff American Sales Corp.**
(201) 262-7211
*pfaffusa.com*

**Philips Lighting Co.**
(800) 555-0050
*lighting.philips.com/nam*

**Pozzi Wood Windows**
(800) 547-6880
*pozzi.com*

**Proctor & Gamble Co.**
(513) 945-8787
*pg.com*

**Prudential Property & Casualty Co.**
(800) 437-5556

**Rubbermaid**
(330) 264-6464, ext. 2502
*rubbermaid.com*

**Sherwin-Williams Co.**
(800) 474-3794
*sherwin-williams.com*

**Stanley Hardware (Division of the Stanley Works)**
(800) 622-4393

**Velux-America Inc.**
(800)-88-VELUX
*velux-america.com*

**Wood-Mode Inc.**
(717) 374-2711
*wood-mode.com*

## Government Agencies and Allied Organizations

### Sources of General Information

The Consumer Information Center (CIC) publishes the free *Consumer Information Catalog*, which lists more than 200 free and low-cost government booklets on a wide variety of consumer topics. Copies of the catalog can be obtained by contacting the Web address *www.pueblo.gsa.gov*, writing to *Consumer Information Catalog*, Pueblo, CO 81009, or calling (719) 948-4000.

The Federal Information Center (FIC), which is administered by the General Services Administration (GSA), can help you find information about United States government agencies and programs. The FIC can also tell you which office to contact for help with problems. You can contact the FIC online or by calling (800) 688-9889.

### Federal Offices, Hot Lines, and Databases

**Consumer Product Safety Commission**
(800) 628-2772 (Product Safety Hotline)
*cpsc.gov*

**Consumer Resource Handbook**
*pueblo.gsa.gov*

**Department of Energy**
(800) 342-5363
*energy.com*

**Office of Energy Efficiency and Renewable Energy**
(800) 363-3732
*eren.doe.gov*

**Department of Health and Human Services**
(877) 696-6775
*dhhs.gov*

**National Center for Injury Prevention & Control**
(770) 448-1506
*cdc.gov/ncipc*

**National Institute on Aging**
(800) 222-2225
*nih.gov/hia*

**Department of Housing and Urban Development**
(202) 708-1112
*hud.gov*

**Office of Fair Housing and Equal Opportunity**
(800) 669-9777
*hud.gov*

**Department of Labor**
(866) 4USA-DOL
*dol.gov*

**Bureau of Labor Statistics**
*bls.gov*

**Dictionary of Occupational Titles**
*wave.net/upg/immigration/dot_index.html*

**Occupational Information Network (O*NET)**
*online.onetcenter.org*

**Occupational Outlook Handbook**
*bls.gov/oco/*

**Occupational Safety and Health Administration**
(202) 693-1999
*osha.gov*

**Online Career Center**
(800) 666-7837
*occ.com/occ*

**Federal Trade Commission**
202-326-2222
*ftc.gov*

**Cybershopping**
*pueblo.gsa.gov/*

**Government Printing Office**
Publications Office
(202) 512-1800
*gpo.gov*

**Small Business Administration**
(800) 827-5722
*sba.gov*

## Educational Resources

The following list of various companies may serve as resources for additional teaching materials. Most provide videos and/or computer software, and many provide printed materials. Contact these organizations for their latest catalogs.

**AAVIM**
(800) 228-4689
*aavim.org*

**AGC Educational Media**
(800) 323-9084
*agcmed.com*

**Cambridge Educational**
(800) 468-4227
*cambridgeeducational.com*

**Concept Media**
(800) 233-7078
*conceptmedia.com*

**Creative Educational Video**
(800) 922-9965
*cev-inc.com/*

**Distinctive Home Video Productions**
(415) 344-7756
*distinctivehomevideo.com*

**Durrin Productions**
(800) 536-6843
*durrinproductions.com*

**ETR Associates**
(831) 438-4060
*etr.org*

**Karol Media**
(800) 526-4773
*karolmedia.com*

**Learning Seed**
(800) 634-4941
*learningseed.com*

**NIMCO Inc.**
(800) 962-6662
*lnimcoinc.com*

**RMI Media Productions**
(800) 4821-5480
*rmimed.com*

## Goodheart-Willcox Welcomes Your Comments

We welcome your comments or suggestions regarding *Housing Decisions* and its ancillaries as we are continually striving to publish better educational materials. Please send any comments you may have by visiting our Website at *g-w.com* or writing to the following address:

Editorial Department
Goodheart-Willcox Publisher
18604 West Creek Drive
Tinley Park, IL 60477-624

Reproducible Master

# Evaluation of Individual Participation

Name _____ Date _____ Period _____

The rating scale below shows an evaluation of your class participation. It indicates what levels you have passed and what levels you can continue to try to reach.

**Criteria:**

### 1. Attentiveness

| 1 | 2 | 3 | 4 | 5 |
|---|---|---|---|---|
| Completely inattentive. | Seldom attentive. | Somewhat attentive. | Usually attentive. | Extremely attentive. |

### 2. Contribution to Discussion

| 1 | 2 | 3 | 4 | 5 |
|---|---|---|---|---|
| Never contributes to class discussion. | Rarely contributes to class discussion. | Occasionally contributes to class discussion. | Regularly contributes to class discussion. | Frequently contributes to class discussion. |

### 3. Interaction with Peers

| 1 | 2 | 3 | 4 | 5 |
|---|---|---|---|---|
| Often distracts others. | Shows little interaction with others. | Follows leadership of other students. | Sometimes assumes leadership role. | Respected by peers for ability. |

### 4. Response to Teacher

| 1 | 2 | 3 | 4 | 5 |
|---|---|---|---|---|
| Unable to respond when called on. | Often unable to support or justify answers when called on. | Supports answers based on class information, but seldom offers new ideas. | Able to offer new ideas with prompting. | Often offers new ideas without prompting. |

**Total Points:** _____ out of 20

**Comments:**

_____

_____

*Introduction*

Reproducible Master

# Evaluation of Individual Reports

Name _____ Date _____ Period _____

The rating scale below shows an evaluation of your oral or written report. It indicates what levels you have passed and what levels you can try to reach on future reports.

Report title _____ Oral _____ Written _____

**Criteria:**

### 1. Choice of Topic

| 1 | 2 | 3 | 4 | 5 |
|---|---|---|---|---|
| Slow to choose topic. | Chooses topic with indifference. | Chooses topic as assigned, seeks suggestions. | Chooses relevant topic without assistance. | Chooses creative topic. |

### 2. Use of Resources

| 1 | 2 | 3 | 4 | 5 |
|---|---|---|---|---|
| Unable to find resources. | Needs direction to find resources. | Uses fewer than assigned number of resources. | Uses assigned number of resources from typical sources. | Uses additional resources from a variety of sources. |

### 3. Oral Presentation

| 1 | 2 | 3 | 4 | 5 |
|---|---|---|---|---|
| No notes or reads completely. Poor subject coverage. | Has few good notes. Limited subject coverage. | Uses notes somewhat effectively. Adequate subject coverage. | Uses notes effectively. Good subject coverage. | Uses notes very effectively. Complete coverage. |

### 4. Written Presentation

| 1 | 2 | 3 | 4 | 5 |
|---|---|---|---|---|
| Many grammar and spelling mistakes. No organization. | Several grammar and spelling mistakes. Poor organization. | Some grammar and spelling mistakes. Fair organization. | A few grammar and spelling mistakes. Good organization. | No grammar or spelling mistakes. Excellent organization. |

**Total Points:** _____ out of _____

*Housing Decisions*

Reproducible Master

# Evaluation of Group Participation

**Group Members** _____  _____
_____  _____
_____  _____
_____  _____

The rating scale below shows an evaluation of the efforts of your group. It indicates what levels you have passed and what levels you can try to reach on future group projects.

**Criteria:**

### 1. Teamwork

| 1 | 2 | 3 | 4 | 5 |
|---|---|---|---|---|
| Passive membership. Failed to identify what tasks needed to be completed. | Argumentative membership. Unable to designate who should complete each task. | Independent membership. All tasks completed individually. | Helpful membership. Completed individual tasks and then assisted others. | Cooperative membership. Worked together to complete all tasks. |

### 2. Leadership

| 1 | 2 | 3 | 4 | 5 |
|---|---|---|---|---|
| No attempt at leadership. | No effective leadership. | Sought leadership from outside group. | One member assumed primary leadership role for the group. | Leadership responsibilities shared by several group members. |

### 3. Goal Achievement

| 1 | 2 | 3 | 4 | 5 |
|---|---|---|---|---|
| Did not attempt to achieve goal. | Were unable to achieve goal. | Achieved goal with outside assistance. | Achieved assigned goal. | Achieved goal using added materials to enhance total effort. |

**Total Points:** _____ **out of 15**

Members cited for excellent contributions to group's effort are:

_____

_____

Members cited for failing to contribute to group's effort are:

_____

_____

# Correlation of National Standards for Housing, Interiors, and Furnishings with *Housing Decisions*

In planning your program, you may want to use the chart shown here. It correlates the Family and Consumer Sciences Education National Standards with the content of *Housing Decisions*. The chart lists the competencies for each content standard within the "Housing, Interiors, and Furnishings" area. Also listed are the text topics that relate to each competency and the chapters in which they are found (with numbers shown in bold).

After studying the content of this text, students will be able to achieve the following comprehensive standard:

**11.0** Integrate knowledge, skills, and practices required for careers in housing, interiors, and furnishings.

| Content Standard 11.1 Analyze career paths within the housing, interiors, and furnishings industry. ||
|---|---|
| **Competencies** | **Text Concepts** |
| **11.1.1** Determine the roles and functions of individuals engaged in housing, interiors, and furnishings careers. | **5:** A place to buy<br>**23:** Who provides housing? career clusters; career opportunities in housing; effect of technology on housing careers; career levels |
| **11.1.2** Explore opportunities for employment and entrepreneurial endeavors. | **23:** Career opportunities in housing; housing careers in planning, engineering, and design; housing careers in construction; housing careers in sales and service; entrepreneurial careers in housing and design; housing careers in allied fields; effect of technology on housing careers |
| **11.1.3** Examine education and training requirements and opportunities for career paths in housing, interiors, and furnishings | **23:** Career opportunities in housing; housing careers in planning, engineering, and design; housing careers in construction; housing careers in sales and service; housing careers in allied fields; effect of technology on housing careers<br>**24:** Setting career goals; finding a job |
| **11.1.4** Examine the impact of housing, interiors, and furnishings occupations on local, state, national, and global economies. | **1:** Housing and the quality of life; quality of life for society; human ecology<br>**2:** How housing affects the economy<br>**23:** Who provides housing? |

*Introduction* 29

## Content Standard 11.2 Evaluate housing decisions in relation to available resources and options.

| Competencies | Text Concepts |
|---|---|
| **11.2.1** Determine the principles and elements of design. | **10:** Design characteristics; elements of design; line; form; space; mass; texture<br><br>**11:** Understanding color; the color wheel; color harmonies<br><br>**12:** The principles of design; proportion and scale; balance; emphasis; rhythm |
| **11.2.2** Determine the psychological impact the principles and elements of design have on the individual. | **11:** Using color harmonies<br><br>**12:** Goals of design; harmony with unity and variety; beauty; sensory design<br><br>**17:** The properties of light; functions of lighting |
| **11.2.3** Determine the effects the principles and elements of design have on aesthetics and function. | **11:** Using color harmonies; choosing the right colors; using color correctly<br><br>**12:** Goals of design; function and appropriateness; sensory design<br><br>**17:** The properties of light; lighting for visual comfort; lighting for safety; lighting for beauty |

## Content Standard 11.3 Evaluate the use of housing and interior furnishings and products in meeting specific design needs.

| Competencies | Text Concepts |
|---|---|
| **11.3.1** Research product information including but not limited to floor coverings, wall coverings, textiles, window treatments, furniture, lighting fixtures, kitchen and bath fixtures and equipment, accessories, and building materials. | **8:** Materials used for exterior construction; windows and doors<br><br>**9:** Plumbing systems; heating systems; cooling systems<br><br>**13:** Understanding fibers, yarns, and fabrics; textiles for home use; textiles for floor treatments; textiles for upholstered furniture; textiles for window treatments; textiles for kitchen, bath, and bed<br><br>**14:** Floor treatments; wall treatment<br><br>**15:** Evaluating furniture construction; wood in furniture<br><br>**17:** Window treatments; choosing accessories<br><br>**18:** Appliance considerations; choosing kitchen appliances; choosing laundry appliances |

| | |
|---|---|
| **11.3.2** Select manufacturers, products, and materials considering care, maintenance, safety, and environmental issues. | **9:** Conserving energy<br>**13:** Textiles for home use; appearance; durability; maintenance; comfort; ease of construction<br>**14:** Planning your background treatments, planning your floors; planning your walls; planning your countertops<br>**16:** Selecting furniture<br>**18:** Choosing kitchen appliances; choosing laundry appliances; choosing climate-control appliances; choosing other appliances<br>**21:** Resources for home care |
| **11.3.3** Review measuring, estimating, ordering, purchasing, and pricing skills. | (The competencies for this content standard are applicable for more advanced texts.) |
| **11.3.4** Appraise various interior furnishings, appliances, and equipment which provide cost and quality choices for clients. | **14:** Planning your background treatments; planning your floors; planning your walls; planning your countertops<br>**16:** Selecting furniture; prioritizing furniture needs; determining how much you can afford; identifying your lifestyle; identifying your furniture style; determining your design preferences; stretching your furniture dollars; using multipurpose furniture; reusing furniture; creating the eclectic look<br>**17:** Choosing accessories<br>**18:** Appliance considerations; purchase price; energy cost; features; size; safety; quality; consumer satisfaction |

### Content Standard 11.4 Demonstrate computer-aided drafting design, blueprint reading, and space planning skills required for the housing, interiors, and furnishings industry.

| Competencies | Text Concepts |
|---|---|
| **11.4.1** Read information provided on blueprints. | **7:** Architectural drawings for a house; prints of architectural drawings; views for architectural drawings |
| **11.4.2** Examine floor plans for efficiency and safety in areas including but not limited to zones, traffic patterns, storage, electrical, and mechanical systems. | **7:** The space within; grouping by function; traffic patterns; survey the storage space<br>**9:** Electrical systems; gas as an energy source; plumbing systems; heating systems; cooling systems<br>**21:** Meeting storage needs; organize for storage; space savers |

| | |
|---|---|
| **11.4.3** Draw an interior space to scale using correct architecture symbols and drafting skills. | **7:** Architectural drawings for a house; prints of architectural drawings; views of architectural drawings<br><br>**16:** Developing a scale floor plan |
| **11.4.4** Arrange furniture placement with reference to principles of design, traffic flow, activity, and existing architectural features. | **7:** The space within; grouping by function; traffic patterns; survey the storage space<br><br>**16:** Arranging furniture; developing a scale floor plan; factors to consider when arranging furniture |
| **11.4.5** Utilize applicable building codes, universal guidelines, and regulations in space planning. | **4:** Zoning regulations and other restrictions; natural restraints; legal restraints; housing for special needs; considerations for senior citizens; considerations for people with disabilities; considerations for families with children<br><br>**19:** Completing a scaled plan<br><br>**20:** Equipping a home for people with disabilities; universal design; features for special needs |
| **11.4.6** Create floor plans using computer design software. | **2:** High tech<br><br>**8:** Computer applications in construction<br><br>**16:** Developing a scale floor plan; computer-aided drafting and design (CADD) |

## Content Standard 11.5 Analyze influences on architectural and furniture design and development.

| Competencies | Text Concepts |
|---|---|
| **11.5.1** Explore features of furnishings that are characteristic of various historical periods. | **15:** Choosing furniture styles; traditional furniture styles; twentieth century furniture styles; late twentieth century styles; twenty-first century furniture styles; antiques, collectibles, and reproductions |
| **11.5.2** Consider how prosperity, mass production, and technology are related to the various periods. | **2:** Housing during the 1700s and 1800s; housing in the 1900s; finding affordable housing; planning for leisure time; working at home; a mobile society; early technology; industrialization<br><br>**6:** Traditional houses; modern houses; contemporary houses<br><br>**15:** Traditional furniture styles; twentieth century furniture styles; late twentieth century styles; twenty-first century furniture styles; antiques, collectibles, and reproductions |

| | |
|---|---|
| **11.5.3** Examine the development of architectural styles throughout history. | **2:** Historical influences on housing; cultural influences on housing; societal influences on housing; environmental influences on housing; economic influences on housing; technological influences on housing; governmental influences on housing<br><br>**6:** Traditional houses; modern houses; contemporary houses |
| **11.5.4** Compare historical architectural details to current housing and interior design trends. | **6:** Contemporary houses; solar houses; earth-sheltered houses; housing trends<br><br>**15:** Twentieth century furniture styles; contemporary; traditional; casual; country; eclectic<br><br>**16:** Determining your design preferences; creating the eclectic look<br><br>**20:** Equipping a home for people with disabilities; universal design; features for special needs<br><br>**22:** Innovative solutions in housing; universal design; green buildings; planned communities; new living spaces |
| **11.5.5** Consider future trends in architectural and furniture design and development. | **6:** Contemporary houses; solar houses; earth-sheltered houses; housing trends<br><br>**9:** Electricity in the house; energy conservation through computer power<br><br>**15:** Twenty-first century furniture styles; wood in furniture; plastic, metal, rattan, wicker, bamboo, and glass furniture<br><br>**22:** Recent developments in housing; automated houses; housing concerns; sources of energy; conserving energy; a clean environment; solving environmental concerns |

## Content Standard 11.6 Evaluate clients' needs, goals, and resources in creating design plans for housing, interiors, and furnishings.

| Competencies | Text Concepts |
|---|---|
| **11.6.1** Assess human needs, safety, space, and technology as they relate to housing and interior design goals. | **1:** People and their housing; meeting needs through housing; personal priorities; housing needs vary; personal quality of life<br><br>**2:** Societal influences on housing; technological influences on housing; environmental protection |

*Introduction* 33

|  | |
|---|---|
|  | **20:** A safe home; a secure home; equipping a home for people with disabilities |
|  | **21:** Keeping the home clean and well-maintained; meeting storage needs; redecorating; remodeling |
| **11.6.2** Assess community, family, and financial resources needed to achieve clients' housing and interior goals. | **1:** Housing needs vary; households; life cycles; life cycles and housing needs; quality of life for society |
|  | **4:** Location; housing for special needs; considerations for senior citizens; considerations for people with disabilities; considerations for families with children |
|  | **5:** Acquiring a place to live; to rent or to buy? a place to rent; a place to buy; condominium ownership; cooperative ownership |
| **11.6.3** Assess a variety of available resources for housing and interior design. | **2:** Legislation |
|  | **3:** Resources for housing decisions; human resources; nonhuman resources; the decision-making process |
|  | **13:** Textile laws |
|  | **16:** Information sources |
|  | **21:** Resources for home care |
| **11.6.4** Critique design plans that address clients' needs, goals, and resources. | **1:** Personal priorities; roles; lifestyle; housing needs vary; personal quality of life |
|  | **3:** The decision-making process |
|  | **7:** The space within; grouping by function; traffic patterns; survey the storage space; housing modifications for people with physical disabilities |
|  | **14:** Planning your background treatments; planning your floor; planning your walls; planning your countertops |
|  | **16:** Developing a scale floor plan; factors to consider when arranging furniture |

### Content Standard 11.7 Demonstrate design ideas through visual presentation.

(The competencies for this content standard are applicable for more advanced texts.)

### Content Standard 11.8 Demonstrate general procedures for business profitability and career success.

(The competencies for this content standard are applicable for more advanced texts.)

# Scope and Sequence

In planning your program, you may want to use this Scope and Sequence chart to identify the major concepts presented in each chapter of *Housing Decisions*. Refer to the chart to select topics that meet your curriculum needs. Bold numbers indicate chapters in which concepts are found.

## Part One  Housing for You

### Factors Influencing Housing Decisions
**1:** People and their housing; Meeting needs through housing; Factors affecting housing choices; Personal priorities; Space; Costs; Roles; Lifestyle; Housing needs vary; Households; Life cycles and housing needs; Housing and the quality of life; Human ecology.

### Forces Affecting Housing
**2:** Historical influences on housing; Cultural influences on housing; Societal influences on housing; Household size; Household composition; An older population; People with disabilities; Finding affordable housing; Planning for leisure time; Working at home; A mobile society; Environmental influences on housing; Economic influences on housing; How housing affects the economy; Technological influences on housing; Governmental influences on housing.

### Financial and Legal Aspects of Housing
**1:** Factors affecting housing choices; Costs.

**2:** Economic influences on housing; How housing affects the economy; How the economy affects housing; Governmental influences on housing; Legislation; Funding for housing; Environmental protection.

### Creating Interior/Exterior Living Spaces
**2:** Environmental influences on housing; The natural environment; The constructed environment; The behavioral environment; Interaction of the environments.

### Safety
**1:** Meeting needs through housing.

**2:** New immigrants; Societal influences on housing; Environmental influences on housing.

### New Technology, Trends, and Housing Issues
**1:** Lifestyle; Housing and the quality of life; Quality of life for society.

**2:** New immigrants; Societal influences on housing; An older population; People with disabilities; Finding affordable housing; Planning for leisure time; Working at home; Technological influences on housing; Early technology; Industrialization; High tech; Governmental influences on housing; Legislation; Environmental protection.

### Leadership and Citizenship
**1:** People and their housing; Factors affecting housing choices; Lifestyle; Housing and the quality of life; Quality of life for society; Human ecology.

**2:** Societal influences on housing; Governmental influences on housing.

## Part Two  Making Housing Choices

### Factors Influencing Housing Decisions
**3:** Types of decisions; Decisions made with thought and care; Interrelated decisions; Resources for housing decisions; Human resources; The decision-making process.

**4:** Location; Community; Neighborhood; Site; Multifamily housing; Single-family houses; Housing for special needs; Housing considerations for senior citizens; Housing considerations for people with disabilities; Housing considerations for families with children; Moving to a new home.

**5:** Needs, wants, and housing costs.

### Financial and Legal Aspects of Housing
**3:** Nonhuman resources; The decision-making process.

Introduction  35

**5:** Acquiring a place to live; Human and nonhuman costs; Costs involved in method of paying; To rent or to buy; A place to rent; Assigning or subletting a lease; Responsibilities and rights in rental housing; Renter's insurance; A place to buy; The right price; To build or to buy; Shopping for a place to buy; Steps in buying a house; Condominium ownership; Cooperative ownership.

### Home Construction
**4:** Location; Community; Neighborhood; Site; Single-family houses; Housing for special needs; Housing considerations for senior citizens; Housing considerations for people with disabilities.

### Safety
**4:** Housing for special needs; Housing considerations for senior citizens; Housing considerations for people with disabilities; Housing considerations for families with children.

### Careers: Options and Preparation
**3:** Types of decisions; The decision-making process.

**4:** Moving to a new home.

**5:** A place to buy.

### Leadership and Citizenship
**3:** Types of decisions; Decisions made with thought and care; Interrelated decisions; The decision-making process.

## Part Three  From the Ground Up

### Forces Affecting Housing
**9:** Conserving energy; Energy conservation through computer power.

### Creating Interior/Exterior Living Spaces
**6:** Traditional houses; Modern houses; Contemporary houses.

**7:** The space within; Grouping by function; Traffic patterns; Survey the storage space; Housing modifications for people with physical disabilities.

### Home Construction
**7:** Architectural drawings for a house; Prints; Views for architectural drawing; The space within; Grouping by function; Traffic patterns; Survey the storage space; Housing modifications for people with physical disabilities.

**8:** The foundation and the frame; Materials used for exterior construction; Wood siding; Manufactured siding; Masonry siding; Windows and doors; Computer applications in construction; Managing the construction.

**9:** Electrical systems; Gas as an energy source; Plumbing systems; Heating systems; Conventional heating systems; Solar heating systems; Fireplaces and stoves; Cooling systems; Insulation.

### Interior/Exterior Design
**6:** Traditional houses; Modern houses; Contemporary houses; Housing trends.

### Selecting Furnishings and Equipment
**9:** Plumbing fixtures; Fireplaces and stoves.

### Safety
**7:** Housing modifications for people with physical disabilities.

**9:** Electrical systems; Electricity in the house; Heating systems.

### Care and Maintenance
**9:** Electrical systems; Plumbing systems; Heating systems; Cooling systems; Conserving energy; Energy conservation through computer power.

### New Technology, Trends, and Housing Issues
**6:** Contemporary houses; Solar houses; Earth-sheltered houses; Housing trends.

**7:** Housing modifications for people with physical disabilities.

**8:** Computer applications in construction; Analyzing components of construction; Selecting components of construction; Managing the construction.

**9:** Solar heating systems; Conserving energy; Energy conservation through computer power.

## Part Four  The Inside Story

### Factors Influencing Housing Decisions
**16:** Factors to consider when arranging furniture; Selecting furniture; Prioritizing furniture needs; Identifying your lifestyle; Identifying your furniture style; Determining your design preferences.

**17:** Lighting for visual comfort; Lighting for safety; Lighting for beauty.

**18:** Appliance considerations; Features; Size; Safety; Quality; Consumer satisfaction.

### Financial and Legal Aspects of Housing
**13:** Textile laws; Textile Fiber Products Identification Act; Wool Products Labeling Act; Flammable Fabrics Act.

**15:** Consumer protection.

**16:** Determining how much you can afford; Information sources; Stretching your furniture dollars; Shopping for bargains.

**18:** Appliance considerations; Energy cost; Safety; Consumer satisfaction.

### Creating Interior/Exterior Living Spaces
**14:** Floor treatments; Flooring materials; Floor coverings; Walls; Wall treatments; Planning your background treatments.

**16:** Developing a scale floor plan; Factors to consider when arranging furniture; Determining your design preferences.

**17:** Window treatments; Artificial light; Lighting for visual comfort; Lighting for safety; Lighting for beauty; Structural and nonstructural lighting; Choosing accessories.

### Home Construction
**14:** Floor treatments; Flooring materials; Floor coverings; Walls; Wall treatments; Ceiling treatments.

### Interior/Exterior Design
**10:** Design characteristics; Elements of design; Line; Form; Space; Mass; Texture.

**11:** Understanding color; Color characteristics; Neutrals; Warm and cool colors; Color harmonies; Using color harmonies; Choosing the right colors; Using color correctly.

**12:** The principles of design; Proportion and scale; Balance; Emphasis; Rhythm; Goals of design; Function and appropriateness; Harmony with unity and variety; Beauty; Sensory design.

**16:** Determining your design preferences; Creating the eclectic look.

**17:** Window treatments; Draperies and curtains; Decorative window-top treatments; The properties of light; Lighting for beauty.

### Selecting Furnishings and Equipment
**13:** Understanding fibers, yarns, and fabrics; Fabric construction; Fabric modifications; Textiles for home use; Textiles for floor treatments; Textiles for upholstered furniture; Textiles for window treatments; Textiles for kitchen, bath, and bed.

**15:** Choosing furniture styles; Antiques, collectibles, and reproductions; Evaluating furniture construction; Wood, plastic, metal, rattan, wicker, bamboo, and glass in furniture; Upholstered furniture; Beds.

**16:** Selecting furniture; Prioritizing furniture needs; Determining how much you can afford; Identifying your lifestyle; Identifying your furniture style; Determining your design preferences; Deciding where and how to shop; Deciding when to shop; Information sources; Stretching your furniture dollars; Shopping for bargains; Using multipurpose furniture.

**17:** Window treatments; Draperies and curtains; Shades, shutters, and blinds; Decorative window-top treatments; Structural and nonstructural lighting; Choosing accessories.

**18:** Appliance considerations; Features; Size; Safety; Quality; Consumer satisfaction; Choosing kitchen appliances; Choosing laundry appliances; Choosing climate-control appliances; Choosing other appliances; Personal computers; Portable appliances.

### Safety
**16:** Arranging furniture; Factors to consider when arranging furniture.

**17:** Lighting for safety.

**18:** Appliance considerations; Safety.

Introduction  37

**Care and Maintenance**

**13:** Textiles for home use; Maintenance; Textiles for window treatments; Cost and care.

**14:** Flooring materials; Floor coverings; Planning your background treatments; Planning your countertops.

**17:** Choosing accessories.

**18:** Appliance considerations; Features.

## Part Five   A Safe and Attractive Environment

**Factors Influencing Housing Decisions**
**20:** A safe home; Keeping children safe in your home; Controlling noise pollution; Security from home intruders; Equipping a home for people with disabilities.

**Financial and Legal Aspects of Housing**
**21:** Remodeling; Getting your money's worth.

**Creating Interior/Exterior Living Spaces**
**19:** Planning the landscape; Landscape elements; Designing the outdoor living spaces; Landscape backgrounds; Accents; Other landscape features; Lighting the outdoor living space; Completing a scaled plan; Developing the landscape design.

**21:** Exterior home maintenance and cleaning; Meeting storage needs; Organize for storage; Space savers; Redecorating; Remodeling; Resources for home care; Help with home maintenance.

**Home Construction**
**20:** Equipping a home for people with disabilities; Universal design; Features for special needs.

**Interior/Exterior Design**
**19:** Designing the outdoor living spaces; Landscape backgrounds; Accents; Other landscape features.

**21:** Redecorating; Remodeling.

**Selecting Furnishings and Equipment**
**19:** Furnishing your outdoor living space.

**20:** Equipping a home for people with disabilities; Universal design; Features for special needs.

**Safety**
**19:** Planning the landscape; Lighting the outdoor living space.

**20:** A safe home; Preventing accidents; Keeping children safe in your home; Keeping the air safe and clean; Controlling noise pollution; A secure home; Security from carbon monoxide poisoning; Security from fire; Security from home intruders; Equipping a home for people with disabilities; Features for special needs.

**21:** Keeping the home clean and well maintained; Yard maintenance; Making common home repairs.

**Care and Maintenance**
**19:** Planning the landscape; Landscaping for conservation.

**20:** Keeping the air safe and clean; Controlling noise pollution; Equipping a home for people with disabilities.

**21:** Keeping the home clean and well maintained; Interior home maintenance and cleaning; Exterior home maintenance and cleaning; Outdoor and lawn care; Tools for outdoor tasks; Yard maintenance; Making common home repairs; The basic tools; Plumbing repairs; Installing nails and screws; Electrical repairs; Meeting storage needs; Organize for storage; Space savers; Redecorating; Remodeling; Resources for home care; Help with home maintenance.

**New Technology, Trends, and Housing Issues**
**19:** Landscaping for conservation; Water and soil conservation; Energy conservation.

**20:** A safe home; Keeping the air safe and clean; Controlling noise pollution; A secure home; Security from home intruders; Equipping a home for people with disabilities; Universal design.

# Part Six  Progress in Housing

### Forces Affecting Housing
**22:** Recent developments in housing; Automated houses; Housing concerns; Sources of energy; Conserving energy; Innovative solutions in housing.

### Financial and Legal Aspects of Housing
**22:** Housing concerns; Conserving energy; Innovative solutions in housing; Universal design.

### Interior/Exterior Design
**23:** Housing careers in planning, engineering, and design; Entrepreneurial careers in housing and design.

### Safety
**22:** Recent developments in housing; Automated houses; Housing concerns; A clean environment; Solving environmental concerns.

**24:** Staying safety conscious.

### Care and Maintenance
**22:** Recent developments in housing; Automated houses; Conserving energy; A clean environment; Solving environmental concerns; Green buildings.

### New Technology, Trends, and Housing Issues
**22:** Recent developments in housing; Automated houses; Housing concerns; Sources of energy; Conserving energy; A clean environment; Solving environmental concerns; Innovative solutions in housing; Universal design; Green buildings; Planned communities; New living spaces.

**23:** Who provides housing? Entrepreneurial careers in housing and design; Effect of technology on housing careers; Computer usage by housing professionals; Lifelong learning.

### Careers: Options and Preparation
**23:** Who provides housing? Career clusters; Career opportunities in housing; Housing careers in planning, engineering, and design; Housing careers in construction; Housing careers in sales and service; Entrepreneurial careers in housing and design; Housing careers in allied fields; Effect of technology on housing careers; Computer usage by housing professionals; Career levels; Professional positions; Midlevel positions; Entry positions; Career ladders; Lifelong learning.

**24:** Setting career goals; Examining career interests; Determining abilities and aptitudes; The goal-setting process; Making a career plan; Finding a job; Applying for a job; Job application forms; The job interview; Evaluating job offers; Maintaining the job; Work habits; Attitude on the job; Communication skills on the job; Ethical behavior on the job; Interpersonal skills; Leadership skills; Staying safety conscious; Terminating the job; Careers and lifestyle; Career satisfaction and lifestyle; Balancing family and work.

### Leadership and Citizenship
**22:** A clean environment; Solving environmental concerns; Innovative solutions in housing; Planned communities.

**23:** Entrepreneurial careers in housing and design; Career levels.

**24:** Interpersonal skills; Leadership skills; Career satisfaction and lifestyle; Balancing family and work.

# Basic Skills Chart

The chart below identifies activities in the *Student Activity Guide* and the *Teacher's Resources* for *Housing Decisions* that specifically encourage the development of basic skills. The following abbreviations are used in the chart:

- **SAG** designates activities in the *Student Activity Guide* (identified by letter).
- **TR** designates strategies described in the *Teacher's Resources* (referred to by number).
- **Verbal** activities include the following types: role-playing, conducting interviews, making oral reports, debating, and active listening.
- **Reading** activities may involve actual reading inside and outside the classroom. However, many of these activities are designed to improve reading comprehension of the concepts presented in each chapter. Some are designed to improve understanding of vocabulary terms.
- **Writing** activities allow students to practice composition skills, such as letter writing, informative writing, and creative writing.
- **Math/Science** activities require students to use computation skills in solving typical problems they may come across in their everyday living. Any activities related to the sciences are also listed.
- **Analytical** activities involve the higher-order thinking skills of analysis, synthesis, and evaluation. Activities that involve decision making, problem solving, and critical thinking are included in this section.

**Note:** The activities at the end of each chapter in the text (*In Your Community, To Think About,* and *Using Technology*) are meant to promote discussion and use higher-order thinking skills. Therefore, all these activities would fall under the *Verbal* and *Analytical* categories.

|  | **Verbal** | **Reading** | **Writing** | **Math/Science** | **Analytical** |
|---|---|---|---|---|---|
| **Chapter 1** | **SAG:** C, G<br>**TR:** 1, 5-9, 11, 16, 29, 33, 39, 42-48 | **SAG:** A, D, E, H<br>**TR:** 2, 3, 10, 14, 21-23, 30, 34, 37, 40, 51 | **SAG:** A, B, D, E, F, G<br>**TR:** 15-17, 24-28, 31, 32, 35, 36, 49, 50, 52 |  | **SAG:** A, D<br>**TR:** 4, 5, 10, 13, 20, 38, 49 |
| **Chapter 2** | **SAG:** A<br>**TR:** 2, 3, 6, 9-13, 15, 16, 22, 26, 33, 35, 36, 38, 39, 44, 47 | **SAG:** B, C, D<br>**TR:** 1, 3, 5, 6, 10, 13, 27, 28, 30, 31, 39, 40, 46, 47, 54 | **SAG:** B, C, D, E<br>**TR:** 4, 17, 18, 20, 23, 40, 46 | **TR:** 6, 7, 18, 19, 21, 24, 26, 32-37, 41-43 | **TR:** 2, 13, 15, 26, 32, 45, 46, 50, 52, 53 |
| **Chapter 3** | **TR:** 3, 14 | **SAG:** A, B, C, D, F<br>**TR:** 1, 2, 5, 10, 17, 18 | **SAG:** B<br>**TR:** 9, 17 | **SAG:** D | **SAG:** A, E<br>**TR:** 1, 4-8, 11-13, 15 |
| **Chapter 4** | **SAG:** A, F<br>**TR:** 5, 7, 13-15, 23, 25, 28, 32, 34, 36 | **SAG:** D, E, G<br>**TR:** 3, 5, 9, 11, 22, 27, 35, 37, 38 | **SAG:** B, E<br>**TR:** 8, 16, 29, 35 | **TR:** 36 | **SAG:** B, C, D<br>**TR:** 1, 2, 8, 10, 14, 17, 18, 20, 26, 27, 30, 31, 33, 35 |
| **Chapter 5** | **SAG:** A, D<br>**TR:** 1, 3-6, 10, 13, 17, 18, 20, 26, 27, 29, 30, 32, 33, 35, 36 | **SAG:** A, B, C, F<br>**TR:** 1, 2, 6-9, 14-16, 19, 27, 28, 33, 34, 38 | **TR:** 10, 21, 25, 35, 38 | **SAG:** E<br>**TR:** 25, 30 | **TR:** 20, 25, 28 |

| | Verbal | Reading | Writing | Math/Science | Analytical |
|---|---|---|---|---|---|
| Chapter 6 | **TR:** 1, 2, 5-8, 12, 14, 17, 20, 23, 24, 26-30 | **SAG:** A, B, C, D **TR:** 2-4, 10-13, 15, 16, 18, 19, 21, 22, 24, 26 | **SAG:** E **TR:** 6, 7, 10, 21, 24, 30 | **TR:** 24, 26 | **TR:** 24, 26, 30 |
| Chapter 7 | **TR:** 1, 2, 4-9, 14-16, 20-23, 31, 33, 37, 40, 41 | **SAG:** A, B, E **TR:** 3, 5, 6, 9, 16-18, 24, 25, 38 | **TR:** 13, 38, 42 | **SAG:** B **TR:** 2, 12, 19, 34, 35 | **SAG:** C, D **TR:** 1, 12, 25-30, 39, 40, 42 |
| Chapter 8 | **TR:** 1, 4, 5, 7, 11, 12, 14-20, 23-26 | **SAG:** A, B **TR:** 3, 9, 15, 17-19, 26 | **SAG:** A, B **TR:** 2, 9, 11, 22, 26 | **TR:** 13, 23, 24 | **SAG:** C **TR:** 2, 10 |
| Chapter 9 | **TR:** 7, 8, 11, 14, 16-19, 21, 23, 26-29, 33, 38, 41 | **SAG:** B, C, D **TR:** 1-5, 9, 15, 18, 23, 25, 27, 31, 32, 34-37, 39 | **SAG:** A **TR:** 4, 11, 13, 17, 22, 39 | **SAG:** B, C **TR:** 1, 3, 5, 7-10, 13-15, 18-21, 23, 25, 28, 29, 34, 40, 41 | **TR:** 3, 9, 18, 27, 40, 41 |
| Chapter 10 | **TR:** 1, 4, 6, 8, 10, 11, 14, 16, 23, 24 | **SAG:** B, C, D **TR:** 2, 3, 9, 11, 13-15, 18, 21, 22, 26 | **TR:** 3, 25, 26 | **SAG:** A, D **TR:** 17-19 | **SAG:** A, C **TR:** 6, 9, 17, 22 |
| Chapter 11 | **TR:** 1, 4, 6-8, 12, 14-16, 18, 22, 25 | **SAG:** B, D, E **TR:** 6, 7, 9, 21, 25, 26 | **TR:** 23 | **SAG:** A, C, F **TR:** 2, 3, 12-15 | **SAG:** C, F **TR:** 1, 4, 12, 16, 19, 21 |
| Chapter 12 | **TR:** 1, 3, 6, 8, 9, 11, 12, 15-19, 21 | **SAG:** A, B, D **TR:** 2, 3, 5-9, 11, 12, 14, 15, 18 | **TR:** 13, 14 | **SAG:** A **TR:** 5, 18 | **SAG:** B, C, D **TR:** 6-8, 18 |
| Chapter 13 | **TR:** 1, 2, 9-11, 13, 19, 21, 23, 27, 30, 32, 33, 36 | **SAG:** A, B, C, D, E **TR:** 1-6, 9, 10, 14-16, 20-22, 24, 34-36 | **SAG:** A, B, C **TR:** 1, 17, 25, 26, 28, 31, 35, 36 | | **TR:** 1, 9, 11, 16, 19, 24, 26, 32, 36 |
| Chapter 14 | **TR:** 1, 3, 4, 6, 9, 12, 16-18, 21, 23, 24, 26-28 | **SAG:** C **TR:** 3, 6-10, 12, 15, 18, 19, 21, 25, 27, 28 | **SAG:** A, D **TR:** 5, 7, 13 | | **SAG:** A, B, D **TR:** 1, 2, 13, 14, 16, 20, 26 |
| Chapter 15 | **TR:** 2-4, 9, 10, 12-14, 17-21 | **SAG:** A, C, E **TR:** 1-5, 7-9, 13, 14, 16-18, 20, 23-25, 28 | **SAG:** B **TR:** 4, 16, 19, 26, 28 | **TR:** 23, 25 | **SAG:** A, B, D **TR:** 8, 10, 17, 18, 24, 28 |
| Chapter 16 | **TR:** 1-4, 8, 9, 15, 19, 22, 23, 26, 27 | **SAG:** E **TR:** 2, 6, 8, 9, 15, 16, 20, 21, 26, 27 | **SAG:** A, B, C, D, F **TR:** 4, 10, 11, 21, 22, 24 | **SAG:** A, B, C **TR:** 12, 14, 20, 25 | **SAG:** A, B, C, D, F **TR:** 6, 11, 19, 22, 25 |
| Chapter 17 | **TR:** 1-3, 9, 19-21, 23, 28, 32 | **SAG:** B **TR:** 1-5, 9, 10, 12-17, 24, 25, 27, 31 | **SAG:** B, C **TR:** 8, 12, 24, 27, 31 | **TR:** 10-17, 20, 25 | **SAG:** A, C, D, E, F **TR:** 19-21, 30 |

*Introduction* 41

|  | **Verbal** | **Reading** | **Writing** | **Math/Science** | **Analytical** |
|---|---|---|---|---|---|
| **Chapter 18** | **TR:** 1, 2, 4-7, 21, 25, 26, 29, 31, 35 | **SAG:** D, E **TR:** 1-3, 6, 10, 12-15, 19, 23, 24, 35 | **SAG:** A, B, C **TR:** 3, 10, 11, 13, 18, 20, 24, 27, 30, 31, 33, 35 | **TR:** 17, 28, 30 | **SAG:** A, B, C **TR:** 5, 7, 21, 27 |
| **Chapter 19** | **TR:** 1-3, 8, 9, 11, 16-20, 22, 24 | **TR:** 1, 2, 4, 6, 7, 11, 14, 16, 17, 22, 24 | **SAG:** C, D **TR:** 4, 13, 19, 21, 24 | **SAG::** E | **SAG:** A, B, C, E **TR:** 7, 9, 19, 22, 24 |
| **Chapter 20** | **TR:** 1-4, 7, 8, 10, 13, 14, 18, 20, 23, 24 | **SAG:** B, C, E **TR:** 2-4, 6, 8, 10, 13, 14, 17, 19, 22-24 | **SAG:** A **TR:** 6, 7, 11, 18, 22 | | **SAG:** C, D, E **TR:** 3, 8, 11, 17, 23 |
| **Chapter 21** | **TR:** 1-3, 5, 10, 12, 14, 15, 24, 27, 29, 30, 33, 35, 40-42 | **SAG:** B **TR:** 1, 3, 8, 11, 12, 16-20, 22, 26, 34, 36-38, 41, 42 | **SAG:** B, C **TR:** 4, 8-10, 16, 18-20, 26, 37, 39, 42 | **SAG:** B, D **TR:** 5, 6, 10, 15, 17, 23, 28-30, 34 | **SAG:** A, C, D **TR:** 2, 8, 9, 21, 22, 28, 31 |
| **Chapter 22** | **SAG:** A, C **TR:** 1-4, 6-8, 10, 12, 15, 16, 21, 23-28, 30, 33, 34, 36 | **SAG:** B, D, E **TR:** 2-5, 8, 9, 12-14, 18, 19, 26, 27, 30-32, 34 | **SAG:** D **TR:** 1, 5, 12-14, 19, 22 | **SAG:** A, B **TR:** 1, 7, 8, 28, 30, 32, 34 | **SAG:** C **TR:** 8, 12, 18, 20, 25, 28, 30 |
| **Chapter 23** | **TR:** 2, 3, 9, 13, 16, 18, 20, 21, 23 | **SAG:** B, C, D **TR:** 1-4, 7, 12, 13, 15, 17, 19, 21-23 | **SAG:** B **TR:** 4, 6-8, 12, 14, 19, 22 | | **SAG:** A **TR:** 1, 18, 19 |
| **Chapter 24** | **SAG:** B **TR:** 1, 2, 5-7, 9, 12, 14, 18, 19, 24, 27, 29, 31, 32 | **SAG:** D **TR:** 1, 2, 5, 8, 10, 14, 16, 19-21, 26, 33 | **SAG:** C, D **TR:** 1, 5, 6, 8, 10, 11, 13, 19, 20, 22, 25, 27, 29, 30, 33, 34 | **TR:** 17 | **SAG:** A, C, D **TR:** 4, 9, 16, 30, 33 |

# PART 1

# Housing for You

**Goals:** Students will view housing in terms of the satisfaction it provides in meeting human needs. Students will also learn to recognize the many factors influencing housing.

## Bulletin Board

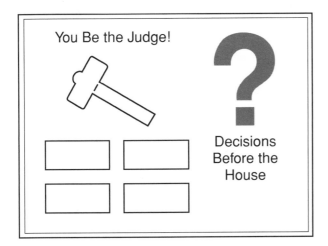

**Title:** *You Be the Judge*

Under the title, diagonally place a large judge's gavel made of construction paper. Below it, place pictures of four different types of housing. On the right, place a large question mark, labeled as shown.

## Teaching Materials

**Text**
Chapters 1 and 2, pages 20-73
*To Know*
*To Review*
*In Your Community*
*To Think About*
*Using Technology*

**Teacher's Resources**
*Getting Acquainted Through Housing*, reproducible master I-A
*Housing for You*, transparency master I-B
*Housing for You*, transparency master overlay I-C

## Introductory Activities

1. *Getting Acquainted Through Housing*, reproducible master I-A, TR. Use this master to help students become acquainted with each other and with various aspects of housing.
2. Introduce students to the glossary and index in the student text. To demonstrate ways of using these resources, assign students various words to find. Have students find the assigned terms in both the glossary and the index to compare the types of information found. You may also introduce some terms that are not listed in the glossary but are included in the index. Have students start card files, with 3-inch x 5-inch cards to list and define important terms related to the study of housing.
3. *Housing for You*, transparency master I-B, TR. Use this transparency to introduce some of the concepts in Chapter 1. Briefly introduce the terms *needs, personal priorities, self-actualization, households, life cycle, lifestyles,* and *quality of life*. Discuss with students how life situations affect housing needs as well as housing satisfaction. (This transparency is also used in Item 4.)
4. *Housing for You*, transparency master overlay I-C, TR. Superimpose this transparency on *Housing for You*, transparency master I-B. Use the combined image to contrast the concepts already covered with those upcoming in Chapter 2. Briefly discuss history, culture, society, environment, economy, technology, and government as they influence housing. Discuss with students how housing has changed because of these various influences.
5. Have students discuss the meaning of the following quote by Winston Churchill: "We shape our buildings, and then they shape us."

Reproducible Master I-A

# Getting Acquainted Through Housing

Name _____ Date _____ Period _____

Match class members with descriptions of their housing. No person's name may appear more than twice in the spaces provided. Try to fill in all the blanks.

| **Classmate's Name** | | **Classmate's Home** |
|---|---|---|
| _____ | 1. | Has a large kitchen. |
| _____ | 2. | Has a fireplace. |
| _____ | 3. | Has a basement. |
| _____ | 4. | Has an attic. |
| _____ | 5. | Has five or more people living in it. |
| _____ | 6. | Is two stories high. |
| _____ | 7. | Is built of stone or brick. |
| _____ | 8. | Is built of wood. |
| _____ | 9. | Has more than two bedrooms. |
| _____ | 10. | Was built by one or more family members. |
| _____ | 11. | Has a two-car garage. |
| _____ | 12. | Faces east. |
| _____ | 13. | Faces west. |
| _____ | 14. | Faces south. |
| _____ | 15. | Faces north. |
| _____ | 16. | Was painted within the past year. |
| _____ | 17. | Is located on a busy street. |
| _____ | 18. | Is more than 15 years old. |
| _____ | 19. | Is less than 3 years old. |
| _____ | 20. | Is an apartment. |

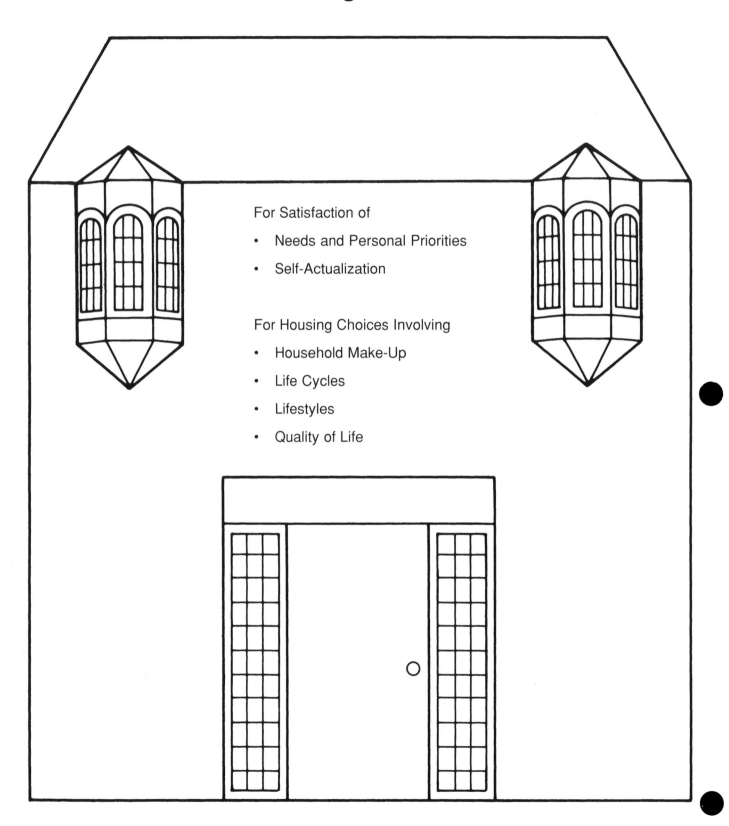

Transparency Master Overlay I-C

# Housing for You

Influences on
Housing

- History
- Culture
- Society
- Environment
- Economy
- Technology
- Government

*Chapter 1   Housing and Human Needs*

CHAPTER 1

# Housing and Human Needs

## Objectives

After studying this chapter, students will be able to

- explain how they interact with their housing.
- show how they move toward self-actualization through housing.
- explain how their housing helps them satisfy needs and personal priorities.
- describe how housing needs change with the life cycle.
- compare housing needs with various lifestyles.
- determine how housing affects the quality of life.
- explain human ecology.

## Bulletin Boards

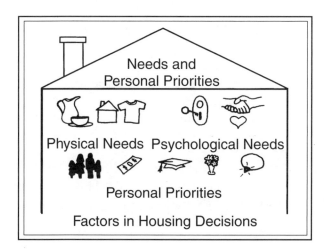

Title: *Needs and Personal Priorities–Factors in Housing Decisions*

Draw the outline of a house. Draw or collect pictures that depict physical and psychological needs and personal priorities. Place these inside the house with the appropriate labels.

Title: *Life Situations: Factors in Housing Decisions*

Under the title, draw or mount pictures that depict households with different lifestyles. Label them and place them inside a large drawing or picture of a house.

Title: *Family Life Cycle and Housing Needs*

Under the title, divide the bulletin board into the sections shown in Figure 1-18 of the text and label them. Ask students to find pictures of housing that would be suitable for families in each of the stages. Place these in the appropriate sections.

## Teaching Materials

**Text**, pages 20-42
   *To Know*
   *To Review*
   *In Your Community*
   *To Think About*
   *Using Technology*

**Student Activity Guide**
   A. *Human Needs*
   B. *Your Housing Needs and Personal Priorities*
   C. *Space and Privacy Needs*
   D. *Lifestyles*
   E. *Households*
   F. *Family Life Cycles*
   G. *Family Stages*
   H. *Human Needs and Housing Crossword Puzzle*

**Teacher's Resources**
   *Who Lives in Your Home?* reproducible master 1-1
   *Maslow's Hierarchy*, color transparency CT-1
   *Maslow's Theory of Human Needs*, transparency master 1-2

*Personal Priorities Relating to Housing*, reproducible master 1-3
*Housing Needs*, reproducible master 1-4
*Types of Households*, color transparency CT-2
*Individual Life Cycle*, transparency master 1-5
*The Family Life Cycle*, color transparency CT-3
*Stages of the Family Life Cycle*, reproducible master 1-6
Chapter 1 Test

# Introductory Activities

1. *Who Lives in Your Home?* reproducible master 1-1, TR. Have each student give his or her survey to an adult to fill out. Ask students to share their findings and help tabulate the results. Refer to the survey findings as you discuss Chapter 1.
2. Have students find and discuss the glossary and/or dictionary definitions of key terms listed in the *To Know* section of the text. Have them add these to their card files.

# Strategies to Reteach, Reinforce, Enrich, and Extend Text Concepts

## People and Their Housing

3. **RT** Have students define the term *near environment* and list the related factors that influence the way they live.
4. **RF** Have each student list ways that people have produced negative results in his or her near environment. Ask students to suggest ways to overcome or reverse these negative effects.
5. **RF** Have students list five ways their feelings are affected by their housing.
6. **RF** Have students discuss how the types of houses and the furnishings inside them influence people's feelings and behavior.
7. **RF** Have students discuss books, television shows, or movies that indicate how housing is used to satisfy people.

## Meeting Needs Through Housing

8. **RT** *Maslow's Hierarchy*, color transparency CT-1, TR. Use this transparency to introduce and discuss Maslow's hierarchy of human needs.
9. **ER** Have students list their physical needs and their psychological needs. Have students compare their lists of needs.
10. **RF** *Maslow's Theory of Human Needs*, transparency master 1-2, TR. Use this master to explain what each level of the pyramid means. Have students brainstorm which levels match the following terms: *air, beauty, economy, family unity, creativity, shelter, food, space, privacy, self-expression, water,* and *rest*.
11. **RT** Have students discuss in pairs why one level of needs must be at least partially met before the next level of needs can be sought. Ask each pair to provide an example, and share these in whole-class discussion.
12. **RF** *Human Needs*, Activity A, SAG. Have students complete the pyramid of human needs. Then have students define each need and explain how they believe housing can help fulfill it.
13. **ER** Have students draw their own pyramids, arranging needs and personal priorities in ways that are logical to them.

## Factors Affecting Housing Choices

14. **RT** Have students define the term *personal priorities*.
15. **RF** Have students list items that some people possess as a result of their personal priorities.
16. **ER** *Personal Priorities Relating to Housing*, reproducible master 1-3, TR. Have students work in small groups to compile a report on how personal priorities relate to housing.
17. **ER** Have students work in small groups to develop a survey form to use with students outside the class. The form should focus on the students' housing-related personal priorities.
18. **RF** Show students slides or pictures of several different types of houses. Have students discuss which needs and personal priorities are satisfied by each type of home.
19. **ER** *Your Housing Needs and Personal Priorities*, Activity B, SAG. Students are

50   Chapter 1   *Housing and Human Needs*

asked to select or draw pictures of rooms that reflect their personal priorities. They are then asked to describe three needs addressed by the rooms in the pictures and identify a personal priority associated with each need.
20. **ER** *Space and Privacy Needs*, Activity C, SAG. Have students interview people of various ages about their needs for personal space. After comparing results, have students draw some conclusions about how age, hobbies, interests, and family size affect the needs for personal space.
21. **RT** Have students explain the difference between the terms *household* and *family* as defined in the chapter. When might a household not be a family?
22. **RF** Ask students to describe how housing costs and a household's financial resources influence the housing options available.
23. **RF** Ask students to list all the roles held by each person in their household and reflect on how these roles influence the person's housing needs.
24. **RF** Have students write a paragraph describing how changes in roles over time can affect a person's housing needs.
25. **RF** Have students select pictures from magazines and use other materials to create collages that depict certain lifestyles. Students will summarize the main focus of the lifestyle shown. Have students share with the class why they included certain aspects.
26. **ER** *Lifestyles*, Activity D, SAG. Students are asked to clip and mount two housing advertisements that reflect two different lifestyles. For each ad, students should identify and describe the lifestyle represented. Then they should list the advantages and disadvantages of each lifestyle.
27. **ER** Have students view pictures of different house exteriors and describe the types of households that might live in each. Try to have students identify the life cycle and lifestyle of the household within. Use pictures from magazines, your personal photo/slide collection, or the text.
28. **ER** Ask each student to write a paragraph describing the lifestyle of his or her household and explaining how this lifestyle affects housing needs.
29. **EX** Invite a guest who has traveled to various parts of the country or world to speak to the class about differences in housing. Have the guest speaker discuss how differences in housing are affected by varying lifestyles.

## Housing Needs Vary

30. **RF** Have students identify different types of households and explain how housing can satisfy each type.
31. **EX** Have students list some possible types of households other than those described in the text. Have students explain what the housing needs of those households might be.
32. **ER** *Housing Needs*, reproducible master 1-4, TR. Students are asked to list possible housing needs of various types of living units.
33. **ER** Have students visit a dwelling for group living, such as a dorm, camp, or nursing home. Have them describe how the living arrangements differ from their own homes. Ask them to describe the private areas and the shared living areas. Have students tell why they would or would not want to live in the group dwelling.
34. **RT** *Types of Households*, color transparency CT-2, TR. Use this transparency to review the various types of households.
35. **ER** Have each student draw a diagram showing the size and composition of his or her household. Underneath, have students write ways in which their housing fits the size and composition of their households.
36. **ER** *Households*, Activity E, SAG. Students are asked to draw or mount two cartoon examples of households. Underneath each, students are to describe the members of each household.
37. **RT** Have students define the term *individual life cycle*.
38. **RF** *Individual Life Cycle*, transparency master 1-5, TR. Use the transparency to show students one way of representing the different stages of life. Point out the relative length of each stage for the average person. Have students list possible substages for the *Infancy*, *Childhood*, and *Adulthood* stages.

39. **RF** Have students name the stage and substage of the individual life cycle through which they are passing. Then ask students to think of someone they know in each life stage and substage.
40. **RT** Have students define the term *family life cycle*.
41. **RT** *The Family Life Cycle*, color transparency CT-3, TR. Use this transparency to discuss the stages and substages of the family life cycle.
42. **RF** Have students name the stage(s) and substage(s) of the family life cycle through which their households are passing.
43. **ER** *Family Life Cycle*, reproducible master 1-6, TR. Students are asked to show—through drawings or mounted pictures—how one aspect of housing changes during the family life cycle. Some possibilities are the beds, clothes, storage, chairs, or size of house.
44. **RF** *Family Life Cycles*, Activity F, SAG. Students are asked to complete an illustration of the family life cycle by listing the substages. They are then asked to describe the housing needs of each stage.
45. **EX** *Family Stages*, Activity G, SAG. Each student is asked to interview one or two members of a family to learn about the family's stage and housing needs. Students should record the information and speculate on how the family's housing needs might change in the future.
46. **EX** Have students describe how the use of a spare room may change, depending on whether the household includes: small children, teenagers, people with hobbies, or retirees.

## Housing and the Quality of Life

47. **RF** Have students discuss the term *quality of life* and relate the meaning to housing for individuals and society as a whole.
48. **ER** Arrange a field trip for students to visit a model home. Have students try to determine what effect the home may have on the quality of life of its future residents.
49. **EX** Ask each student to develop a written plan for one or more ways to use housing to improve the quality of life for his or her household. Have students implement their plans, if possible, and report their progress to the class.
50. **ER** Have students write a paper explaining how human ecology will affect the quality of life for future societies.

## Chapter Review

51. **RF** *Human Needs and Housing Crossword Puzzle*, Activity H, SAG. Have students fill in the crossword puzzle to review important concepts and terms in the chapter.
52. **ER** Have each student write a story titled "My Home Talks." The story will be written as though the student's home is telling the story, explaining who lives in it and how it meets the needs, roles, and personal priorities of the residents.

# Answer Key

## Text

### *To Review*, page 40

1. near
2. A
3. (List three:) shelter, food, water, rest
4. security, love/acceptance, esteem, and self-actualization
5. as a result of past experiences, people known, and activities
6. (Student response. See pages 25-27 of the text.)
7. (List five:) living alone, having a private room, having a private space in a room, doing solitary activities, doing activities that require concentration, setting a chair apart from the other furnishings, using a sound to drown out all other sounds
8. (Student response. See pages 28-29 of the text.)
9. (Student response.)
10. household
11. several generations living together, such as grandparents, parents, and children; members of the same generation living together, such as brothers and sisters
12. infancy, childhood, youth, and adulthood
13. (Student response. See pages 36-37 of the text.)

14. In the beginning stage, the couple is establishing a home and a new life with each other. In the aging stage, the couple has an established home and home life, and probably a family, but eventually one spouse will be alone after the death of the other.

## Student Activity Guide

### *Human Needs,* Activity A

1. physical needs
2. security
3. love and acceptance
4. esteem
5. self-actualization
   (Definitions and explanations are student response.)

### *Family Life Cycles,* Activity F

beginning stage—married couple, couple making adjustments
childbearing stage—childbearing, caring for young children
parenting stage—school-age children, teenagers
launching stage—children leave home
midyears stage—couple is alone again
aging stage—retirement, one spouse is left alone after death of other spouse
   (Housing needs of each stage are student response.)

### *Human Needs and Housing Crossword Puzzle,* Activity H

## Teacher's Resources
### Chapter 1 Test

1. B
2. C
3. A
4. L
5. K
6. F
7. E
8. I
9. J
10. G
11. T
12. T
13. T
14. F
15. F
16. T
17. T
18. T
19. T
20. F
21. F
22. F
23. B
24. C
25. B
26. B
27. C
28. B
29. D
30. A
31. B
32. A
33. C
34. D
35. B
36. A
37. B
38. D
39. C
40. D

41. (List three. Student response. See pages 20-27 of the text.)
42. Personal priorities determine how the needs are met.
43. (Student response. See pages 30-31 of the text.)
44. (List four:) single-person, single-parent family, nuclear family, extended family, stepfamily (Student response for examples. See pages 30-34 of the text.)
45. beginning stage, childbearing stage, parenting stage, launching stage, midyears stage, aging stage (Examples are student response. See pages 34-37 of the text.)

Reproducible Master 1-1

# Who Lives in Your Home?

**Name** _____ **Date** _____ **Period** _____

Give the following survey to someone to fill out. Then bring the completed survey to class.

••••••••••••••••••••••••••••••••••••••••••••••••••••••••••••••••••••

**Directions:** Please complete the following survey about the people in your home. The information will be used in class to establish general housing trends. Please do not identify yourself on this form.

1. How many people live in your home? _____
2. How many people in your home are in the following age ranges?
    - _____ 0-5
    - _____ 6-12
    - _____ 13-18
    - _____ 19-29
    - _____ 30-49
    - _____ 50 or older
3. What are the occupations of the wage earners living in your home?
   _____
   _____

4. List some of the leisure activities of the people living in your home.
   _____
   _____
   _____
   _____
   _____

5. How would you rank the following priorities related to housing? Rank from high (1) to low (10).
    - _____ Security
    - _____ Self-expression
    - _____ Privacy
    - _____ Beauty
    - _____ Social interaction
    - _____ Esteem
    - _____ Family unity
    - _____ Prestige
    - _____ Economy
    - _____ Creativity

# Maslow's Theory of Human Needs

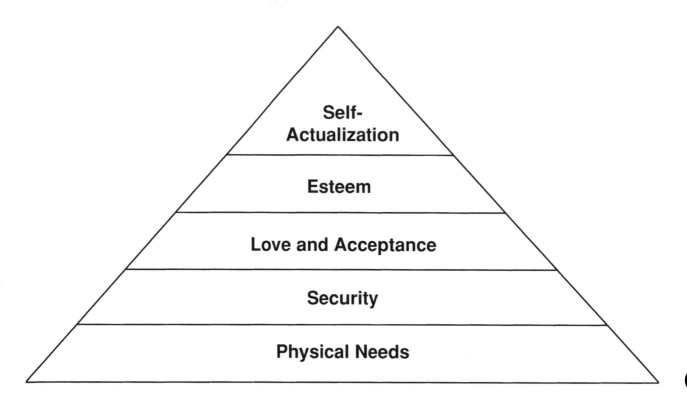

## Explanation

1. **Physical needs.** Your physical needs, such as food, water, shelter, and clothing, must be at least partially satisfied before you can think about anything else.
2. **Security.** Next, you need to feel safe in your surroundings and know what to expect. You need protection from physical harm and economic disaster.
3. **Love and acceptance.** At this point, you want to gain affection. You need to be praised and accepted by others. A small failure can make you feel rejected as a person. You need much support, assurance, and personal warmth.
4. **Esteem.** Not only do you want to be liked, but you also want to be respected. In this way, you gain confidence and feel necessary in the world.
5. **Self-actualization.** To reach this level, all other needs must be fulfilled to some degree. You feel a need to develop your full potential. You learn because you want to be a "well-rounded" person. You have pride and self-respect. You can show individuality despite social pressures. You have your own opinions and are able to express them.

# Personal Priorities Relating to Housing

Name _____ Date _____ Period _____

**Group Members:**
_____
_____

1. List the personal priorities related to housing that any two members consider important.

   _____
   _____
   _____
   _____
   _____
   _____
   _____
   _____

2. Evaluate the list and choose the 10 personal priorities your group considers most important. (These priorities do not need to be ranked.)

   _____           _____
   _____           _____
   _____           _____
   _____           _____
   _____           _____

3. Explain why your group decided on this list of personal priorities.

   _____
   _____
   _____
   _____
   _____
   _____

Reproducible Master 1-4

# Housing Needs

Name _____ Date _____ Period _____

Complete the chart by providing your thoughts on the housing needs of the individuals or groups listed below. Compare your answers to those of your classmates.

| Household | Housing Needs |
|---|---|
| Young single (under 30) | |
| Older single adult (over 40) | |
| Young couple (planning for children) | |
| Older couple (with an ailing grandparent) | |
| Nuclear family with one-year-old twins | |
| Single-parent family with two children in college | |
| Extended family with four young children and two grandparents | |
| Active retirees | |
| Inactive retirees | |

Chapter 1   *Housing and Human Needs*

# Individual Life Cycle

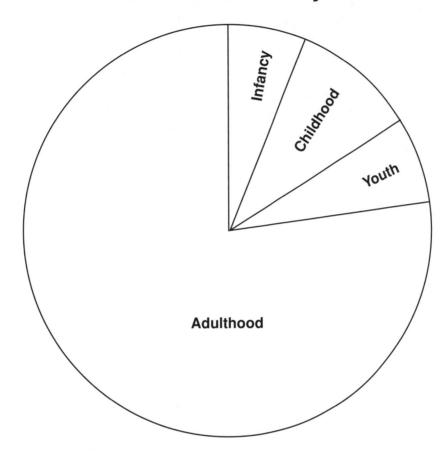

| Infancy | Childhood | Youth | Adulthood |
|---|---|---|---|
|  |  | Preteens<br>Early teens<br>Middle teens<br>Late teens |  |

Reproducible Master 1-6

# Stages of the Family Life Cycle

Name _____ Date _____ Period _____

Use drawings or mount pictures to show how one aspect of housing changes during the family life cycle.

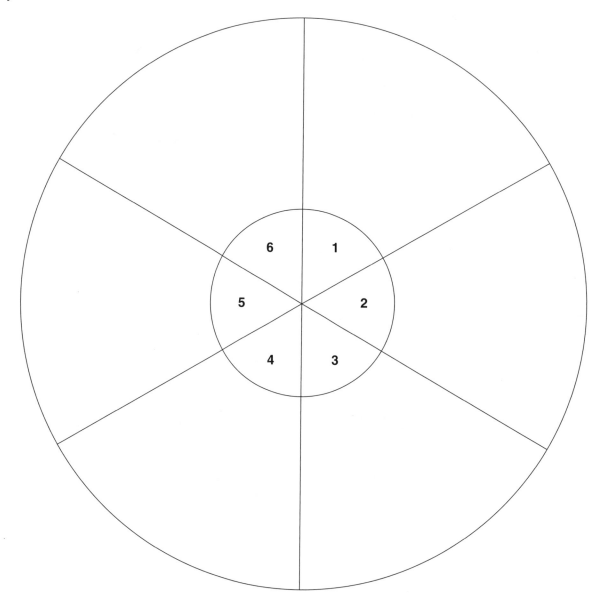

**Stages**

1. Beginning
2. Childbearing
3. Parenting
4. Launching
5. Midyears
6. Aging

Reproducible Test Master

# Housing and Human Needs

Name _____

Date _____ Period _____ Score _____

**Chapter 1 Test**

❑ Matching: Match the following terms and identifying phrases.

_____ 1. Having the respect, admiration, and high regard of others.

_____ 2. Group of people living together and sharing the same dwelling.

_____ 3. Having new or original ideas.

_____ 4. Highest level of human needs.

_____ 5. Patterns of behavior that people display.

_____ 6. A way of life.

_____ 7. Series of stages through which an individual or family passes during a lifetime.

_____ 8. Strong beliefs or ideas about what is important.

_____ 9. The degree of satisfaction obtained from life.

_____ 10. The immediate housing environment.

A. creativity
B. esteem
C. household
D. human ecology
E. life cycle
F. lifestyle
G. near environment
H. needs
I. personal priorities
J. quality of life
K. roles
L. self-actualization
M. self-expression

❑ True/False: Circle T if the statement is true or F if the statement is false.

T  F  11. Housing environments influence the feelings and behavior of humans.

T  F  12. All humans have the same basic needs.

T  F  13. Archaeologists are social scientists who study ancient cultures by unearthing dwelling places of past civilizations.

T  F  14. Air and food are psychological needs.

T  F  15. People who consider privacy a high personal priority like to have many areas of the house designed for group living.

T  F  16. Housing can help satisfy needs for self-expression, beauty, and esteem.

T  F  17. Self-actualization is the highest level of human need.

T  F  18. A household can contain one person or a group of people.

T  F  19. Every person is in some stage of the individual life cycle.

T  F  20. As a family moves from one stage of the family life cycle to another, needs for living space stay the same.

T  F  21. A life cycle is a living pattern or way of life.

T  F  22. Adults may have several roles but teenagers have just one.

(Continued)

Reproducible Test Master

❏ Multiple Choice: Choose the best response. Write the letter in the space provided.

_____ 23. A near environment is best described as _____.
   A. a group of people who live near you
   B. one small part of your total surroundings
   C. the relationship between people and their homes
   D. the total surroundings

_____ 24. An example of a physical need is _____.
   A. a vacation home
   B. entertainment
   C. food
   D. transportation

_____ 25. An example of a psychological need is _____.
   A. air
   B. self-esteem
   C. shelter
   D. water

_____ 26. Something a person believes and considers important is called a _____.
   A. basic need
   B. personal priority
   C. physical need
   D. psychological need

_____ 27. _____ helps an individual feel safe and protected.
   A. Acceptance
   B. Esteem
   C. Security
   D. Space

_____ 28. If money for housing is extremely limited, people often place a special emphasis on _____.
   A. basic needs
   B. creativity
   C. esteem
   D. space

_____ 29. Displaying one's own personality and style preference through housing is best described as _____.
   A. creativity
   B. self-actualization
   C. self-esteem
   D. self-expression

_____ 30. When a person expresses unique ideas to others, this is an example of _____.
   A. creativity
   B. self-actualization
   C. self-esteem
   D. self-expression

_____ 31. Being respected and admired by others helps fulfill the need for _____.
   A. economy
   B. esteem
   C. privacy
   D. security

_____ 32. Self-actualization is best described as _____.
   A. becoming the best person you can be
   B. being held in high regard
   C. having new or original ideas
   D. showing your true personality

(Continued)

_____ 33. A _____ includes at least one spouse who already has children.
   A. extended family
   B. nuclear family
   C. stepfamily
   D. None of the above.

_____ 34. An extended family may include _____.
   A. aunts and uncles
   B. cousins
   C. grandparents
   D. All of the above.

_____ 35. The family life cycle includes the _____ stage.
   A. adult
   B. launching
   C. infancy
   D. All of the above.

_____ 36. All of the following are true about a household's need for space *except* _____.
   A. Furnishings have no effect on the perception of space in a room.
   B. Having adequate space helps people avoid feeling crowded.
   C. Having too much space can make people feel lonely.
   D. Hobbies and activities can influence the need for space.

_____ 37. Which of the following offers the most privacy?
   A. Having separate bedrooms.
   B. Living in a single-person household.
   C. Separating chairs in the family room.
   D. Using sound to block out the sounds of others.

_____ 38. Which of the following influences lifestyle?
   A. everyday activities
   B. income
   C. occupation
   D. All of the above.

_____ 39. The term used to express the degree of satisfaction obtained from life is _____.
   A. human ecology
   B. self-esteem
   C. quality of life
   D. social status

_____ 40. The study of humans and their environment is called _____.
   A. astrology
   B. geography
   C. geology
   D. human ecology

❑ Essay Questions: Provide complete responses to the following questions or statements.

41. Give three examples of ways in which housing can meet human needs.

42. Explain how needs and personal priorities relate to each other when making housing decisions.

43. Explain how a person's roles can influence his or her housing needs.

44. Identify four types of households. Explain how housing needs vary with each type.

45. List the stages in the family life cycle. Give an example of how housing needs change for each stage.

# CHAPTER 2
# Influences on Housing

## Objectives

After studying this chapter, students will be able to

- relate historical events to housing.
- describe various cultures and housing characteristics.
- determine the relationship between societal changes and housing.
- analyze concerns about environmental aspects of housing.
- relate the effects of economy and housing on each other.
- summarize the impact of technology on housing.
- identify the role of government in housing decisions.

## Bulletin Boards

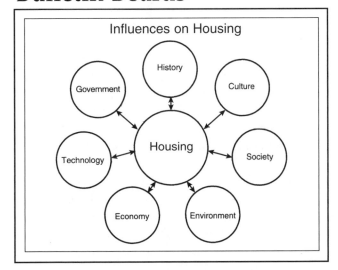

Title: *Influences on Housing*

Make eight circles of different colored construction paper, with one circle slightly larger than the others. Place the word *Housing* on the larger circle. Place each of the following terms on separate circles: *History, Culture, Society, Environment, Economy, Technology,* and *Government*. Arrange the circles and place arrows as shown. Have students discuss how each influence affects housing as well as how housing affects each influence. (If space permits, use large circles so students can develop a collage within each.)

Title: *Housing and the Environment Affect Each Other*

For the background, use the color of the circle labeled *Environment* in Bulletin Board I. Draw an equilateral triangle with each side indicating a type of environment (natural, constructed, or behavioral). Inside the triangle, write *Housing and the Environment*. Have students discuss each type of environment, its relationship to housing, and the interaction of the environments. (See pages 58-61 of the text.)

## Teaching Materials

**Text,** pages 43-73
 *To Know*
 *To Review*
 *In Your Community*
 *To Think About*
 *Using Technology*
**Student Activity Guide**
  A. *Housing in My Community*
  B. *Culture and Society Influence Housing*
  C. *Housing Environments*
  D. *Housing and the Economy*
  E. *Filling a House with High Tech*
**Teacher's Resources**
 *Influences on Housing,* color transparency CT-4
 *Environment Chains,* transparency master 2-1
 *Trivia Game Review,* reproducible master 2-2
 Chapter 2 Test

## Introductory Activities

1. *Influences on Housing,* color transparency CT-4, TR. Use this transparency to introduce the concepts in Chapter 2.
2. Have students brainstorm how each of the influences in Bulletin Board I affects and is affected by housing.

3. Have students find and discuss the glossary and/or dictionary definitions of key terms listed in the *To Know* section of the text. Have them add these to their card files.

# Strategies to Reteach, Reinforce, Enrich, and Extend Text Concepts

## Historical Influences on Housing

4. **ER** Have students prepare one-page reports on one type of Native American housing—Eskimo igloo or seal or bearskin tent; Chippewa bark tent; Algonquin bark wigwam; Pueblo adobe apartment; Chinook driftwood lodge; or another basic type. Have students research the geographic location, climate, food, and water supplies. Reports should contain information about the cultural and societal influences on the housing, the materials and technology used, and how the houses were built.
5. **EX** Have students find or draw pictures depicting typical housing from 1600 to the present. Have students mount the pictures in historical order on a bulletin board. The pictures should form a collage to represent the history of housing. (Note: Some will fit in more than one place.)
6. **EX** Have students find information about some aspect of lighting in early homes. Suggested topics include types of candles used, gas and oil lamps, and the beginning of electrical lighting. Have students report to the class.
7. **ER** Have students draw the typical lot and layout of the tenement houses described on page 47 of the text. Have students determine the space a two-room apartment would occupy with 116 apartments in a building.
8. **EX** *Housing in My Community*, Activity A, SAG. Invite a city planner and/or local historian to discuss growth in your community. Students are to ask questions regarding the topics listed. Then students are asked to write a summary of the speaker's comments.
9. **ER** Plan a field trip to local historical houses. Observe facilities for cooking, bathing, sleeping, and socializing. Discuss modifications made since the houses were constructed.

## Cultural Influences on Housing

10. **RF** Have students look at the illustrations in the chapter and discuss the ways culture influences housing designs.
11. **RF** Discuss ways religion and customs have influenced housing.
12. **ER** Show students a map of Europe. Compare the cultures of the North and West with those of the South and East. Tell how cultures influence housing in the areas.
13. **EX** Have students choose an activity that takes place in the home. Research how people in various parts of the world or nation differ in the way they carry out this activity. Have students report to the class.

## Societal Influences on Housing

14. **RF** *Culture and Society Influence Housing*, Activity B, SAG. Students are asked to describe various cultural and societal influences on housing.
15. **EX** Have students find U.S. Census Bureau information about population increase, types of housing, and household size and composition. List the implications related to housing needs. Discuss the effects that trends in marriage and divorce rates, family size, and life expectancy have on housing.
16. **RF** Discuss the advantages and disadvantages of having homogeneous populations living in close proximity, such as housing developments for elderly people, low-income neighborhoods, and apartment buildings for singles.
17. **ER** Have students look at pictures of houses and write stories about the people they imagine living there.
18. **ER** Have each student keep a journal for a week to record how much leisure time they have and how it is spent. Have them determine how their housing affects their leisure time.
19. **RF** Have students list the number of times they have moved and determine the

average for the class. Compare it to the national average given in the chapter. Also determine whether the moves have been short or long distances.

20. **ER** Divide a bulletin board or poster in two columns. Label the left column *Cultural and Societal Influences* and the other column *Housing Characteristics*. In the first column, have students list or mount pictures of 10 cultural and societal influences. In the second column, have students mount pictures of resulting housing characteristics.

## Environmental Influences on Housing

21. **RF** Have students discuss the natural environment by looking at a map depicting climates.
22. **RF** Have students describe housing in terms of its natural, constructed, and behavioral environments.
23. **ER** *Environment Chains*, transparency master 2-1, TR. Have students make their own chains showing how one type of environment affects another.
24. **ER** Have students make a poster or model to show how the natural, constructed, and behavioral environments affect one another.
25. **RF** *Housing Environments*, Activity C, SAG. Students are asked to evaluate natural, constructed, and behavioral environments using the form provided.
26. **EX** Have students investigate and report on local housing laws designed to protect the environment.
27. **EX** Have students organize a project to improve the housing environment in your community.
28. **EX** Using Bulletin Board II, *Housing and the Environment Affect Each Other*, have students determine if the various housing environments exert equal influence. Ask students to redraw the triangle to show the degree of influence on housing from each environment.

## Economic Influences on Housing

29. **ER** *Housing and the Economy*, Activity D, SAG. Students are asked to brainstorm and list all of the jobs involved in building, selling, and decorating a home.
30. **EX** Have students find magazine and newspaper articles about ways people cope when housing becomes too expensive. Suggested topics include: smaller houses, manufactured housing, fewer luxuries, and shared housing.
31. **RF** Have students make mini-collages on large paper circles that match the color of the *Economy* circle in Bulletin Board I. The collages should show ways the economy influences housing. (Save for use in Item 52.)
32. **RF** Have students list and discuss factors in the general economy that affect housing.
33. **EX** Use the most recent gross national product (GNP) report and find the impact of the housing industry. Discuss housing costs.
34. **ER** Make photocopies of a federal income tax form. Have students find and discuss the items that are related to housing costs.
35. **ER** Invite a real estate agent to speak to the class. Ask for estimates of a median-priced house in 1960, 1970, 1980, 1990, 2000, and today. Using Census Bureau reports, discuss the median income in those years. Compare the cost of housing and the ability to pay for it at the different times.

## Technological Influences on Housing

36. **RF** Have students discuss how technological advancements have improved housing.
37. **RF** Have students make mini-collages on large paper circles that match the color of the *Technology* circle in Bulletin Board I. The collages should show ways that technology influences housing. (Save for use in Item 52.)
38. **RF** Have students discuss which housing technologies use methods similar to basket weaving and pottery making.
39. **RF** Have students look through housing magazines and locate advertisements for new materials used in housing or new uses for older materials. Have students discuss the advantages and possible disadvantages of the products found.
40. **ER** Have students research an application of CADD for interior or exterior

design and write a report on their findings. Students should focus on applications that improve the efficiency of housing.
41. **RF** *Filling a House with High Tech*, Activity E, SAG. Have students mount pictures of high-tech products in the space provided and explain how the products can improve the quality of housing.
42. **EX** Visit a manufactured housing dealer. Observe materials and construction techniques used. Indicate where synthetic materials have replaced natural materials and discuss the reasons. List technology measures that make construction easier and faster.
43. **ER** Have an architect or a student familiar with computer design demonstrate how CADD equipment is used in designing a house.

## Governmental Influences on Housing

44. **RF** Discuss ways housing legislation is designed to help people face circumstances such as racial discrimination, low income, natural catastrophes, physical disabilities, or homelessness.
45. **ER** Have students study a local zoning map to see which areas are industrial, commercial, residential, or other. Have students locate their homes, school, and other familiar places on the map.
46. **ER** Have students study Appendix A on housing legislation in the text. Have each student select one piece of legislation to research and report. Ask them to provide the purpose, jurisdiction, and provisions of the Act. Have students explore the effect their respective legislation has had in the community.
47. **EX** Have students find out what laws have been enacted to provide access to public buildings for people with physical disabilities. Discuss if the same laws are applicable to private housing.
48. **RF** Have students make mini-collages on large paper circles that match the color of the *Government* circle in Bulletin Board I. The collages should show ways that government influences housing. (Save for use in Item 52.)
49. **ER** Invite a local government official to speak to the class about the housing agencies represented in the community and the services performed.
50. **EX** Attend a meeting of a local zoning board to see the processes involved in regulating housing.
51. **ER** Invite a legislator to class to explain how housing laws are passed and how individuals and community groups can influence legislation.
52. **EX** Have students compare the mini-collages saved from Items 31, 37, and 48. Have students determine which areas of influence seem to be the greatest and create circles of various sizes to indicate the differences.

## Chapter Review

53. **EX** Have students find photographs of houses where their parents and grandparents grew up. Have students point out the differences between these houses and modern houses. Identify the historical, cultural, societal, environmental, economical, technological, and governmental influences.
54. **RF** *Trivia Game Review*, reproducible master 2-2, TR. Have teams of students try to provide as many correct questions as possible to the answer cards. The cards ask questions on the seven basic areas of influence affecting housing.

# Answer Key

## Text

### *To Review*, pages 71-72

1. (List three:) rock overhang or cliff, hut, tepee, wigwam, adobe
2. copied Native American dwellings
3. because it used tree logs, which were common in the Northeast and many other parts of the country
4. the search for jobs during the Industrial Revolution
5. (List two:) a housing shortage, substandard housing, crowded homes in high density areas
6. tenement houses—small, crowded, multi-story buildings originally built without windows, toilets, and running water; row

houses—a group of more spacious dwellings connected by common sidewalls
7. (List three:) Industrial Revolution, World War I, the Great Depression, World War II
8. The towns combine residences and commercial areas within walking distance. They also produce most of the energy needed and/or use minimum natural resources.
9. (List one:) Doors on Navajo and Crow Indian dwellings face east. European settlers desired home ownership. Early colonists copied styles of their homelands. Spanish settlers copied mission architecture.
10. (List three:) size, composition, ages, disabilities and other special needs, income, mobility
11. (List two:) hearing loss, sight loss, loss of physical abilities, sensitivity to temperature changes
12. because housing costs are rising faster than income, making single-family houses less affordable
13. It influences the type of housing selected such as housing with on-site recreational facilities, or with low- versus high-maintenance requirements.
14. four
15. constructed environment
16. a positive impact
17. supply and demand, which is the number of existing houses versus the number needed by the population
18. (List two:) create designs, change plans, conserve materials, improve energy efficiency, meet client needs and desires
19. (List two:) makes policy concerning housing; helps certain groups get affordable housing; insures housing loans; promotes a decent, safe, and sanitary home and suitable living environment for every American

## Student Activity Guide

### Culture and Society Influence Housing, Activity B

1. Doors faced east.
2. Views contrasted to those of Native Americans.
3. Architecture was copied in Spanish houses.
4. Settlers copied houses from their homelands.
5. Less space is needed.
6. Housing developments focus on the specific needs of singles.
7. Housing needs change.
8. Modifications are necessary to address their needs.
9. Affordable housing is difficult for many.
10. Houses need to have time-saving conveniences and features.
11. Hobby rooms, swimming pools, and tennis courts are added.
12. People change housing often.

### Housing Environments, Activity C

1. B
2. N
3. C
4. B
5. N
6. B
7. B
8. C
9. B
10. N

(Part 2 is student response.)

## Teacher's Resources

### Trivia Game Review, reproducible master 2-2

#### C—Culture
C1. What is *culture*?
C2. What are *hogans*?
C3. What is *common property*?
C4. What is *private ownership*?
C5. What is *east*?
C6. What is *dirt*?
C7. What is *typical of Spanish architecture*?
C8. What is *wood*?
C9. What is *a cliff dweller*?
C10. Who are *the Hispanic*?

#### EC—Economy
EC1. What are *the production and consumption of goods and services*?
EC2. What are *resources*?
EC3. What are *housing starts*?
EC4. What is *two million*?
EC5. What is *the housing industry*?
EC6. What is *the housing market*?
EC7. What is *gross domestic product*?
EC8. What is *mortgage interest rates*?

Chapter 2   Influences on Housing   69

EC9. What is *one-third*?
EC10. What is *housing*?

**EN—Environment**
EN1. What is *environment*?
EN2. What is *natural environment*?
EN3. What is *climate*?
EN4. What is *topography*?
EN5. Who is *Frank Lloyd Wright*?
EN6. What is *the constructed environment*?
EN7. What is *dysfunctional*?
EN8. What is *a chain reaction*?
EN9. What are *human resources*?
EN10. What are *elements of the natural environment*?

**G—Government**
G1. What are *federal, state, and local*?
G2. What is *colonial times*?
G3. What are *zoning regulations*?
G4. What are *Uniform Building Codes*?
G5. What is *the U.S. Department of Housing and Urban Development*?
G6. What are *building codes*?
G7. What is a *residential zone*?
G8. What are *rent supplements*?
G9. What are *the Environmental Protection Agency (EPA) and the Consumer Product Safety Commission (CPSC)*?
G10. What is *air and water quality*?

**H—History**
H1. Who are *Native Americans*?
H2. What are *caves and dugouts*?
H3. What are *tepees and wigwams*?
H4. What is *a house raising*?
H5. What is *the log cabin*?
H6. Who are *agrarians*?
H7. What is *density*?
H8. What is a *census*?
H9. What are *tract houses*?
H10. What is *a new town*?

**S—Society**
S1. What is *two*?
S2. What is *the single-person household*?
S3. Who are *baby boomers*?
S4. Who are *people with disabilities*?
S5. What is *middle income*?
S6. What is *dual income*?
S7. What is *demographics*?
S8. What is *four*?
S9. What is *the Sunbelt*?
S10. What is *a mobile society*?

**T—Technology**
T1. What is *farming*?
T2. What is *technology*?
T3. What is *the Industrial Revolution*?
T4. What is *the railroad*?
T5. What is *a computer*?
T6. What is *the microwave oven*?
T7. What is *computer-aided drafting and design*?
T8. Who are *architects and interior designers*?
T9. What is *high tech*?
T10. Who are *cave dwellers*?

## Chapter 2 Test

1. B
2. F
3. C
4. D
5. K
6. E
7. J
8. A
9. H
10. I
11. T
12. F
13. F
14. T
15. F
16. F
17. T
18. T
19. T
20. T
21. B
22. C
23. D
24. C
25. D
26. A
27. B
28. B
29. D
30. C
31. D
32. B
33. C
34. C
35. A

36. (List three:) smaller households, increase in single-person households, fewer married couples owning houses, increasing divorce rate, more people postponing marriage for careers, an aging population, more people with physical disabilities
37. natural environment, constructed environment, behavioral environment (Examples are student response.)
38. (List four. Student response.)
39. (List three:) physically disabled, elderly, low income, homeless

Transparency Master 2-1

# Environment Chains

**Name** _____ **Date** _____ **Period** _____

In the two empty chains below, give two different examples of how one environment affects another. (The first chain is provided as an example.)

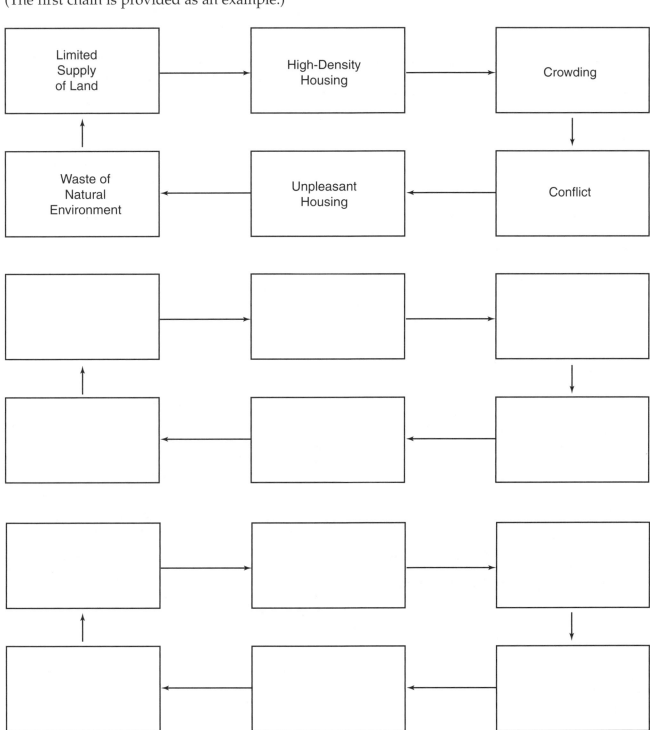

Chapter 2  *Influences on Housing*  71

Reproducible Master 2-2

# Trivia Game Review

Photocopy and cut "cards" apart on dotted lines. Provide separate, labeled containers for each category and place cards in the corresponding containers. (The game can be played with a few categories or with all seven categories.) The class will divide into two or more teams, with each choosing a captain. Captains will serve as spokespersons for their teams. A team will take its turn by its captain drawing an answer card from the category selected. After conferring with team members, the captain should respond in the form of a question. A limit may be set on the amount of time allowed to respond. If the team responds correctly, it keeps the card. If incorrectly, the card is placed back in the container. A team will continue drawing cards until a question is missed. Then the next team repeats the process. The object is to end the game with the most cards.

## Trivia Cards

### C–Culture

C1. The beliefs, social customs, and traits of a group of people.

C2. Navajo Dwellings made of logs and mud.

C3. View of Native Americans that land belongs to everyone.

C4. Type of ownership Europeans sought in North America.

C5. Direction that the door faced in Navajo dwellings.

C6. Floor types of early housing.

C7. Red tile roofs.

C8. Traditional building material of the Pilgrims' homeland.

C9. The Native Americans who dwelled in cliffs or rock overhangs.

C10. They settled in the South and Southwest.

(Continued)

Reproducible Master 2-2 (Continued)

| EC–Economy | EN–Environment |
|---|---|
| EC1. Two basic economic influences on housing. | EN1. The condition, objects, places, and people around you. |
| EC2. Objects, qualities, and personal strengths that can be used to reach goals. | EN2. Environment provided by nature. |
| EC3. The term for the number of houses being built in a year. | EN3. Weather conditions in a region. |
| EC4. Average number of housing starts in a year. | EN4. The lay of the land. |
| EC5. Type of industry that employs planners, developers, and builders. | EN5. Architect who designed homes that visually fit with their natural environment. |
| EC6. Term to describe the transfer of dwellings from producers to consumers. | EN6. An environment changed by human effort. |
| EC7. Value of all goods and services produced in a country. | EN7. Term to describe a negative behavioral environment. |
| EC8. An aspect of home mortgages that seems to increase at the same rate as inflation. | EN8. Result of one environment affecting another. |
| EC9. The portion of income that the average family pays for housing. | EN9. Resources such as intelligence, talent, and energy. |
| EC10. The first major sector of the economy to normally rebound after an economic slump. | EN10. Land, water, trees, and items in nature. |

(Continued)

Reproducible Master 2-2 (Continued)

| G–Government | H–History |
|---|---|
| G1. Levels at which government influences housing. | H1. They were here before the Colonists. |
| G2. Period of first housing laws. | H2. Shelter of early humans. |
| G3. Restrictions that control land use. | H3. Dwellings of the early Native Americans. |
| G4. National guide for building standards. | H4. Event where neighbors would come over to help build a house. |
| G5. The full name of the department called HUD. | H5. A housing symbol of the early United States. |
| G6. Minimum standards for building materials and construction. | H6. People who earned their living from the land. |
| G7. Zone where only houses can be built. | H7. The number of people in a given area. |
| G8. Help with housing for low-income people. | H8. An official count of the population taken by the government. |
| G9. Two federal agencies concerned with the safety and protection of housing environments. | H9. Similarly designed houses built in the same development. |
| G10. Environmental concerns in the constructed environment. | H10. A planned urban development. |

(Continued)

74   Chapter 2   *Influences on Housing*   Copyright Goodheart-Willcox Co., Inc.

Reproducible Master 2-2 (Continued)

| S–Society | T–Technology |
|---|---|
| S1. Maximum number of members in the majority of U.S. households. | T1. The occupation that prompted people to abandon caves and build structures for housing. |
| S2. The household group that includes never-marrieds and single-again adults. | T2. The type of knowledge people need to adapt to their environment. |
| S3. People born after World War II through 1964. | T3. Event in the late 1800's having a large technological impact on housing. |
| S4. Those who most need housing free of physical restrictions. | T4. The primary method of moving goods during the Industrial Revolution. |
| S5. The income group that represents the largest U.S. category. | T5. The type of technology responsible for many high-tech items in the home. |
| S6. Term to describe a family where both partners work. | T6. High-tech appliance found in kitchens. |
| S7. Statistical facts about the human population. | T7. What CADD means. |
| S8. The average number of years between moves. | T8. Two groups of housing professionals who use CADD. |
| S9. Term for Southern and Southwestern states. | T9. Another term for *technology*. |
| S10. Type of society where people travel often. | T10. The people who first used technology. |

Reproducible Test Master

# Influences on Housing

Name _____

Date _____ Period _____ Score _____

**Chapter 2 Test**

❑ Matching: Match the following terms and identifying phrases.

_____ 1. Living off the land.
_____ 2. Number of people who live in a given area.
_____ 3. Interaction among people.
_____ 4. Created when a dwelling is built.
_____ 5. Land and trees.
_____ 6. Beliefs and customs.
_____ 7. Record of houses and units.
_____ 8. Goal of HUD.
_____ 9. Total value of all goods and services produced in the country.
_____ 10. An era of modern processes, materials, and tools, especially the computer.

A. affordable housing
B. agrarian
C. behavioral environment
D. constructed environment
E. culture
F. density
G. dysfunctional
H. gross domestic product (GDP)
I. high tech
J. housing census
K. natural environment
L. subdivision
M. topography
N. zoning regulations

❑ True/False: Circle *T* if the statement is true or *F* if the statement is false.

T F 11. The first shelters of the European settlers were copied after Native American dwellings.

T F 12. The thatched roof became the symbol of early United States.

T F 13. During the Industrial Revolution, agriculture grew as a way of life.

T F 14. Overcrowding is one reason that urban housing in the 1800s became slums.

T F 15. The beliefs, customs, and traits of a group of people form their environment.

T F 16. Household size is on the increase.

T F 17. Housing needs for the disabled and elderly differ from the housing needs of others.

T F 18. Behavioral environment is the interaction among people.

T F 19. The housing market is the transfer of housing from producers to consumers.

T F 20. CADD is used to create designs by computer.

(Continued)

☐ Multiple Choice: Choose the best response. Write the letter in the space provided.

_____ 21. The earliest forms of shelter were used because they _____.
   A. had plenty of room
   B. provided protection and safety
   C. used imported materials
   D. All of the above.

_____ 22. The first log cabins were built by _____.
   A. Native Americans
   B. slumlords
   C. Swedish and Finnish colonists
   D. tenement house developers

_____ 23. People who earned their living from the land lived in _____.
   A. log cabins
   B. plantation houses
   C. sod houses
   D. All of the above.

_____ 24. The forerunners of modern apartments were _____.
   A. dugouts and cliffs
   B. log and sod houses
   C. tenement and row houses
   D. tract houses

_____ 25. The Industrial Revolution caused _____.
   A. a slump in the housing industry
   B. homes to become family work centers
   C. mass movement from the cities
   D. mass movement to the cities

_____ 26. From 1940 to 2000, households headed by married couples _____.
   A. decreased
   B. disappeared
   C. increased
   D. remained the same

_____ 27. The age group with the largest increase in population growth is _____.
   A. children
   B. baby boomers
   C. young adults
   D. the elderly

_____ 28. The average household moves every _____ years.
   A. five
   B. four
   C. six
   D. seven

(Continued)

Reproducible Test Master

_____ 29. Water, trees, and solar energy are resources of the _____ environment.
   A. behavioral
   B. chemical
   C. constructed
   D. natural

_____ 30. A highway through the mountains involves _____ environments.
   A. behavioral and constructed
   B. behavioral, constructed, and natural
   C. constructed and natural
   D. natural and behavioral

_____ 31. To measure the economy, include the number of _____.
   A. housing starts
   B. people who can afford to buy housing
   C. people employed in the housing industry
   D. All of the above.

_____ 32. Technology dates back to _____.
   A. Frank Lloyd Wright
   B. the cave dwellers
   C. the Great Depression
   D. the Industrial Revolution

_____ 33. Government affects housing at the _____ level(s).
   A. federal
   B. federal and state
   C. federal, state, and local
   D. state and local

_____ 34. Zoning regulations control _____.
   A. funding for housing
   B. housing for people in need
   C. land and density
   D. standards for construction

_____ 35. The federal agencies that focus on safety issues affecting the housing environment are _____.
   A. EPA and CPSC
   B. EPA and HUD
   C. FHA and HUD
   D. HUD and CPSC

❑ Essay Questions: Provide complete responses to the following questions or statements.
36. List three changes in society that have affected housing.
37. Name and give an example for each of the three types of environments.
38. Name four ways technology has affected you and your housing.
39. Name three groups of people who may need special consideration in housing.

# PART 2
# Making Housing Choices

**Goal: Students will be able to make informed decisions concerning the location, form, and acquisition of housing.**

## Bulletin Board

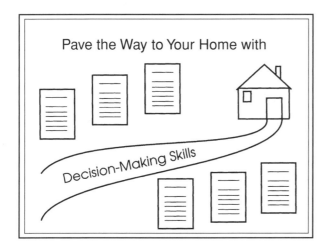

Title: *Pave the Way to Your Home with Decision-Making Skills*

Draw a path, labeled as shown, to an outline of a house. Under the title, place pages from newspapers or real estate listings that advertise various forms of housing for sale and for rent. Under the path, place copies of a lease, property deed, and mortgage.

## Teaching Materials

**Text**
  Chapters 3-5, pages 74-153
  *To Know*
  *To Review*
  *In Your Community*
  *To Think About*
  *Using Technology*

**Teacher's Resources**
  *Making Housing Choices*, transparency master II-A
  *Decisions*, reproducible master II-B
  *Making Housing Choices*, transparency master overlays II-C and II-D

## Introductory Activities

1. *Making Housing Choices*, transparency master II-A, TR. Use this transparency to contrast the concepts covered in Chapters 1 and 2 with those upcoming in Chapter 3. Introduce students to the types of decisions they can make, the resources available, and the steps in decision making. (This transparency is also used in Items 3 and 4.)

2. *Decisions*, reproducible master II-B, TR. Have students work in small groups, each group with one copy of this master. Ask groups to cut apart the strips and sort them into two categories—housing-related decisions and miscellaneous decisions. (You may wish to provide additional "decisions" that students write into the blank strips.) When groups finish, have members share with the class how they categorized each strip.

3. *Making Housing Choices*, transparency master overlay II-C, TR. Superimpose this transparency on *Making Housing Choices*, transparency master II-A. Use the combined image to introduce the concepts in Chapter 4. Explain that many choices are involved in acquiring housing, and decision-making skills can help students make satisfying choices. (This transparency overlay is also used in Item 4.)

4. *Making Housing Choices*, transparency master overlay II-D, TR. Superimpose this transparency on two others—*Making Housing Choices*, transparency master II-A, and *Making Housing Choices*, transparency master overlay II-C. Use the combined image to introduce the concepts in Chapter 5. Briefly discuss the processes of renting, buying, building, and financing housing. Relate these options to decision making.

# Answer Key
## Teacher's Resources

***Decisions,*** reproducible master II-B

Housing-related decisions: 1, 2, 3, 4, 6, 8, 9, 10, 11, 12, 13, 14, 15, 18, 19, 20, 22, 24

(Students may include any of the remaining strips if they justify their answers.)

Transparency Master II-A

## Housing for You

- Housing and Human Needs
- Influences on Housing

## Making Housing Choices

Decision-Making Skills

- Types of Decisions
- Resources (Human and Nonhuman) for Housing Decisions
- Steps in Decision Making

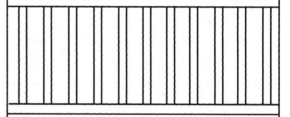

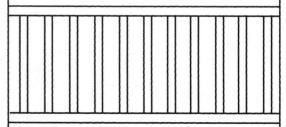

Chapter 3  *Using Decision-Making Skills*  81

Reproducible Master II-B

# Decisions

Work as a group to cut apart the following strips and arrange them according to your teacher's instructions.

| | |
|---|---|
| 1. Add a sunroom. | 13. Provide for solar heat. |
| 2. Buy fade-resistant drapes. | 14. Plant a lawn. |
| 3. Rent a moving van. | 15. Get a home improvement loan. |
| 4. Get the television repaired. | 16. Buy a car. |
| 5. Get a second job. | 17. Make a homework schedule. |
| 6. Determine sunroom location. | 18. Install a swimming pool. |
| 7. Take a night class. | 19. Move. |
| 8. Purchase building materials. | 20. Buy or make building plans. |
| 9. Wallpaper the hall. | 21. Hire someone to babysit. |
| 10. Repair a leaky faucet. | 22. Choose paint colors. |
| 11. Look at lamps for sale. | 23. Use vacation time working at home. |
| 12. Purchase indoor-outdoor furniture. | 24. Install a home security alarm. |
| | |
| | |
| | |

82  Chapter 3  *Using Decision-Making Skills*

Transparency Master Overlay II-C

A Place to Live
- Region
- Community
- Neighborhood
- Site
- House

Special Needs
- Moving

Chapter 3  *Using Decision-Making Skills*  **83**

Transparency Master Overlay II-D

**Acquiring Housing**
- Renting—Rights and Responsibilities

**Acquiring Housing**
- Building
- Buying
- Financing

# CHAPTER 3
# Using Decision-Making Skills

## Objectives

After studying this chapter, students will be able to

- define the different types of decisions.
- list their human and nonhuman resources.
- explain the steps of the decision-making process.
- demonstrate how to make wise decisions.

## Bulletin Boards

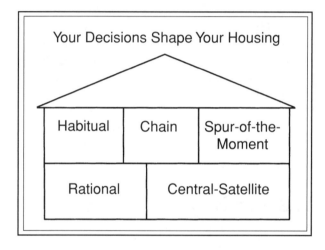

Title: *Your Decisions Shape Your Housing*

Draw the shape of a house on the board under the title. Divide the house into rooms labeled *Habitual, Chain, Spur-of-the-Moment, Central-Satellite,* and *Rational.*

Title: *Take the Decision-Making Steps*

Draw five large steps on the board. On each step, list one of the five steps in the decision-making process.

## Teaching Materials

*Text*, pages 76-89
  *To Know*
  *To Review*
  *In Your Community*
  *To Think About*
  *Using Technology*
**Student Activity Guide**
  A. *Thought Involved in Making Decisions*
  B. *Decision Groupings*
  C. *Resources*
  D. *Human Resources*
  E. *Decision Making*
  F. *Resources and Decisions*
**Teacher's Resources**
  *Types of Decisions*, transparency master 3-1
  *Central-Satellite Decisions*, reproducible master 3-2
  *Chain Decisions*, reproducible master 3-3
  *Decision-Making Steps*, color transparency CT-5
  Chapter 3 Test

## Introductory Activities

1. Have students read an article about how a home or room was redecorated or remodeled. Then have them identify and discuss various decisions that were made during the redecorating or remodeling process.
2. Have students find and discuss the glossary and/or dictionary definitions of the key terms listed in the *To Know* section of the text. Have them add these to their card files.

## Strategies to Reteach, Reinforce, Enrich, and Extend Text Concepts

### Types of Decisions

3. **RF** *Types of Decisions*, transparency master 3-1, TR. Use the master to outline the types of decisions presented in the text. Have students give examples of each type.
4. **RF** *Central-Satellite Decisions*, reproducible master 3-2, TR. Students are asked to select a housing-related issue and

identify its central-satellite decisions on the worksheet.
5. **RF** *Thought Involved in Making Decisions*, Activity A, SAG. Students are asked to read and analyze an example of a rational decision, a spur-of-the-moment decision, and habitual behavior.
6. **ER** *Chain Decisions*, reproducible master 3-3, TR. Students are asked to use the diagram to write a complete chain of decisions related to a housing decision.
7. **ER** *Decision Groupings*, Activity B, SAG. Students are asked to read a hypothetical situation and diagram a possible decision chain and group of central-satellite decisions that fit the situation.

## Resources for Housing Decisions

8. **RT** Have students list 10 different resources they could use to make housing decisions. Students should label each resource *human, nonhuman,* or *community*.
9. **ER** Ask students to write a paragraph describing resources used by a fictitious household to make housing decisions.
10. **EX** Have students develop a list of community resources related to housing. Students should include the name, street and Web addresses, phone number, and a short description of each resource. Compile the resources into a brochure and give copies to a community newcomers' association or local businesses to distribute.
11. **ER** *Resources*, Activity C, SAG. Students are asked to separate a list into human and nonhuman resources. They are then asked to list 15 community resources.
12. **ER** *Human Resources*, Activity D, SAG. Students are asked to assess the human resources of two families and analyze their ratings.

## The Decision-Making Process

13. **RT** Have students choose a housing situation that requires a decision and list all the steps involved in the decision-making process for that decision.
14. **ER** *Decision-Making Steps*, color transparency CT-5, TR. Use this transparency to review the steps in decision making. Discuss with students the possible consequences of skipping any of the steps in decision making.
15. **EX** *Decision Making*, Activity E, SAG. Each student is asked to solve a housing dilemma or challenge facing his or her family by using the steps in the decision-making process. They are then asked to answer questions designed to evaluate the decision.
16. **ER** Invite a school counselor to speak to the class on decision making. Have the speaker relate as many examples as possible to housing.

## Chapter Review

17. **ER** Have students read an article about how a home was designed and built. Then have students write a paper on the article discussing the types of decisions made, resources used, decision-making steps involved, and categories of housing decisions affected through the design and building process.
18. **RF** *Resources and Decisions*, Activity F, SAG. Students are asked to complete statements about decision-making skills by filling in the blanks.

## Answer Key

### Text

*To Review*, page 87
1. rational
2. false
3. true
4. B
5. (List five:) libraries, parks, recreation departments, schools, hospitals, fire stations, police departments, shopping centers, sports facilities
6. time
7. (List three:) ability, knowledge, energy, health, money, property
8. true
9. Identify the challenge. List possible solutions. Make a decision. Take action. Evaluate results.

# Student Activity Guide

## *Thought Involved in Making Decisions*, Activity A

1. rational decision
2. spur-of-the-moment decision
3. rational decision
4. spur-of-the-moment decision
5. (Student response.)
6. (Student response.)
7. habitual decision
8. (Student response.)
9. (Student response.)
10. (Student response.)

## *Resources*, Activity C

Human resources—ambition, coordination, creativity, excellent health, friends, high energy level, math skills, photographic memory, positive attitude

Nonhuman resources—car, employment, house, library, money, savings, telephone, time, tools and equipment

(Community resources are student response.)

## *Resources and Decisions*, Activity F

1. rational
2. spur, moment
3. habitual
4. chain
5. satellite
6. resources
7. human
8. nonhuman
9. community
10. skill
11. attitude
12. energy
13. time
14. money
15. property
16. identification
17. satisfaction

# Teacher's Resources

## Chapter 3 Test

1. E
2. B
3. H
4. C
5. G
6. T
7. F
8. T
9. F
10. T
11. T
12. F
13. T
14. T
15. T
16. B
17. C
18. A
19. B
20. C
21. D
22. B
23. D
24. D
25. A

26. A rational decision is studied carefully, but a spur-of-the-moment decision is based on impulsive action. A rational decision gives more lasting satisfaction.

27. Central-satellite decisions include one major decision (central decision) with other related decisions (satellite decisions). The central decision can be completed without the others. (Example is student response.)

28. Human resources are personal qualities, but nonhuman resources are those not directly supplied by people. (Example is student response.)

# Types of Decisions

| Grouped According to Amount of Thought Taken to Make the Decision ||
|---|---|
| Rational Decisions | Choices are made only after looking at problems carefully. The consequences are considered. |
| Spur-of-the-Moment Decisions | Choices are made hurriedly. Little thought is given to possible outcomes. |
| Habitual Behavior | Action occurs as a matter of habit. Decisions are made only when new situations arise. |

| Grouped According to Relationships Between Decisions ||
|---|---|
| Central-Satellite Decisions | A major decision is surrounded by related, but independent, decisions. |
| Chain Decisions | One decision creates other choices that must be made to complete the action. |

Reproducible Master 3-2

# Central-Satellite Decisions

Name _____ Date _____ Period _____

Write decisions in the circles below to form a group of central-satellite decisions.

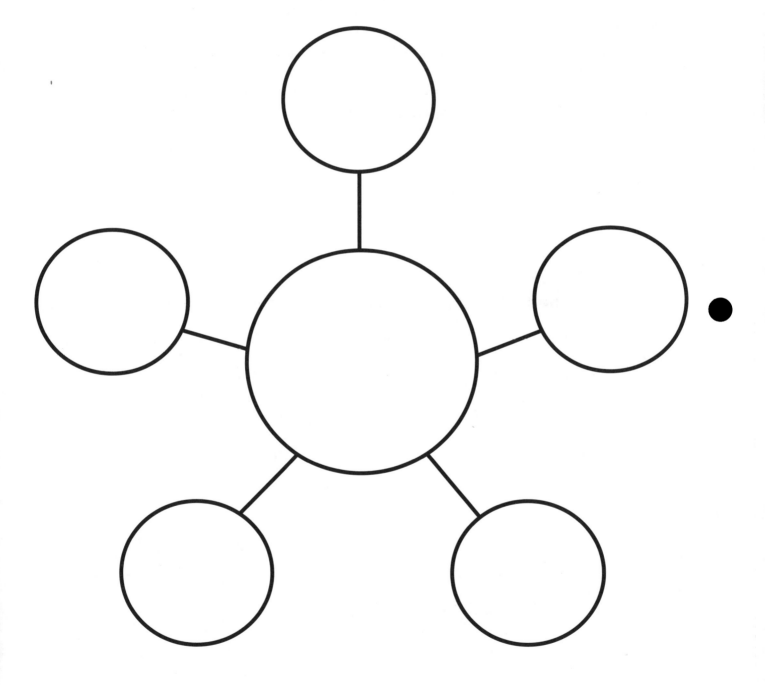

90   *Chapter 3*   *Using Decision-Making Skills*

Reproducible Master 3-3

# Chain Decisions

**Name** _____ **Date** _____ **Period** _____

In chain decisions, additional decisions are needed to complete the action of the first decision. Select a major housing decision and write it on the top link. Then add other decisions that are necessary to complete the chain. Each link should represent a part of the decision-making process.

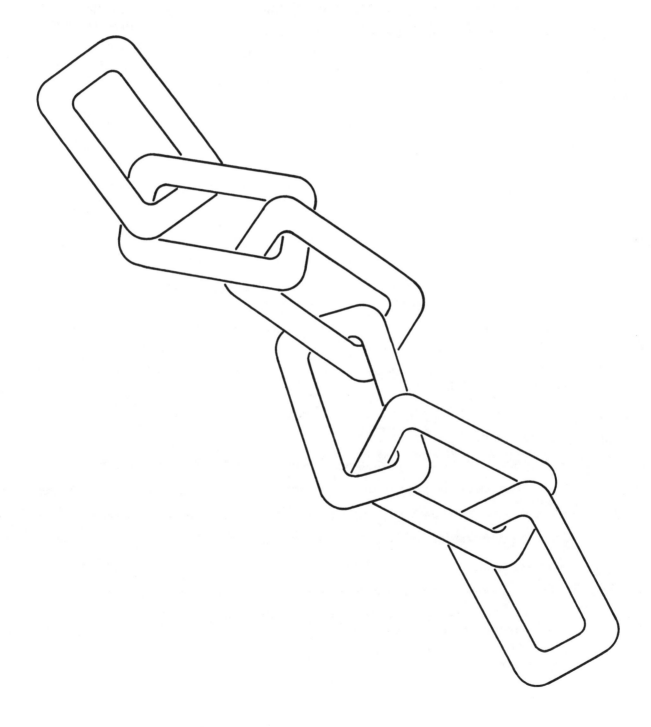

Chapter 3  *Using Decision-Making Skills*  91

Reproducible Test Master

# Using Decision-Making Skills

Name _____

Date _____ Period _____ Score _____

**Chapter 3 Test**

❑ Matching: Match the following terms and identifying phrases.

_____ 1. An action automatically done without thinking.

_____ 2. A group of decisions consisting of one major decision and several related but independent ones.

_____ 3. A decision made without consideration for the consequences.

_____ 4. A series of decisions in which one decision triggers another.

_____ 5. A decision made after careful examination of a problem.

A. acquisition
B. central-satellite decision
C. chain decision
D. conscientious decision
E. habitual behavior
F. irresponsible decision
G. rational decision
H. spur-of-the-moment decision

❑ True/False: Circle *T* if the statement is true or *F* if the statement is false.

T  F  6. Decisions are classified into two main groups.

T  F  7. Spur-of-the-moment decisions are made after studying a problem closely and considering all the possible consequences.

T  F  8. Central-satellite decisions can be described as one major decision surrounded by related but independent decisions.

T  F  9. In habitual decisions, one decision triggers other choices that must be made to complete an action.

T  F  10. Knowledge is a human resource.

T  F  11. Time is a nonhuman resource.

T  F  12. The first step in the decision-making process is seeking alternative solutions.

T  F  13. A decision should be judged for both its short-term and long-range consequences.

T  F  14. Once you have made a wise housing decision, you may still decide to change it.

T  F  15. Housing decisions are related to your needs and personal priorities.

❑ Multiple Choice: Choose the best response. Write the letter in the space provided.

_____ 16. A spur-of-the-moment decision is likely to be a result of _____.
  A. considering all possible consequences
  B. impulsive action
  C. related decisions
  D. studying a problem closely

(Continued)

_____ 17. _____ is *not* a human resource.
   A. Attitude
   B. Knowledge
   C. Property
   D. Skill

_____ 18. The public library is a good example of a _____ resource.
   A. community
   B. human
   C. personal
   D. satellite

_____ 19. A person with a high energy level has a valuable _____ resource.
   A. community
   B. human
   C. nonhuman
   D. satellite

_____ 20. The decision-making process starts with _____.
   A. human resources
   B. nonhuman resources
   C. problem identification
   D. taking action

_____ 21. Some decisions are changed because _____.
   A. necessary resources are not available
   B. the person views the problem differently
   C. the person could not foresee the outcome
   D. All of the above.

_____ 22. Making a decision and taking action _____.
   A. is a skill that comes naturally
   B. is difficult for some people
   C. should only be done by the head of the household
   D. All of the above.

_____ 23. _____ is the resource everyone has in equal amount.
   A. Energy
   B. Money
   C. Skill
   D. Time

_____ 24. Housing decisions are related to _____.
   A. environmental and governmental influences
   B. life situations
   C. needs and personal priorities
   D. All of the above.

_____ 25. Decisions that are grouped according to the relationships between the decisions are _____.
   A. central-satellite and chain
   B. chain and habitual
   C. rational and spur-of-the-moment
   D. All of the above.

(Continued)

❑ Essay Questions: Provide complete responses to the following questions or statements.

26. What is the difference between a rational decision and a spur-of-the-moment decision? What outcome can be expected of each type of decision?

27. What are central-satellite decisions? Give an example of a situation requiring this type of decision and show how the satellite decisions are related to the central one.

28. Compare human and nonhuman resources. Give examples of the way resources affect your housing.

# CHAPTER 4
# Choosing a Place to Live

## Objectives

After studying this chapter, students will be able to

- describe different regions in which people live.
- list factors people consider when choosing a community or neighborhood.
- describe different types of housing
- identify decisions involved in choosing a site and house.
- determine special needs to consider when choosing housing.
- compare the different ways to move.

## Bulletin Boards

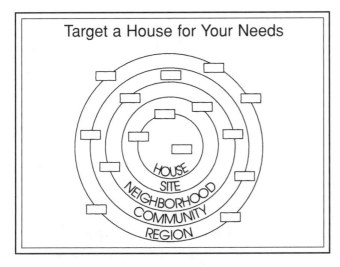

Title: *Target a House for Your Needs*

Make five concentric circles as shown and place a different color within each band to resemble a target. Add the following labels: *House, Site, Neighborhood, Community,* and *Region*. Then add pictures representing each category within the appropriate band.

Title: *What's in a Location?*

Divide the board into five sections and add the following headings: *House, Site, Neighborhood, Community,* and *Region*. Have students place pictures or words in the sections that describe desirable choices for each.

## Teaching Materials

**Text**, pages 90-119
  *To Know*
  *To Review*
  *In Your Community*
  *To Think About*
  *Using Technology*
**Student Activity Guide**
  A. *Your Community Zoning Rules*
  B. *Evaluating a Place to Live*
  C. *Housing Location*
  D. *Creating Site Zones*
  E. *Choices*
  F. *Special Housing Needs*
  G. *Places to Live*
**Teacher's Resources**
  *Neighborhood Checklist*, reproducible master 4-1
  *Site Zones*, transparency master 4-2
  *Matching Exercise*, reproducible master 4-3
  *A Place to Live Flow Chart*, color transparency CT-6
  *Moving Checklist*, reproducible master 4-4
  Chapter 4 Test

## Introductory Activities

1. *Neighborhood Checklist*, reproducible master 4-1, TR. Have students use the checklist to evaluate their own neighborhoods.
2. Have students list 10 priorities they would set in choosing a place to live. Students should assume that finances, travel, or other constraints are not an issue. As students share their priorities, have them discuss whether each item deals with region, community, neighborhood, site, or house.
3. Have students find and discuss the glossary and/or dictionary definitions of key terms listed in the *To Know* section of the text. Have them add these to their card files.

# Strategies to Reteach, Reinforce, Enrich, and Extend Text Concepts

## Location

4. **RT** Have students list five factors to consider when choosing a region in which to live.
5. **ER** Have students select a region other than their own to research. Students should give a brief oral report on the region, including information on climate, topography, employment opportunities, and the cost of living.
6. **RT** Have students list five factors to consider when choosing a community in which to live.
7. **RF** Have students discuss which communities within their regions are suited for contact or noncontact people.
8. **ER** Have students choose a community beyond their own to evaluate in terms of the items listed in Chart 4-3 of the text. Have students write a paper discussing the strengths and weaknesses of the community.
9. **EX** Have students research a successful community project in a community other than their own. Some possible examples are programs for recycling, cleanup, and food banks. (Students might consider proposing a project for their own community and creating visuals for the presentation.)
10. **RF** Have students differentiate between physical and social neighborhoods.
11. **RT** Have students define the term *planned neighborhood*.
12. **RT** Have students list five factors to consider when choosing a site on which to live.
13. **RF** Have students describe three types of natural restraints that affect a site.
14. **ER** *Site Zones*, transparency master 4-2, TR. Ask for a volunteer to color one of the zones with a colored pen for overhead transparencies. Then have the student name at least one function for the site. Repeat with the other zones and name each zone.
15. **EX** Have students check with local authorities on the zoning regulations and building codes in effect for their neighborhoods. They should label the regulations *local*, *state*, or *federal*. Students should list the authorities they contacted and explain how the authorities are involved with establishing or enforcing these regulations and codes. Have students report their findings to the class.
16. **ER** *Your Community Zoning Rules*, Activity A, SAG. Invite a member of a zoning authority or city council to present information about zoning rules in your community. Students are to record information by answering the questions provided.
17. **ER** *Evaluating a Place to Live*, Activity B, SAG. Make arrangements for the class to visit a subdivision and tour a house model. Students are asked to evaluate the subdivision using the form provided.
18. **ER** *Housing Location*, Activity C, SAG. Students are asked to design and evaluate a site and neighborhood for a house.
19. **ER** *Creating Site Zones*, Activity D, SAG. Students are asked to sketch a lot design around a house floor plan and identify the public, private, and service zones.

## Types of Housing

20. *Matching Exercise*, reproducible master 4-3, TR. Students match housing terms with their descriptions and summarize the type of housing in which they prefer to live as adults.
21. **RT** Have students list five factors to consider when choosing a house in which to live.
22. **RT** Have students define the terms *multi-family housing* and *single-family housing*.
23. **RF** Have students differentiate between rental, cooperative, and condominium units.
24. **RF** Have students describe five types of single-family homes.
25. **ER** Have students tour their community and identify a unique type of housing. Each student should interview one of the residents of the housing to report to the class why the person chose that type of housing.
26. **EX** *Choices*, Activity E, SAG. Students are asked to find and list businesses that supply various housing choices, then answer questions about housing choices.

96 Chapter 4 *Choosing a Place to Live*

27. **EX** Have students describe an imaginary family. They should list the number of members, their sexes, their ages, the type of hobbies the family enjoys, and jobs held by the head(s) of the household. Then have students describe a home suitable for this family based on their likely needs. Have students look through housing magazines or classified ads to find a suitable home.
28. **RF** *A Place to Live Flow Chart*, color transparency CT-6, TR. Use the transparency to show that one decision relates to the next when choosing a place to live. Have students share with the class concepts they have learned about choosing a place to live.
29. **ER** Have students use the flow chart in Item 28 as an outline for writing a one-page report on the choices made in selecting their current home. Have them include reasons for each of the choices.
30. **EX** Select different house types—such as multifamily, single-family, detached, attached, and manufactured—from different neighborhoods for students to analyze. Divide the class into small groups and assign a different house to each. Ask each group to locate on an area map its housing unit and the nearest schools, shopping areas, and other community resources. Have students sketch the house on its site, label the site zones, and describe the neighborhood and community by reporting the available services and approximate distances to important places.

## Housing for Special Needs

31. **ER** Have students find pictures of the interior and exterior of housing and discuss whether the housing is suitable for people with special housing needs. Have students list what is important in housing for older people, people with disabilities, and children.
32. **ER** *Special Housing Needs*, Activity F, SAG. Students are asked to interview someone with special housing needs and complete the information requested.

## Moving to a New Home

33. **ER** *Moving Checklist*, reproducible master 4-4, TR. Have students who have moved recently review a checklist of actions to take before and during a move. Encourage students to add any additional steps they feel are needed.
34. **RF** Have students name the advantages of hiring a moving company versus moving one's own possessions.
35. **ER** Have students research what is involved in moving to a new location. Have each student write a case study about an imaginary family planning to move. Students should detail the major decisions that must be made and the steps that must be taken to ensure a well-organized move.
36. **ER** Have students contact a moving company, a truck-trailer rental service, and a person who moved himself or herself. Students should compare the costs in terms of money, time, and effort.
37. **ER** Have students get copies of *U-Haul's Moving Guide*, available at most U-Haul rental agencies. Have students discuss additional points to consider when moving that the booklet includes.

## Chapter Review

38. **RF** *Places to Live*, Activity G, SAG. Students are asked to complete the statements about finding a place to live by filling in the blanks.

## Answer Key

### Text

*To Review*, pages 117-118

1. region, community, neighborhood, population composition, and site
2. (List three:) scenery, climate, family, friends, employment, cost of living, topography
3. neighborhoods
4. A
5. (List two:) topography, soil conditions, water levels, orientation to sun, orientation to wind, orientation to scenery
6. D
7. FHA, the Federal Housing Administration, establishes minimum property standards (MPS).
8. The public zone is part of the site that can be seen from the street. The service zone

includes sidewalks, driveways, and storage areas. The private zone is hidden from public view and used for recreation and relaxation.
9. rental units—landlords; cooperative units—a corporation whose stockholders are usually the occupants; condominium units—the individual occupants
10. A
11. designs, builds
12. A tract house is one of many same-design houses built in a neighborhood before individuals purchase them. A house customized from stock plans is built where the owner wants and with the individualized touches desired.
13. modular, manufactured/mobile, panelized, precut, and kit
14. senior citizens, people with disabilities, and children
15. moving yourself—less expensive, scheduled at your convenience, permits possessions to arrive with you; hiring a professional mover—involves less personal time and effort, allows goods to be insured against damage

## Student Activity Guide

### Places to Live, Activity G

1. region
2. community
3. residential
4. commercial
5. industrial
6. zoning
7. restrictions
8. planned
9. heterogeneous
10. homogeneous
11. site
12. topography
13. landscaping
14. orientation
15. minimum
16. public
17. service
18. private
19. apartment
20. rentals
21. co-op
22. condominium
23. single
24. attached
25. townhouse
26. custom
27. built
28. owner
29. tract
30. factory
31. kit
32. modular
33. universal
34. Fair
35. lading

## Teacher's Resources

### Matching Exercise, transparency master 4-3

1. N
2. D
3. F
4. B
5. C
6. A
7. G
8. E
9. H
10. K
11. L
12. J
13. I

### Chapter 4 Test

1. J
2. D
3. B
4. G
5. H
6. C
7. F
8. I
9. F
10. F
11. T
12. T
13. F
14. T
15. T
16. F
17. T
18. T
19. D
20. D
21. C
22. C
23. C
24. C
25. D
26. C
27. A
28. C
29. D
30. B

31. A physical neighborhood is determined by the way the land and buildings are used.
32. (List two:) number of windows, size of windows, orientation to the sun, the width of the roof overhang, the time of year, trees or built-in features that provide shade
33. Senior citizens receive a monthly payment while they live in the house, but when they leave, the mortgage company assumes ownership.
34. (List three:) retirement, decrease in energy, inability to drive, loneliness, health, cost of living
35. Using a moving company involves more cost, less time, and less energy than moving one's self.

Reproducible Master 4-1

# Neighborhood Checklist

Name _____ Date _____ Period _____

|  | Yes | No | Not Important |
|---|---|---|---|
| **Neighborhood Quality** | | | |
| 1. Are the homes attractive and well-maintained? | ❏ | ❏ | ❏ |
| 2. Are public services (police and fire protection) good? | ❏ | ❏ | ❏ |
| 3. Are roads paved? | ❏ | ❏ | ❏ |
| 4. Are sidewalks clean and well maintained? | ❏ | ❏ | ❏ |
| 5. Is street lighting adequate? | ❏ | ❏ | ❏ |
| 6. Is a city sewer system installed? | ❏ | ❏ | ❏ |
| 7. Is the public water supply safe? | ❏ | ❏ | ❏ |
| 8. Are home prices increasing? | ❏ | ❏ | ❏ |
| 9. Is heavy traffic or loud noise common? | ❏ | ❏ | ❏ |
| 10. Is litter or pollution evident? | ❏ | ❏ | ❏ |
| 11. Are factories or heavy industry nearby? | ❏ | ❏ | ❏ |
| 12. Are many businesses closing or houses becoming vacant? | ❏ | ❏ | ❏ |
| 13. Is crime or vandalism increasing? | ❏ | ❏ | ❏ |
| **Neighborhood Convenience** | | | |
| 1. Are opportunities for employment nearby? | ❏ | ❏ | ❏ |
| 2. Are schools nearby? | ❏ | ❏ | ❏ |
| 3. Are shopping centers accessible via public transportation? | ❏ | ❏ | ❏ |
| 4. Is public transportation available and reliable? | ❏ | ❏ | ❏ |
| 5. Are child care services nearby? | ❏ | ❏ | ❏ |
| 6. Are hospitals, clinics, or doctors close? | ❏ | ❏ | ❏ |
| 7. Is there a park or playground nearby? | ❏ | ❏ | ❏ |
| **Neighbors** | | | |
| 1. Are friends or relatives nearby? | ❏ | ❏ | ❏ |
| 2. Are a variety of people your age nearby? | ❏ | ❏ | ❏ |
| 3. Are the neighbors friendly? | ❏ | ❏ | ❏ |
| 4. Is a community group active? | ❏ | ❏ | ❏ |

|  | Good | Fair | Poor |
|---|---|---|---|
| What is your overall rating of the neighborhood? | ❏ | ❏ | ❏ |

Transparency Master 4-2

# Site Zones

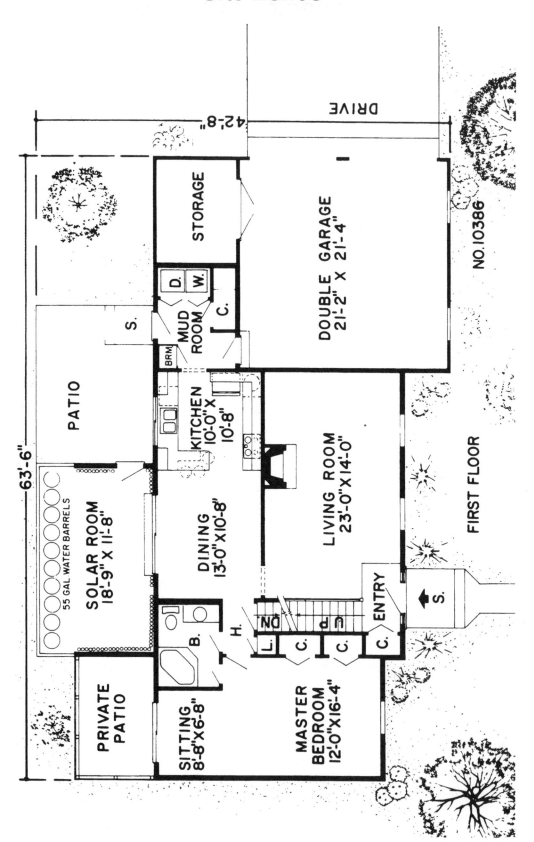

Reproducible Master 4-3

# Matching Exercise

**Name** _____ **Date** _____ **Period** _____

Match the following types of housing with their descriptions. Then describe the housing in which you would like to live most of your adult life and identify the type of housing it is.

**Housing Descriptions**

_____ 1. A house built by a developer who repeats a couple sets of construction plans to build a neighborhood.

_____ 2. A house built to the owner's specifications.

_____ 3. Apartment with a bathroom and one main room having a small kitchen area.

_____ 4. Blend of condominium and cooperative housing.

_____ 5. Housing unit obtained by buying shares in a nonprofit corporation.

_____ 6. Housing unit that an individual owns, inside a building with other such units and common facilities shared with others.

_____ 7. Housing unit built completely in a plant and moved to a housing site in parts or fully finished.

_____ 8. Low-rise building that houses two households.

_____ 9. One-story apartment with landscaped grounds.

_____ 10. Rental suite located at the top of an apartment high-rise.

_____ 11. Type of manufactured housing that arrives at the site as components cut to exact size.

_____ 12. Type of manufactured housing that arrives at the site as panels of floors, ceilings, and walls, complete with windows, doors, plumbing, and wiring.

_____ 13. Type of manufactured housing that arrives at the site as unassembled parts or as a finished shell.

**Types of Housing**

A. condominium
B. co-op
C. cooperative
D. custom-built house
E. duplex
F. efficiency apartment
G. factory-built housing
H. garden apartment
I. kit house
J. panelized housing
K. penthouse
L. precut housing
M. single-sectional housing
N. tract house
O. triplex

As an adult, I would like to live in _____

because _____

_____

_____

_____

_____

_____

Chapter 4  *Choosing a Place to Live*  101

Reproducible Master 4-4

# Moving Checklist

Name _____ Date _____ Period _____

Before moving, you will want to be sure you have taken care of the many details involved. Use this checklist as a reminder of what has to be done before and during a move. Add any stages you feel should be included.

**Renters, have you:**

❏ Given your landlord the notice required in the lease?

❏ Cleaned your apartment and asked the landlord to inspect it?

❏ Returned your key to the landlord?

❏ Arranged to get your security deposit returned?

❏ _____

**Owners and renters, have you:**

❏ Checked the condition of your new house to make sure it is clean inside and outside, and the previous owner's belongings are gone?

❏ Notified all utility companies to disconnect your present service and turn on service at the new address?

❏ Notified your employer, drivers license bureau, credit card companies, magazine companies, etc., of your move?

❏ Filled out the change-of-address form at the post office?

❏ Notified your children's school or child care center?

❏ Made arrangements for your children during the move?

❏ Checked with the moving company about the date of the move, time of pickup and delivery, and cost of the move (in a written estimate)?

❏ Checked with the mover to make sure all your items will be insured?

❏ Checked with the rental company (if you plan to rent a truck or van) about the date and cost of the rental?

❏ Arranged with family or friends to help you with the move?

❏ Stocked plenty of boxes, cartons, rope, tape, and packing materials?

❏ Made a list of items to be moved, marked the contents on the boxes, and identified where they will be placed in the house?

❏ Made a plan regarding which items to move first, such as food, dishes, clothing, and towels?

❏ Checked all the keys to your new house to make sure they work properly?

❏ _____

102   Chapter 4   *Choosing a Place to Live*

Reproducible Test Master

# Choosing a Place to Live

Name _____

Date _____ Period _____ Score _____

**Chapter 4 Test**

❑ Matching: Match the following terms and identifying phrases.

_____ 1. Lot within the neighborhood.

_____ 2. A structure in which people live.

_____ 3. Section of a region.

_____ 4. Examples are residential, commercial, and homogeneous.

_____ 5. Section of the world, country, or state.

_____ 6. A dwelling within a multifamily unit that is owned by the person who lives in it.

_____ 7. Federal rulings that regulate the size of housing lots.

_____ 8. Neighborhood rules that limit such housing choices as the design of buildings or the number and kind of animals kept.

A. area
B. community
C. condominium
D. dwelling
E. metropolis
F. minimum property standards
G. neighborhood
H. region
I. restrictions
J. site
K. subdivision

❑ True/False: Circle *T* if the statement is true or *F* if the statement is false.

T  F   9. The specific part of a state or country in which you live is a community.

T  F  10. A region is divided into neighborhoods.

T  F  11. A community volunteer is considered a "contact" person.

T  F  12. Density refers to the number of people living on a specific amount of land.

T  F  13. A neighborhood with people who are very similar to one another is heterogeneous.

T  F  14. Space within a site but outside a dwelling can be divided into three main zones.

T  F  15. A dwelling designed for more than one household is called a multifamily dwelling.

T  F  16. A landlord can refuse to rent to families with children.

T  F  17. Moving expenses may qualify as an income tax deduction.

T  F  18. The dollar cost of moving is usually lowest when people move themselves.

❑ Multiple Choice: Choose the best response. Write the letter in the space provided.

_____ 19. The _____ is *not* an important factor when considering orientation.
  A. direction of prevailing winds
  B. location of the sun
  C. scenic view
  D. location of the moon

(Continued)

_____ 20. A type of physical neighborhood is _____.
   A. commercial
   B. industrial
   C. residential
   D. All of the above.

_____ 21. A neighborhood that has an overall design for development before any construction begins is called a _____ neighborhood.
   A. heterogeneous
   B. homogeneous
   C. planned
   D. social

_____ 22. The social neighborhood is determined by the _____.
   A. limits set by developers
   B. size of the household
   C. type and number of people living there
   D. type of zoning

_____ 23. A location within a neighborhood is called a _____.
   A. boundary
   B. community
   C. site
   D. zone

_____ 24. Limits set by developers are called _____.
   A. boundaries
   B. property lines
   C. restrictions
   D. zones

_____ 25. The slope or lay of the land is a natural feature called _____.
   A. earthology
   B. ecology
   C. geology
   D. topography

_____ 26. The _____ zone is *not* considered a zone within the site.
   A. private
   B. public
   C. sanitation
   D. service

_____ 27. A _____ is a multifamily house.
   A. condominium
   B. kit house
   C. mobile home
   D. tract house

_____ 28. An example of manufactured housing is a _____.
   A. row house
   B. condominium
   C. kit house
   D. townhouse

(Continued)

_____ 29. Life situations that may require special housing considerations include _____.
  A. having a senior citizen in the family
  B. having a physical disability
  C. having impaired eyesight
  D. All of the above.

_____ 30. Hiring a moving company instead of moving yourself _____.
  A. costs less money
  B. costs less time and energy
  C. involves little planning
  D. is the best plan for everyone

❏ Essay Questions: Provide complete responses to the following questions or statements.

31. Explain the term *physical neighborhood*.

32. List two factors that affect the amount of sunlight that enters a home.

33. Explain how a reverse mortgage works.

34. Give three reasons older people may have special needs when considering housing.

35. Compare using a moving company to moving yourself.

CHAPTER 5

# Acquiring Housing

## Objectives

After studying this chapter, students will be able to

- determine the advantages and disadvantages of renting and buying houses.
- contrast the impact of needs and wants on housing costs.
- list several items to check before signing a lease.
- explain the steps in buying a house.
- define legal and financial terms related to acquiring housing.
- describe what to examine when buying condominium or cooperative units.

## Bulletin Boards

Title: Credit: *A Trap or a Tool?*

Under the title, draw a large mousetrap and a hammer. Use the board to start a discussion about the use of credit.

Title: *Rent, Build, or Buy?*

Divide the board into three sections labeled *Renting, Building,* and *Buying.* Under each section, place the column headings *Advantages* and *Disadvantages.* Have students list comments on the board during the discussion of this chapter as appropriate. (Pictures of rental property, houses being built, and finished houses can be added for visual appeal.)

## Teaching Materials

**Text**, pages 120-153
 *To Know*
 *To Review*
 *In Your Community*
 *To Think About*
 *Using Technology*

**Student Activity Guide**
 A. *A Place to Rent*
 B. *The Written Lease*
 C. *Buying or Renting*
 D. *Real Estate*
 E. *Buying a House*
 F. *The Details of Acquiring Housing*

**Teacher's Resources**
 *Hunting for Housing*, reproducible master 5-1
 *The Right Price*, reproducible master 5-2
 *Housing Inspection*, transparency master 5-3
 *Steps in Acquiring Housing*, color transparency CT-7
 *Housing Selection*, reproducible master 5-4
 Chapter 5 Test

## Introductory Activities

1. Have students find and discuss the glossary and/or dictionary definitions of key terms listed in the *To Know* section of the text. Have them add these to their card files.
2. *Hunting for Housing*, reproducible master 5-1, TR. Supply students with real estate ads from the local newspaper or real estate brochure. Have each student choose an ad to paste to his or her worksheet. Students should answer the questions to analyze their ads. Point out that reading ads is only a small first step in acquiring housing.
3. Distribute copies of a publication explaining the rights and responsibilities of landlords

Chapter 5   Acquiring Housing   107

and tenants. (Such a publication may be obtained from a state or local renter's association.) Have students discuss the various rights and responsibilities.

4. Have students role-play members of households trying to select housing. While many household arrangements are possible, some examples include the following:
   A. husband, wife, and two teenage children
   B. two recent graduates who want to share living space
   C. young couple with a newborn
   D. recently retired couple

   Groups should use newspaper ads or real estate catalogs in their role-play. (You may want to supply more details about each role, such as salaries, hobbies, or personal tastes.)

# Strategies to Reteach, Reinforce, Enrich, and Extend Text Concepts

## Acquiring a Place to Live

5. **RT** Have volunteers describe the process their families followed to acquire their current housing.
6. **EX** Collect literature on various credit cards including letters of solicitation, brochures, and credit agreements. Ask students to read the information and explain which credit card offers the best deal and why. Discuss any information students do not understand, such as the computation of finance charges.

## A Place to Rent

7. **RF** Have students name three advantages of renting a home.
8. **RT** Ask students to list eight items that should be included in a written lease.
9. **RF** Have students explain how subletting and assigning a lease differ.
10. **ER** Have students prepare a presentation on selecting an apartment and present it to a consumer education class in your school. The presentation should include visual aids and handouts. Students should cover the information in Figure 5-5 of the text.
11. **EX** *A Place to Rent*, Activity A, SAG. Outside of class time, students are asked to visit an apartment and evaluate it according to the renter's checklist and the questions for landlords.
12. **ER** *The Written Lease*, Activity B, SAG. Students are instructed to answer the questions provided concerning the lease in Figure 5-6 of the text.
13. **ER** Invite both landlords and tenants for a panel discussion on their rights and responsibilities. Before the discussion, have students prepare questions for the panelists.

## A Place to Buy

14. **RF** Have students name three advantages of owning a home.
15. **RT** Ask students to explain three methods of determining how much money they can afford to pay for housing.
16. **RT** Have students describe the major steps that must be taken in order to build a new house.
17. **EX** Have students talk to two homeowners: one with a newly built house and one with a previously owned house. Students should compare the differences in work involved in moving into each. Have students discuss their findings in class.
18. **EX** Arrange for students to tour property for sale or rent in your community. Include an older house, a newly built house from stock plans, a custom-built house, an apartment, a condominium, and a cooperative unit, if possible. Have students discuss the differences among the various types of housing.
19. **RT** Have students list two serious defects for which they should check carefully before buying a previously owned house.
20. **ER** Ask students to look through real estate listings and compare costs of houses. Students should try to determine what factors affect housing costs, such as house size, number of bathrooms, and location. Have students discuss which features they consider essential and which they would forego to save money.
21. **EX** Have students make a chart showing the price range of different types of houses in the community. Various sources to

contact for this information include landlords, tenants, homeowners, real estate agents, newspaper ads, contractors, and architects. Have students determine what amount of household income would be needed to afford each type of house.
22. **ER** *Buying or Renting*, Activity C, SAG. Students are asked to clip and mount two ads for available housing—one for sale and one for rent—and list the advantages and disadvantages of each.
23. **ER** *Real Estate*, Activity D, SAG. Invite a real estate agent to speak to the class about the availability of housing in the community. Have students record information from the presentation on the form provided.
24. **RF** *Buying a House*, Activity E, SAG. Students are asked to individually estimate their likely income in 10 years and, working a budget around that figure, find a house today that each could afford.
25. **ER** *The Right Price*, reproducible master 5-2, TR. Have students answer the questions and solve the problems according to information in the text.
26. **ER** *Housing Inspection*, transparency master 5-3, TR. Have students discuss what to explore when inspecting a house in each of the areas listed on the transparency.
27. **RF** *Steps in Acquiring Housing*, color transparency CT-7, TR. Have students list and describe the steps to take in buying a house. As each step is listed, write it on the transparency master. (Use erasable ink so the transparency can be reused.)
28. **EX** Distribute copies of a mortgage application form to your class. (You should be able to obtain a form from a bank.) Have students read the form and list what they would need to do to become eligible for a mortgage loan.
29. **RF** Discuss each of the ways of financing a house shown in Figure 5-18 of the text. Have students discuss possible advantages and disadvantages of each way.
30. **ER** Have students discuss the kinds of losses covered by homeowners' insurance, as shown in Figure 5-20 of the text. To develop an idea of the type of coverage a homeowner needs, students should estimate the possible costs of losses.
31. **ER** Invite an insurance agent to discuss renters' and homeowners' insurance with the class.
32. **EX** Have students work in groups to role-play the transactions involved in buying a house.

## Condominium and Cooperative Ownership

33. **RF** Have students describe, compare, and contrast condominium ownership and cooperative ownership.
34. **RF** Have students list some advantages and disadvantages of condominium or cooperative ownership.
35. **ER** Have students interview people who live in either a condominium or cooperative arrangement. Ask students to use their findings to write a report.

## Chapter Review

36. **EX** *Housing Selection*, reproducible master 5-4, TR. Have students work in small groups and list the pros and cons of each housing choice. Have students share their responses with the class.
37. **RF** *The Details of Acquiring Housing*, Activity F, SAG. Students are asked to complete statements about housing by filling in the blanks.
38. **ER** Have students write a summary of the processes and costs involved in renting versus buying housing. They may choose any two examples covered in the text.

## Answer Key

### Text

*To Review*, pages 151-152

1. (List four:) less expensive than buying, more freedom to move, no worry about property's value or buying and selling concerns, clear idea of total housing costs, no responsibility for repairs, no expenses for home improvements
2. (List eight. See pages 125-131 of the text.)
3. false
4. breach of contract
5. multiply annual gross income by $2\frac{1}{2}$
6. B, C, D, F, G
7. C
8. (List five. See page 142 of the text.)

9. for protection against financial loss caused by errors in the abstract of title
10. (Student response. See pages 143-144 of the text.)
11. (List two:) lower monthly payments, take advantage of lower interest rates, make home improvements, pay college tuition or other expenses
12. A deed is a legal document by which a title is transferred from one owner to another.
13. C

# Student Activity Guide

## *The Written Lease*, Activity B

1. The landlord can keep all or part of the security deposit.
2. an itemized statement of the damage and the estimated or actual cost of repairs
3. the condition you found when moving in, except for ordinary wear and tear
4. no
5. not without the written consent of the landlord
6. not without the written consent of the landlord
7. not without the written consent of the landlord
8. not without the written consent of the landlord
9. not without the written consent of the landlord
10. not without the written consent of the landlord
11. not without the written consent of the landlord
12. no
13. no
14. all reasonable hours; for examining or showing the apartment or making any necessary repairs
15. no
16. You are responsible for paying the rent until the lease expires.
17. You can be evicted.
18. You can be evicted.

## *The Details of Acquiring Housing*, Activity F

1. process
2. down payment
3. installment
4. cost
5. finance charge
6. interest
7. finance
8. rent
9. lessor
10. security
11. written lease
12. assign
13. sublet
14. breach
15. eviction
16. equity
17. gross
18. foreclosure
19. bid
20. inspector
21. appraiser
22. down
23. abstract
24. survey
25. insurance
26. mortgage
27. FHA-insured
28. VA-guaranteed
29. closing
30. title
31. deed
32. refinance
33. declaration, ownership
34. maintenance

# Teacher's Resources

## *The Right Price*, reproducible master 5-2

cost of house ÷ 2½ = lowest annual salary a household can earn to qualify for buying it

## Chapter 5 Test

1. A
2. G
3. C
4. I
5. E
6. H
7. T
8. T
9. T
10. F
11. F
12. F
13. T
14. F
15. T
16. F
17. B
18. B
19. B
20. C
21. C
22. B
23. B
24. A
25. A
26. A

27. (Student response.)
28. (List three advantages of each:) renting—freedom to move at any time, no worries about the property's value, a clear idea of housing costs, no responsibility for needed repairs, little temptation to spend money on dwelling improvements buying—can personalize the yard and home to meet individual needs and wants, a potential investment that may increase in value, a way to save money through tax deductions, complete privacy, the achieving of the American dream
29. cracked foundation; rotten or sagging roofs, walls, or supports; insect damage; a deteriorating neighborhood
30. (List three:) a poor paint job, old plumbing, slight damage to walls, slight damage to ceilings, slight damage to floors, broken windows, a roof needing repairs, a shabby yard
31. (List two:) includes convenient facilities and services, can be a good money investment, offers tax deductions
32. (List two:) no closing costs, potential tax deductions, no maintenance worries, good likelihood of residents becoming your friends

Reproducible Master 5-1

# Hunting for Housing

Name _____ Date _____ Period _____

Find an ad for a dwelling to buy or rent and mount it in the space below. Then answer the questions that follow.

[                                                                              ]

1. Is the dwelling for rent or for sale? _____
2. What is its price? _____
3. What words indicate whether the dwelling is new or older? _____
   _____
4. What words indicate the condition of the dwelling? _____
   _____
   _____
5. What words indicate the property's size? _____
   _____
6. Can you identify the property's location? _____ If so, how? _____
   _____
   _____
7. What special features of the housing does the ad promote? _____
   _____
   _____
8. What other information about the housing would you like the ad to include? _____
   _____
   _____

Reproducible Master 5-2

# The Right Price

**Name** _____ **Date** _____ **Period** _____

Find two houses for sale in the classified ads. Attach the ads in the spaces provided and answer the questions that follow. Show your calculations on the back of this page.

**House A**

1. What is the cost of House A? _____

2. What is the lowest annual salary a household can earn to qualify for buying House A? _____
   _____
   _____
   _____
   _____
   _____
   _____

3. What is the cost of House B? _____

**House B**

4. What is the lowest annual salary a household can earn to qualify for buying House B? _____
   _____
   _____
   _____
   _____
   _____
   _____

5. If you could afford both houses, which house would you prefer? Explain. _____
   _____
   _____
   _____
   _____
   _____
   _____

*114  Chapter 5  Acquiring Housing*  Copyright Goodheart-Willcox Co., Inc.

## Housing Inspection

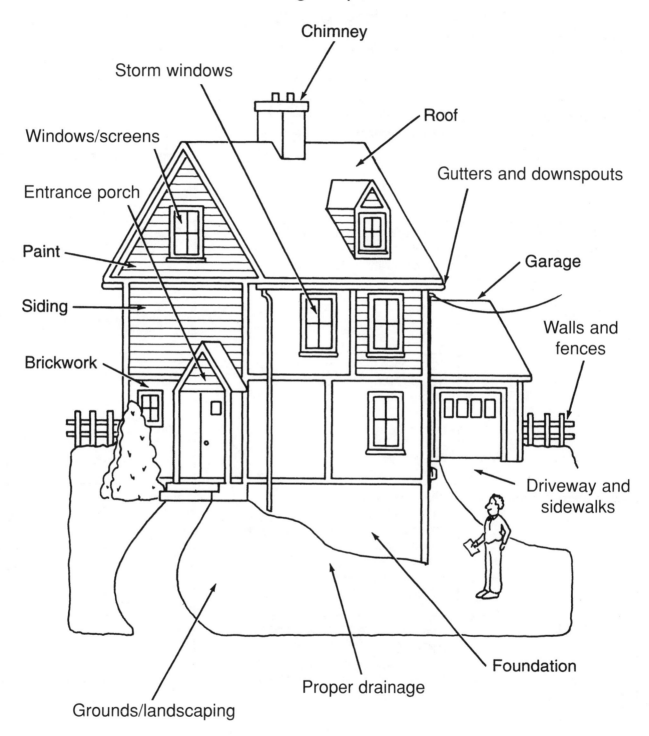

Reproducible Master 5-4

# Housing Selection

**Name** _____ **Date** _____ **Period** _____

In small groups, evaluate the pros and cons of each of the following housing choices. Be prepared to share your responses with the class.

| Housing Choices | Description of Housing | Pros and Cons of Housing Options |
|---|---|---|
| **Rent Furnished Apartment** | Furniture included. Will have private bath. Caretaker has general responsibility of upkeep and repairs. | Pros: |
| | | Cons: |
| **Rent Unfurnished Apartment** | Furniture not included. Will have private bath. Caretaker has general responsibility of upkeep and repairs. | Pros: |
| | | Cons: |
| **Buy Mobile Home** | Put mobile home on a lot for which you pay rent. Upkeep of lot is responsibility of renter. | Pros: |
| | | Cons: |
| **Buy Condominium** | Purchase a specific apartment in a building. Hallways, land, and other common areas are jointly owned by all persons in condominium. Each owner pays a monthly fee to cover maintenance. | Pros: |
| | | Cons: |
| **Rent Duplex** | Rent one of two separate identical apartments in one dwelling. Landlord has major responsibilities of upkeep. Renter may have some responsibilities. | Pros: |
| | | Cons: |

Chapter 5  *Acquiring Housing*

| Housing Choices | Description of Housing | Pros and Cons of Housing Options |
|---|---|---|
| **Rent Furnished Room** | One room with furniture. Usually has cooking facilities. Often has a community bath. | Pros:<br><br>Cons: |
| **Rent Unfurnished House** | Furniture and major appliances not provided. Landlord has major responsibilities of upkeep, repairs, and taxes. A lease may be required. | Pros:<br><br>Cons: |
| **Rent Furnished House** | Furniture is provided. Major appliances are included. Landlord has major responsibility of upkeep, repairs, and taxes. A lease may be required. | Pros:<br><br>Cons: |
| **Buy House** | Furnishings must be provided by the purchaser. Owner is responsible for upkeep, repairs, and taxes on property. | Pros:<br><br>Cons: |
| **Build House** | Pay for and build, or have built, a house of a desired plan. Owner has full responsibility for taxes, upkeep, and repairs. Furnishings must be provided by the owner. | Pros:<br><br>Cons: |

Reproducible Test Master

# Acquiring Housing

Name _____

Date _____ Period _____ Score _____

## Chapter 5 Test

❑ Matching: Match the following terms and identifying phrases.

_____ 1. A copy of all public records concerning a property.

_____ 2. A claim against property given to a lender as security for borrowed money.

_____ 3. The fees for settling the legal and financial matters involved in buying and selling real estate.

_____ 4. A document that gives proof of the rights of ownership and possession of particular property.

_____ 5. Dwellings owned by a corporation whose members are all residents of the dwellings.

_____ 6. A method used to lower monthly mortgage payments.

A. abstract of title
B. agreement of sale
C. closing costs
D. condominium units
E. cooperative units
F. earnest money
G. mortgage
H. refinancing
I. title

❑ True/False: Circle *T* if the statement is true or *F* if the statement is false.

T  F  7. Process, as related to housing, includes operating, maintaining, repairing, and replacing.

T  F  8. Cost, as related to housing, may be in terms of money, time, effort, or other resources.

T  F  9. A finance charge includes both interest and other charges.

T  F  10. About three-fourths of all Americans live in rented homes and are known as lessees.

T  F  11. The amount of a security deposit is commonly two months' rent.

T  F  12. When a person sublets a lease, he or she transfers total interest in a property.

T  F  13. Real estate firms are in the business of selling land and buildings.

T  F  14. An agreement of sale is a claim against property that a buyer gives to the lender of money as security for the borrowed money.

T  F  15. The legal document by which title to a property is transferred is called a deed.

T  F  16. The word *condominium* means high-rise building.

❑ Multiple Choice: Choose the best response. Write the letter in the space provided.

_____ 17. Which of the following best describes a want related to housing?
   A. front door that locks securely
   B. garage door with remote opener
   C. running water
   D. roof that resists leaking

(Continued)

_____ 18. Of the following choices, the most expensive way to pay for a purchase is by _____.
A. using a debit card
B. using an installment buying plan
C. using cash
D. writing a check

_____ 19. The most common breach of contract on the part of the renter is _____.
A. damage
B. failure to pay rent
C. loud noise
D. misuse of facilities

_____ 20. Forcing a renter to leave the property before the rental agreement expires is called _____.
A. assigning the lease
B. breach of contract
C. eviction
D. foreclosure

_____ 21. As a general rule, a person can afford to spend _____ times his or her gross annual income for the purchase price of a home.
A. one-and-one-half
B. two
C. two-and-one-half
D. three

_____ 22. A _____ is likely to have the most space for the least money.
A. custom-built house
B. house that was occupied
C. newly built house
D. studio apartment

_____ 23. When considering buying a pre-owned house, _____ is a serious defect to avoid.
A. broken windows
B. cracked concrete foundation
C. a shabby yard
D. All of the above.

_____ 24. With _____ mortgages, the interest rate goes up or down periodically according to a national interest rate index.
A. adjustable rate
B. conventional
C. graduated payment
D. VA-guaranteed

_____ 25. The _____ deed offers the greatest protection to the buyer.
A. general warranty
B. insured
C. quitclaim
D. special warranty

(Continued)

_____ 26. A declaration of ownership is important when _____.
   A. buying a condominium unit
   B. buying a cooperative unit
   C. buying a single-family house
   D. renting an apartment

❑ Essay Questions: Provide complete responses to the following questions or statements.

27. Contrast the meaning of *needs* versus *wants* using personal examples.

28. List three advantages of each: renting a home and buying a home.

29. What conditions should be avoided when selecting a house?

30. List three housing conditions that can be corrected by spending some money and effort.

31. List two advantages of condominium ownership.

32. List two advantages of cooperative ownership.

PART 3

# From the Ground Up

Goals: Students will examine house styles and develop an understanding of the planning and construction processes.

## Bulletin Board

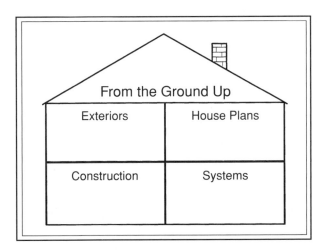

Title: *From the Ground Up*

Create the shape of a two-story house using construction paper. Divide the house into quarters as shown. Label the quarters *Exteriors, House Plans, Construction,* and *Systems*. Develop a collage in each quarter from pictures, articles, and terms provided by the students. Creating the collage can be an ongoing project throughout the unit.

## Teaching Materials

**Text**
Chapters 6-9, pages 154-237
*To Know*
*To Review*
*In Your Community*
*To Think About*
*Using Technology*

**Teacher's Resources**
*From the Ground Up*, transparency master III-A
*From the Ground Up*, transparency master overlays III-B, III-C, and III-D

## Introductory Activities

1. *From the Ground Up*, transparency master III-A, TR. Use this transparency to contrast the concepts covered in Chapters 1-5 with those upcoming in chapter 6. Discuss how a variety of traditional styles as well as modern and contemporary styles are represented in today's architecture. Explain how styles are designed to fit the functions of the time. (This transparency overlay is also used in Items 2, 3, and 4.)

2. *From the Ground Up*, transparency master overlay III-B, TR. Superimpose this transparency on *From the Ground Up* transparency master III-A. Use the combined image to introduce the concepts in Chapter 7. Discuss how understanding house plans allows a person to organize space for rooms, traffic patterns, storage, and the special needs of household members. (This transparency overlay is also used in Items 3 and 4.)

3. *From the Ground Up*, transparency master overlay III-C, TR. Superimpose this transparency on two others—*From the Ground Up*, transparency master III-A, and *From the Ground Up*, transparency master overlay III-B. Use the combined image to introduce the concepts in Chapter 8. Point out that construction of houses involves many steps and materials, all of which can enhance the personality of a house. (This transparency overlay is also used in Item 4.)

4. *From the Ground Up*, transparency master overlay III-D, TR. Superimpose this transparency on three others—*From the Ground Up* transparency master III-A and transparency master overlays III-B and III-C. Use the combined image to introduce the concepts in Chapter 9. Discuss how the systems within a house supply the necessary fuel and water.

Transparency Master III-A

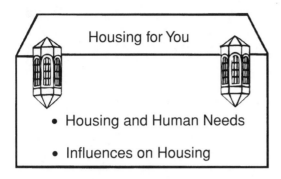

Housing for You
- Housing and Human Needs
- Influences on Housing

Making Housing Choices
- Using Decision-Making Skills
- Choosing a Place to Live
- Acquiring Housing

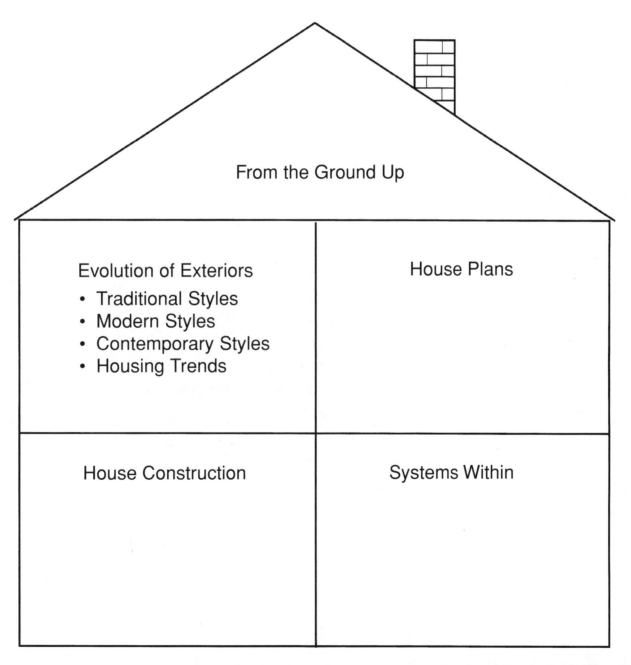

From the Ground Up

Evolution of Exteriors
- Traditional Styles
- Modern Styles
- Contemporary Styles
- Housing Trends

House Plans

House Construction

Systems Within

Transparency Master Overlay III-B

- Architectural Drawings
- Grouping by Function
- Traffic Patterns
- Storage Space
- Modifications for Special Needs

Transparency Master Overlay III-C

- Foundation and Frame
- Exterior Construction
- Windows and Doors

Transparency Master Overlay III-D

- Electrical Systems
- Gas Supply
- Plumbing Systems
- Heating Systems
- Cooling Systems
- Conserving Energy

# CHAPTER 6
# The Evolution of Exteriors

## Objectives

After studying this chapter, students will be able to

- identify Traditional (both folk and classic), Modern, and Contemporary exterior house styles.
- discuss the background of housing styles and current trends.

## Bulletin Boards

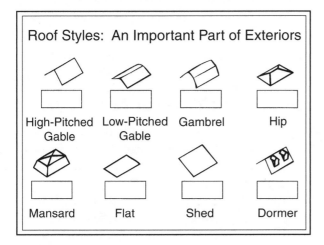

Title: *Roof Styles: An Important Part of Exteriors*

Using Figure 6-28 of the text as a guide, place a drawing and label on the board for each roof style shown. Underneath each drawing, place a picture of a house showing the appropriate roof style.

Title: *Name the Styles*

Under the title, mount pictures of houses that represent various styles. Number each picture. As each style is discussed, have students identify whether the style is represented on the board. If it is, students should identify the picture number(s) that correctly display(s) that style. If no pictures display the style, students should try to find at least one picture that does.

## Teaching Materials

**Text**, pages 156-175
  *To Know*
  *To Review*
  *In Your Community*
  *To Think About*
  *Using Technology*
**Student Activity Guide**
  A. *Roof and Dwelling Styles*
  B. *Origin and Style*
  C. *Housing Styles*
  D. *Evolution of Exteriors Word Puzzle*
  E. *Your Choice of Exteriors*
**Teacher's Resources**
  *Early English Houses*, transparency master 6-1
  *Roof Styles*, color transparencies CT-8A and CT-8B
  *Split-Level Houses*, transparency master 6-2
  Chapter 6 Test

## Introductory Activities

1. Have students work in groups to develop a presentation of different house styles within the community. Students can use slides or photographs or create drawings. Have them discuss the various styles represented.
2. Have students bring to class pictures of house exteriors they admire. Students should try to identify the style represented in each picture. (When students finish the chapter, have them review the pictures again to identify house styles.)
3. Have students find and discuss the glossary and/or dictionary definitions of key terms listed in the *To Know* section of the text. Have them add these to their card files.

# Strategies to Reteach, Reinforce, Enrich, and Extend Text Concepts

## Traditional Houses

4. **RF** Have students look through magazines and identify the Traditional styles they find.
5. **ER** *Early English Houses*, transparency master 6-1, TR. Use this transparency to show how Early English houses developed from the one-room house to the Cape Cod to the saltbox house. Have students discuss how the space in each type of house was probably used.
6. **ER** Have each student write a paper on the Traditional housing style of his or her choice from the text. The paper should describe the style's basic appearance, distinguishing qualities, attractive and unattractive features, and practical and impractical aspects.
7. **ER** Have students make a chart listing the Traditional styles, typical materials used, and distinguishing characteristics.
8. **ER** *Roof Styles*, color transparencies CT-8A and CT-8B, TR. Use these transparencies to show the variety of roof styles. Discuss the differences and why different styles are important. (Reshow these transparencies when discussing Modern and Contemporary house styles later in the chapter.)
9. **RF** *Roof and Dwelling Styles*, Activity A, SAG. Students are asked to label the roof and dwelling styles shown.
10. **ER** Have students choose a Traditional style and write a report on the origin of that style of housing.
11. **EX** Have students make posters showing the relationship between housing and cultural heritage.
12. **RF** *Origin and Style*, Activity B, SAG. Students are asked to read the descriptions provided and list the origins and housing styles described. Upon completion, students may work in small groups to compare answers and make corrections.
13. **ER** Have students find pictures of famous Americans of the past and identify the housing styles that were popular in their eras.

## Modern Houses

14. **ER** Have students give an oral report on Frank Lloyd Wright or another influential designer. The reports should highlight the designer's impact on housing styles.
15. **ER** Have students research bungalows and compare them to ranch houses.
16. **RF** Have students list the advantages and disadvantages of ranch houses.
17. **RF** *Split-Level-Houses*, transparency master 6-2, TR. Use this transparency to point out how the arrangement of levels in split-level houses affects the appearance of the exterior. Also point out the advantages and disadvantages of such a floor plan.
18. **ER** Have students make a chart listing Modern housing styles, typical materials used, and distinguishing characteristics.
19. **RF** Have students list advantages and disadvantages of Modern house styles as compared to Traditional styles.

## Contemporary Houses

20. **ER** Have each student bring to class a picture of a Contemporary house design. Discuss the materials used and distinctive design features of each house pictured.
21. **EX** Have students write a description of a Contemporary house for a classified ad. Have students sketch or find a picture of the house they describe.
22. **ER** Have students make a chart listing Contemporary housing styles, typical materials used, and distinguishing characteristics.
23. **RF** Discuss advantages and disadvantages of Contemporary house styles as compared to Traditional and Modern styles.

## Housing Trends

24. **EX** Have students work in small groups to design a house of the future. They can use their imaginations and the information in the text on future trends. Have students sketch their designs, construct models, and write reports describing them.
25. **RF** *Housing Styles*, Activity C, SAG. Students are asked to define Traditional,

Modern, and Contemporary styles in their own words and mount illustrative pictures. Students may share their examples in small groups.
26. **EX** Have students design their individual dream homes. Students should sketch the exterior, build a model, and list the materials to be used, explaining the reasoning behind the choices made. (If possible, arrange to display a few models in a public area of the school.)
27. **RF** Use a 10-minute video, *American Elegance*, to help students compare Traditional houses with Modern and Contemporary styles. The video is available for purchase from Winterthur Museum and Gardens in Winterthur, Delaware by phoning 302-888-4600.
28. **ER** Arrange for students to visit a variety of houses within or near the community. The tour should include historical and recently built houses. If possible, have a historian discuss the background of some of the houses.
29. **ER** Invite an architect to class to discuss the process of designing the exterior style for a house. Have students prepare questions for the architect in advance.

## Chapter Review

30. **RF** *Evolution of Exteriors Word Puzzle*, Activity D, SAG. Students are asked to complete the word puzzle by filling in the blanks in statements about housing exteriors.
31. **ER** *Your Choice of Exteriors*, Activity E, SAG. Using the questions provided, students are asked to express their opinions regarding the exterior styles presented in the chapter.
32. **ER** Have students discuss ways that housing has changed. Have them give examples of housing in early America versus today. When completed, you may want to have students develop a short play depicting the changes in housing. The play could be presented to other classes within the school or to a nearby elementary school.

# Answer Key

## Text

### To Review, pages 173-174

1. B
2. Scandinavian
3. C
4. garrison
5. Georgian
6. an open space covered with a roof that is supported by columns
7. (List four:) abundance of decorative trim (gingerbread), high porches, steep gable roofs, tall windows, turrets, high ceilings, dark stairways, long halls
8. Frank Lloyd Wright
9. (List one of each:) advantages—easy to maintain, easy to walk through, informal, many variations, few or no stairs; disadvantages—uses much space, expensive to build, not as energy efficient as more compact homes
10. sloped
11. D
12. Contemporary
13. to preserve the best of a society's past architecture for future generations to experience

## Student Activity Guide

### Roof and Dwelling Styles, Activity A

1. hip
2. gambrel
3. flat
4. dormer
5. Mansard
6. gable
7. ranch
8. French Provincial
9. saltbox
10. Dutch Colonial
11. Federal
12. Cape Cod

### Origin and Style, Activity B

1. Native American (Navajo), hogan
2. Native American (Pueblo), adobe
3. South and Southwest, Spanish
4. Swedish and Finnish, log cabin
5. Dutch, Dutch Colonial
6. French, French manor

7. French, French Provincial
8. English, Cape Cod
9. English, saltbox
10. English, garrison
11. English, Georgian
12. English, Federal
13. Greek, Greek Revival
14. Greek, Southern Colonial
15. English, Victorian

## *Evolution of Exteriors Word Puzzle,* Activity D

|  |  |  |  |  |  |  |  |  |  |  |  |  |  |  |  |
|--|--|--|--|--|--|--|--|--|--|--|--|--|--|--|--|
| 1 |   |   |   | A | D | O | B | E |   |   |   |   |   |   |   |
| 2 |   | F | R | E | N | C | H | P | R | O | V | I | N | C | I | A | L |
| 3 |   |   |   |   |   |   |   | L | O | G | C | A | B | I | N |
| 4 | G | R | E | E | K | R | E | V | I | V | A | L |
| 5 |   |   |   |   |   |   |   | D | U | T | C | H | C | O | L | O | N | I | A | L |
| 6 |   |   |   |   |   |   |   | T | R | A | D | I | T | I | O | N | A | L |
| 7 |   |   |   |   | G | A | R | R | I | S | O | N |
| 8 |   |   | K | I | N | G | G | E | O | R | G | E |
| 9 |   |   |   | M | O | D | E | R | N |
| 10 |  |   |   |   |   | P | O | R | T | I | C | O |
| 11 |  |   |   |   | F | E | D | E | R | A | L |
| 12 |  |   |   | T | U | R | R | E | T |
| 13 |  |   | S | A | L | T | B | O | X |
| 14 |  |   |   |   | V | I | C | T | O | R | I | A | N |
| 15 |  |   | P | R | A | I | R | I | E |
| 16 |  |   |   |   |   |   | R | A | N | C | H |
| 17 | F | R | A | N | K | L | L | O | Y | D | W | R | I | G | H | T |
| 18 |  |   |   |   |   |   | C | O | N | T | E | M | P | O | R | A | R | Y |
| 19 |  |   |   | S | O | L | A | R |
| 20 |  |   |   | E | A | R | T | H | S | H | E | L | T | E | R | E | D |

33. (List three:) boxlike shape, two or more stories, symmetrical design, flat roof, balustrade, pediments, portico over the main entrance
34. (List two:) good style for sloping lots; separates traffic into social, quiet, and service areas; separates each level with just a few stairs; involves lower building, heating, and cooling costs than ranch houses
35. partially covered with soil, often designed to use solar energy

# Teacher's Resources

## Chapter 6 Test

1. J
2. H
3. C
4. E
5. M
6. K
7. D
8. F
9. B
10. I
11. T
12. F
13. F
14. F
15. T
16. F
17. T
18. F
19. F
20. F
21. B
22. C
23. D
24. D
25. D
26. D
27. B
28. D
29. B
30. D

31. It has a delicate, dignified, symmetrical appearance; as many as two-and-a-half stories; and dominant windows, with the tops breaking into the eaves line.
32. (Student response. See pages 159-160 of the text.)

# Early English Houses
## Colonial Houses

One-Room House

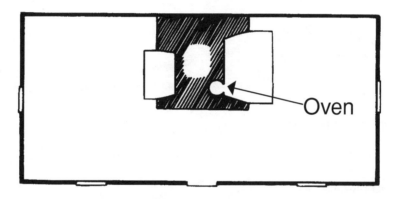

Cape Cod House

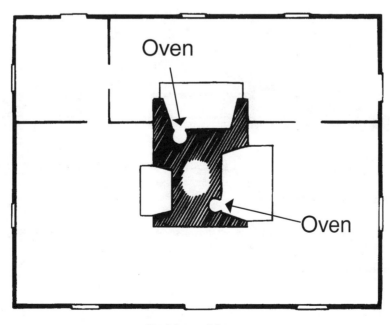

Saltbox House

## Split-Level Houses

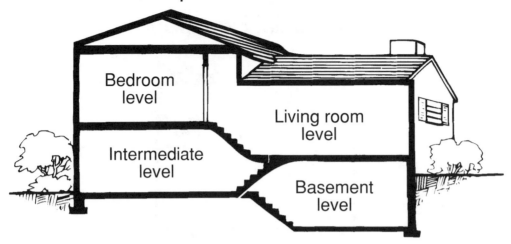

Arrangement 1: House appears to be part one-story and part two-story from front and back view.

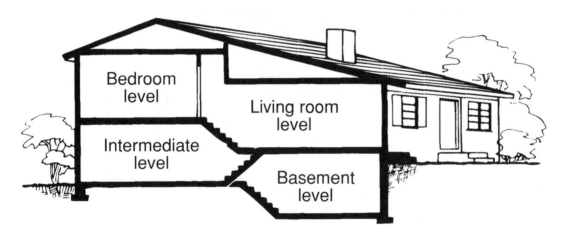

Arrangement 2: House appears to be one-story from front view and two-story from back view.

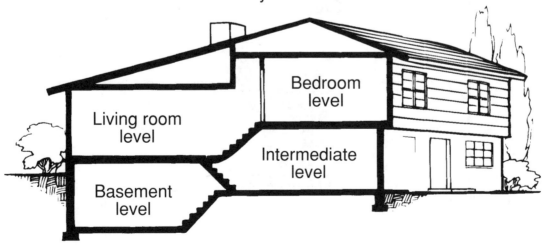

Arrangement 3: House appears to be two-story from front view and one-story from back view.

Reproducible Test Master

# The Evolution of Exteriors

Name _____

Date _____ Period _____ Score _____

**Chapter 6 Test**

❑ Matching: Match the following terms and identifying phrases.

_____ 1. A red tile roof.
_____ 2. A lean-to section.
_____ 3. An overhanging second story.
_____ 4. A two-story portico.
_____ 5. Gingerbread decoration.
_____ 6. Developed for sloping lots.
_____ 7. Hip roof with balustrade.
_____ 8. Inside space usually extends outside.
_____ 9. An eave line broken by the tops of windows.
_____ 10. Passive energy system.

A. Cape Cod
B. French Provincial
C. garrison
D. Georgian
E. Greek Revival
F. Prairie style
G. ranch
H. saltbox
I. solar
J. Spanish
K. split-level
L. turret
M. Victorian

❑ True/False: Circle *T* if the statement is true or *F* if the statement is false.

T F 11. House styles in the recent past are known as Modern.
T F 12. Boxy construction and projecting roof beams are characteristics of hogan dwellings.
T F 13. The log cabin is a strictly American design.
T F 14. The earliest houses in America were large buildings with many rooms.
T F 15. The Georgian style was named after English kings.
T F 16. Victorian houses are plain and simple in design.
T F 17. A ranch-style house has a one-story structure at ground level, with or without a basement.
T F 18. Frank Lloyd Wright designed the California Bungalow.
T F 19. Active solar systems have *no* working parts.
T F 20. Earth-sheltered houses are *not* energy efficient.

❑ Multiple Choice: Choose the best response. Write the letter in the space provided.

_____ 21. The Dutch Colonial style has _____.
  A. a gable roof
  B. dormers in the second story
  C. its origin in Holland
  D. All of the above.

(Continued)

_____ 22. The Mansard roof is typical of the _____ influence.
   A. Dutch
   B. English
   C. French
   D. Swedish

_____ 23. A Cape Cod house _____.
   A. has a gable roof
   B. has one-and-one-half stories
   C. is small and symmetrical
   D. All of the above.

_____ 24. A lean-to section is characteristic of the _____ style.
   A. Cape Cod
   B. Dutch Colonial
   C. Federal
   D. saltbox

_____ 25. A typical feature of the garrison style is a(n) _____.
   A. belvedere
   B. gambrel roof
   C. gingerbread trim
   D. overhanging second story

_____ 26. An open space covered with a roof that is supported by columns is a _____.
   A. balustrade
   B. belvedere
   C. pediment
   D. portico

_____ 27. A small room often on the roof of a Southern Colonial house is called a _____.
   A. balustrade
   B. belvedere
   C. dormer
   D. turret

_____ 28. The style of most "haunted" houses in horror movies is _____.
   A. Georgian
   B. Greek Revival
   C. saltbox
   D. Victorian

_____ 29. In the _____ style, the top part of the basement is above ground.
   A. hillside ranch
   B. raised ranch
   C. ranch
   D. earth-sheltered

_____ 30. The architect of the Prairie-style house is _____.
   A. King George
   B. Queen Victoria
   C. Taliesin
   D. Frank Lloyd Wright

(Continued)

❑ Essay Questions: Provide complete responses to the following questions or statements.
31. Describe the French Provincial house style.
32. Explain how a one-room house grew to the Cape Cod style, then the saltbox style.
33. Name three characteristics of the Federal style.
34. List two advantages of split-level houses.
35. Describe an earth-sheltered house.

# CHAPTER 7
# Understanding House Plans

## Objectives

After studying this chapter, students will be able to

- interpret architectural drawings.
- describe how computers can assist in understanding house plans.
- organize space by grouping rooms according to function.
- plan safe and convenient traffic patterns.
- evaluate storage needs and space.
- list ways to modify housing for people with physical disabilities.

## Bulletin Boards

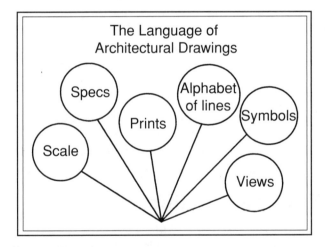

Title: *The Language of Architectural Drawings*

For the background use a print of an architectural drawing, formerly known as blueprint. Add six circles and label them as follows: *Scale, Specs, Prints, Alphabet of Lines, Symbols,* and *Views.*

Title: *Group by Function*

Draw the shape of a house on the board and place the title inside the roof. Divide the house into rooms and label the following: *Quiet Area,* *Work Area,* and *Social Area.* Draw or attach pictures of furnishings that form bedrooms, a bathroom, laundry room, kitchen, dining room, and living room.

Title: *Don't Forget the Storage Space*

Divide the board into four sections. Label the sections *Bedroom, Bathroom, Kitchen,* and *Multipurpose Room.* Have students draw or mount pictures of ideas for storage in the appropriate sections.

## Teaching Materials

**Text**, pages 176-195
   *To Know*
   *To Review*
   *In Your Community*
   *To Think About*
   *Using Technology*
**Student Activity Guide**
   A. *Floor Plan Symbols*
   B. *Drawing a Room to Scale*
   C. *Clothing Storage*
   D. *Floor Plan Evaluation*
   E. *Understanding Plans for a House*
**Teacher's Resources**
   *People Involved from the Ground Up*, color transparency CT-9
   *Interpreting Floor Plan Symbols*, reproducible master 7-1
   *Interpreting Electrical Symbols*, transparency master overlay 7-2
   *Detailed Floor Plan*, reproducible master 7-3
   *Front Elevation Rendering*, reproducible master 7-4
   *Grouping by Function*, color transparency CT-10
   *Variation on Kitchen Arrangement: C-Shape*, transparency master 7-5
   *Variation on Kitchen Arrangement: G-Shape*, transparency master 7-6
   Chapter 7 Test

# Introductory Activities

1. Have each student sketch a rough floor plan of his or her ideal house, including a kitchen, bathroom, living room, and bedrooms. More rooms may be included. Have students work in small groups to present their floor plans and explain why they like them. (Students should save floor plans for Item 42.)
2. To support the concept that everyone needs his or her own space, have two people start at opposite ends of the room and walk toward each other. Students will observe and note the boundaries each person sets. Discuss how the organization of space in houses helps meet the need for personal space.
3. Have students find and discuss the glossary and/or dictionary definitions of key terms listed in the *To Know* section of the text. Have them add these to their card files.

# Strategies to Reteach, Reinforce, Enrich, and Extend Text Concepts

## Architectural Drawings for a House

4. **RT**  Discuss why the various parts of an architectural drawing are necessary.
5. **RF**  Have students study Figures 7-1 through 7-7 in the text and discuss what they are and how they are used.
6. **RT**  Have students explain the difference between a floor plan and a print of an architectural drawing.
7. **RF**  *People Involved from the Ground Up*, color transparency CT-9, TR. Use the transparency to discuss the various professionals involved in planning and constructing a house.
8. **RF**  *Interpreting Floor Plan Symbols*, reproducible master 7-1, TR. Students should use this handout, working individually or as a group, to identify floor plan symbols. (Reuse this master as a transparency in Item 9.)
9. **RF**  *Interpreting Electrical Symbols*, transparency master overlay 7-2, TR. Superimpose this overlay on *Interpreting Floor Plan Symbols*, transparency master 7-1. Combine the images to have students identify the symbols shown. Then have them use Figure 7-3 of the text to check their responses. Discuss how symbols vary slightly on different plans.
10. **RF**  *Floor Plan Symbols*, Activity A, SAG. Students are asked to identify and label the floor plan symbols.
11. **ER**  *Drawing a Room to Scale*, Activity B, SAG. Students are asked to draw their classroom or another room to scale on the graph paper provided and apply the appropriate symbols.
12. **ER**  *Detailed Floor Plan*, reproducible master 7-3, TR. Working in small groups, have students identify the scale used, the lines from the alphabet of lines, and the windows and doors in the detailed floor plan. Have students compare these to Figure 7-4 in the text, which is a less-detailed drawing of the same house.
13. **ER**  *Front Elevation Rendering*, reproducible master 7-4, TR. Have students compare the drawing to various views of the same house, shown in Figures 7-5 and 7-6 of the text. Ask students to summarize in writing the additional facts about the house that are learned after comparing the drawing to the text figures.
14. **EX**  Arrange for the class to visit a building site. Ask the contractor or construction supervisor to explain how architectural drawings are used on the site.

## The Space Within

15. **RT**  *Grouping by Function*, color transparency CT-10, TR. Use the transparency to present the concept of grouping by function. Discuss with students the reasons for the groupings.
16. **RF**  Have students describe how the functions of the quiet area, work area, and social area affect the design of the rooms within these areas.
17. **RF**  Ask students to list possible advantages and disadvantages for grouping rooms with similar functions versus grouping rooms of mixed functions.
18. **RT**  Have students name three ways to separate areas and rooms.
19. **EX**  Have students create a variety of work triangles, using desks or tables to

represent the refrigerator, range, and sink. Students should measure the distances to the three sides of each triangle and go through the motions of preparing a snack. Have students determine what size triangle is too big or too small. Students should also determine which shapes and arrangements of triangles are most convenient and which are most inconvenient.

20. **ER** *Variation on Kitchen Arrangement: C-Shape*, transparency master 7-5, TR. Use this transparency to introduce a variation on typical kitchen arrangements. Discuss the advantages and disadvantages of this arrangement. (This transparency is also used in Item 40.)

21. **ER** *Variation on Kitchen Arrangement: G-Shape*, transparency master 7-6, TR. Use this transparency to introduce another variation on typical kitchen arrangements. Have students discuss the differences in the C-Shape and the G-Shape and tell which they prefer. (This transparency is also used in Item 40.)

22. **EX** Have students look through magazines featuring residential housing and estimate the percentage of houses that show open floor plans. Students should identify the various areas and discuss how the floor plans are designed to improve the quality of life for family members.

23. **RT** Reuse color transparency CT-10, *Grouping by Function*, to introduce the concept of traffic patterns. With a marker, trace the traffic patterns through various parts of the house. Discuss the quality of the traffic flow this floor plan presents.

24. **RT** Have students list eight guidelines for safe and convenient traffic patterns.

25. **RF** Have students trace the major traffic patterns on floor plans. Students should evaluate whether the traffic patterns are safe and convenient. (Use house plan catalogs, housing magazines, or the student text to select floor plans.)

26. **ER** Have each student examine a bedroom for a teen using a floor plan from a house magazine. Have students identify the traffic lanes and determine if the traffic pattern is convenient and direct.

27. **ER** Have students examine a kitchen they like, using a floor plan from a housing magazine. Students will identify the traffic lanes and determine if the traffic pattern is convenient and direct.

28. **ER** Using a floor plan from a housing magazine, have students examine a social area of a house for a young couple that entertains frequently. Students should identify the traffic patterns and determine if they are convenient and direct.

29. **RF** Have students evaluate a floor plan in terms of adequate built-in storage. (Use house plan catalogs, housing magazines, or the student text to select floor plans.)

30. **ER** Ask students to examine a room or a picture of a room. Have them make suggestions for adding storage space or increasing the efficiency of existing storage.

31. **ER** Have students find pictures of built-in storage and storage furniture. Discuss the advantages and disadvantages of different types of storage.

32. **ER** *Clothing Storage*, Activity C, SAG. Students are asked to sketch ways of improving the storage space of the closet illustrated.

33. **EX** Invite an architect or interior designer to discuss the arrangement of space within a house. Students should prepare questions for the guest before the discussion. If possible, arrange to display poster-size floor plans for the guest to discuss.

34. **EX** Have students work in groups to sketch small models of storage furniture that solve storage problems in small houses or apartments.

35. **EX** Have students design and make storage items for their rooms. (Students may want to use free or inexpensive materials.) Ask students to use photos or sketches to present their results to the class.

36. **RF** *Floor Plan Evaluation*, Activity D, SAG. Students are asked to identify the basic areas of the plan, its traffic patterns, the family members who might live there, and the usefulness of the floor plan.

37. **EX** Arrange for the class to visit a store or design studio that features storage components. Have someone in the business discuss different ways storage can be arranged and used.

38. **RF** Have students list the housing modifications that may be made for people with

*Chapter 7 Understanding House Plans* **139**

disabilities. Divide the modifications into two lists: exterior changes and interior changes.

39. **ER** Ask students to study the floor plans in this chapter and determine what changes need to be made to modify the plans for use by a person with physical disabilities.

40. **ER** Have students study the transparencies of kitchens used in Items 20 and 21 to determine if the arrangements are suitable for people with physical disabilities. Have students make suggestions for modifying the kitchens to make them more suitable.

41. **EX** Arrange for students to visit housing designed for a person with physical disabilities. Discuss the exterior and interior features that address the person's special needs.

# Chapter Review

42. **EX** Have students evaluate the floor plans they designed in Item 1. Each student should write a critique of his or her floor plan, addressing its function, traffic patterns, and storage space. Have students redraw their floor plans, using proper scale and symbols and incorporating any improvements as a result of studying this chapter.

43. **RF** *Understanding Plans for a House*, Activity E, SAG. Students are asked to fill in the blanks using terms and concepts from the chapter. Students may work in small groups to check and correct answers.

# Answer Key

## Text

### To Review, pages 193-194

1. information about the size, shape, and location of all parts of the house
2. $\frac{1}{4}" = 3"$, $1" = 12"$, $\frac{1}{12}$
3. C
4. floor plan
5. A. 10 windows
   B. in the closet nearest the front entry
   C. 1,859
   D. two
   E. island
6. quiet, work, and social
7. 22 feet
8. (List two:) separate areas; act as a buffer zone for noise; provide privacy
9. (List five. See page 186 of the text.)
10. (List one of each:) built-in storage—is shown in house plans, does not need to be moved, increases house value; storage furniture—can be moved to other locations in the house, can be moved to other houses, is relatively inexpensive
11. (List two. See pages 190-192 of the text.)
12. (List three. See page 192 of the text.)

## Student Activity Guide

### Floor Plan Symbols, Activity A

1. fireplace and flue
2. single sink
3. refrigerator
4. accordion door
5. picture window
6. toilet
7. stairs
8. stove
9. exterior door
10. built-in shower
11. double sink
12. sliding (regular) door
13. bay window
14. sliding (wall type) door
15. hanging cabinet
16. regular double-hung window
17. interior door
18. bathtub

### Floor Plan Evaluation, Activity D

1. bedrooms, bathrooms, grooming areas, dressing areas
2. kitchen, utility rooms
3. living room, family/game room, dining room, entrance
4. closets, shelves, bookcases, cabinets
5. (Student response.)

### Understanding Plans for a House, Activity E

1. architectural drawing
2. specifications (specs)
3. print
4. alphabet
5. phantom

6. visible
7. hidden
8. center
9. dimension
10. extension
11. break
12. section
13. symbols
14. plan
15. floor plan
16. exterior elevations
17. section
18. detail
19. quiet
20. multipurpose
21. work
22. work triangle

## Teacher's Resources

### *Interpreting Floor Plan Symbols,* reproducible master 7-1

1. toilet
2. bathtub
3. stairs
4. hanging cabinet
5. double sink
6. fireplace
7. window
8. exterior window
9. closet
10. sliding door

### *Interpreting Electrical Symbols,* transparency master overlay 7-2

A. telephone
B. three-way switch
C. light
D. outlet

### Chapter 7 Test

| | | | | | |
|---|---|---|---|---|---|
| 1. | J | 11. | T | 21. | A |
| 2. | L | 12. | F | 22. | D |
| 3. | H | 13. | T | 23. | C |
| 4. | O | 14. | T | 24. | A |
| 5. | I | 15. | F | 25. | C |
| 6. | E | 16. | F | 26. | D |
| 7. | M | 17. | T | 27. | B |
| 8. | K | 18. | T | 28. | D |
| 9. | A | 19. | F | 29. | D |
| 10. | F | 20. | F | 30. | D |

31. A floor plan is a simplified drawing showing the location of rooms, doors, windows, storage areas, and hallways. An architectural drawing is more detailed, giving dimensions, construction specifications, and views.
32. (List three:) locate areas on different ends or levels of the house, use hallways, use alcoves, use balconies, use screens, use freestanding storage units, carefully arrange furniture
33. paths people follow as they move within a room, from room to room, or to the outdoors (List five. See pages 187-188 of the text.)
34. built-in storage, storage units, storage furniture (Advantages and disadvantages are student response.)
35. (List three of each. See pages 190-192 of the text.)

Transparency Master 7-1

# Interpreting Floor Plan Symbols

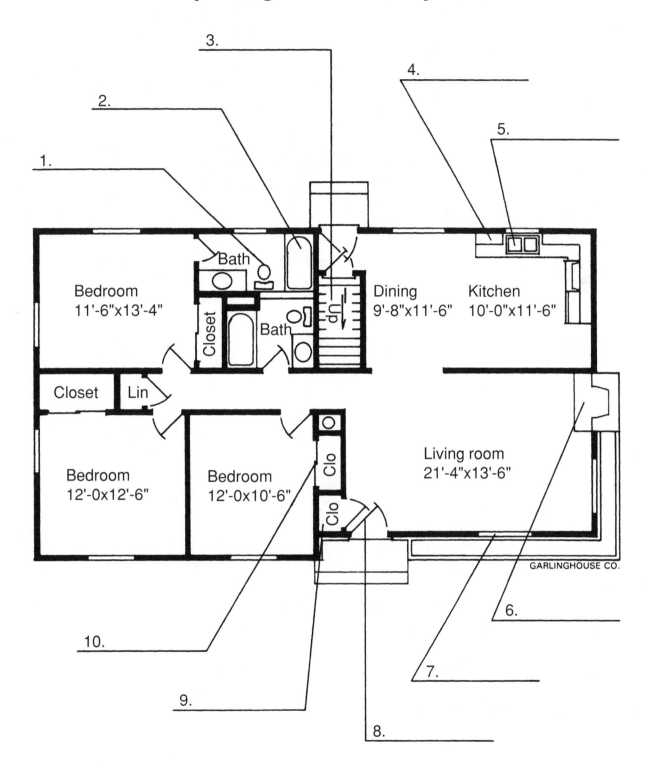

Chapter 7  Understanding House Plans  143

Transparency Master Overlay 7-2

# Interpreting Electrical Symbols

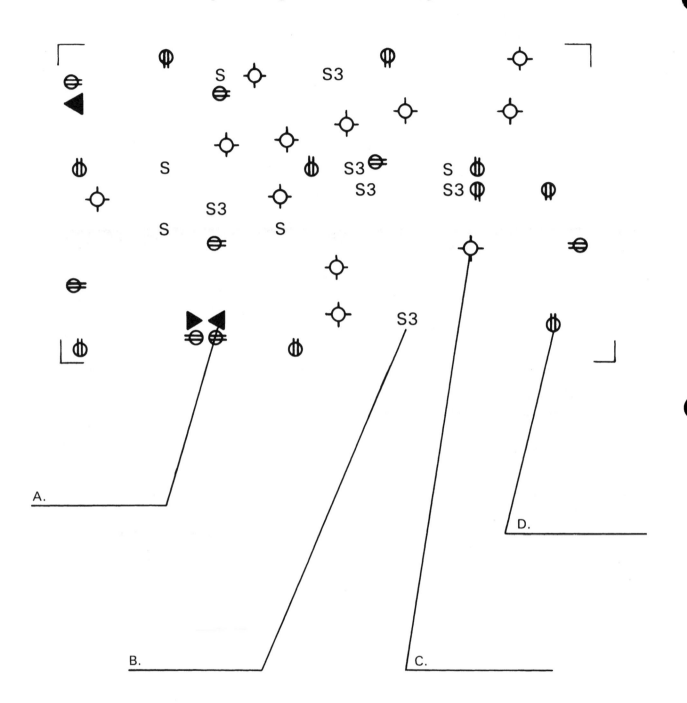

A.

B.

C.

D.

Reproducible Master 7-3

# Detailed Floor Plan

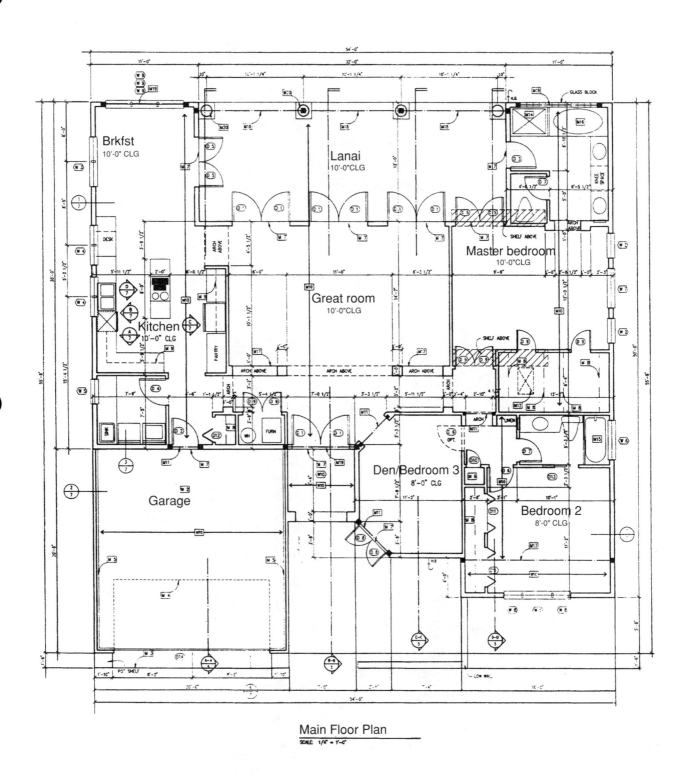

Main Floor Plan
SCALE: 1/4" = 1'-0"

Reproducible Master 7-4

# Front Elevation Rendering

Transparency Master 7-5

# Variation on Kitchen Arrangement: C-Shape

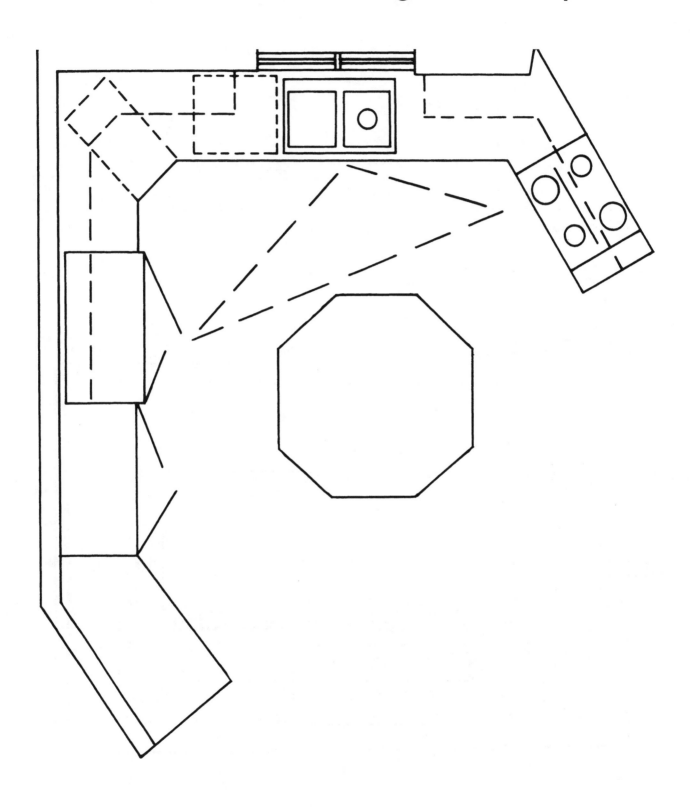

Chapter 7  Understanding House Plans

Transparency Master 7-6

# Variation on Kitchen Arrangement: G-Shape

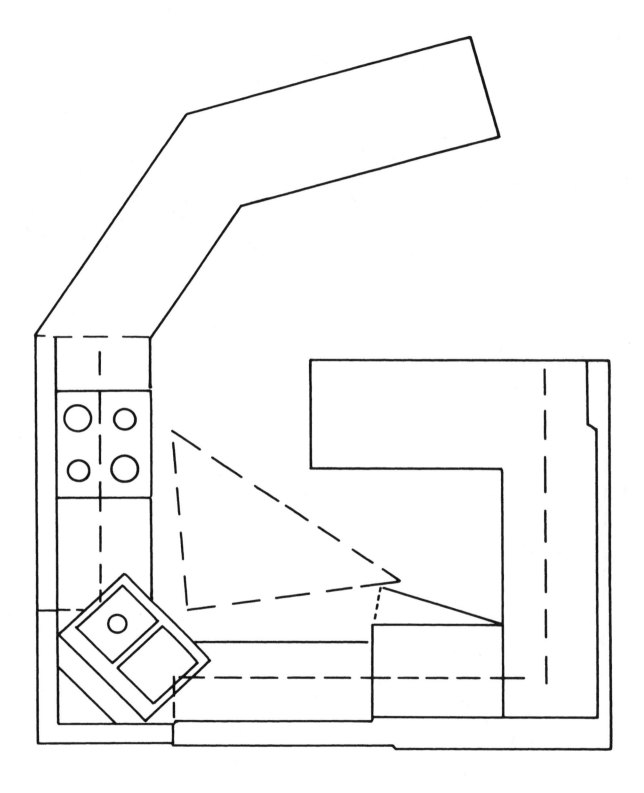

Reproducible Test Master

# Understanding House Plans

Name _____

Date _____ Period _____ Score _____

**Chapter 7 Test**

❏ Matching: Match the following terms and identifying phrases.

_____ 1. Describes types and quality of materials to be used.

_____ 2. Represent plumbing and electrical fixtures, doors, windows, and other common objects in a house.

_____ 3. Includes bedrooms and bathrooms.

_____ 4. Includes the kitchen and utility room.

_____ 5. Includes the living room and family room.

_____ 6. A simplified drawing.

_____ 7. Should be convenient and direct.

_____ 8. Includes desks, chests, and dressers.

_____ 9. Small, recessed section of a room.

_____ 10. Should be four feet wide for wheelchairs.

A. alcove
B. appliances
C. architectural drawings
D. CADD
E. floor plan
F. halls
G. play area
H. quiet area
I. social area
J. specifications
K. storage furniture
L. symbols
M. traffic patterns
N. windows
O. work area

❏ True/False: Circle *T* if the statement is true or *F* if the statement is false.

T F 11. Information about the size, shape, and location of all parts of a house are shown on an architectural drawing.

T F 12. Drawings for a house plan are usually on a scale of $1/4'' = 40'$.

T F 13. A reproduction of an original house plan is a print.

T F 14. The floor plan shows the size and arrangement of rooms, doors, windows, storage areas, and hallways.

T F 15. The social area of a house includes a utility room.

T F 16. The work triangle is an imaginary line drawn from the sink to the refrigerator to the table.

T F 17. Hallways can act as buffer zones for noise.

T F 18. The paths people follow between rooms and to the outdoors are called traffic patterns.

T F 19. Storage shared by all members of a household is called built-in storage.

T F 20. Doors with A- or B-shaped handles are easiest for those with physical disabilities to use.

(Continued)

Reproducible Test Master

❏ Multiple Choice: Choose the best response. Write the letter in the space provided.

_____ 21. The most detailed information about a house can be found in the _____.
   A. architectural drawing
   B. floor plan
   C. layout
   D. scaled drawing

_____ 22. The alphabet of lines used on house plans includes _____.
   A. center lines
   B. hidden lines
   C. visible lines
   D. All of the above.

_____ 23. Written details about house plans are called _____.
   A. alphabet of lines
   B. detail views
   C. specifications
   D. symbols

_____ 24. The _____ area is *not* a major group of rooms in a dwelling.
   A. play
   B. quiet
   C. social
   D. work

_____ 25. The work triangle in a well-designed kitchen is *not* longer than _____.
   A. 10 feet
   B. 17 feet
   C. 22 feet
   D. 27 feet

_____ 26. Hallways _____.
   A. act as a buffer zone for noise
   B. help separate areas within a house
   C. range from 36 to 42 inches in width
   D. All of the above.

_____ 27. Traffic patterns should _____.
   A. go through rooms to save space
   B. provide easy access from entrances to other parts of the house
   C. use the same paths to lead to all three areas of the house
   D. All of the above.

_____ 28. When checking for built-in storage in a dwelling, you should consider _____.
   A. the amount of storage
   B. the way you plan to use a room
   C. your hobbies and activities
   D. All of the above.

(Continued)

_____ 29. Houses for people with physical disabilities can and should be _____.
   A. affordable
   B. attractive
   C. safe
   D. All of the above.

_____ 30. When building or choosing a house for a person with disabilities, make sure _____.
   A. the lot is flat
   B. thresholds are level
   C. entrances face south
   D. All of the above.

❑ Essay Questions: Provide complete responses to the following questions or statements.

31. What is the difference between a floor plan and an architectural drawing?

32. Describe three ways to separate areas and rooms.

33. What are traffic patterns? List five guidelines to consider when evaluating them.

34. Name three ways to provide storage. Give the advantages and disadvantages of each.

35. To make housing safe and convenient for people with physical disabilities, name three ways to modify the interior and three ways to modify the exterior.

# CHAPTER 8
# House Construction

## Objectives

After studying this chapter, students will be able to

- describe how a house is constructed.
- list the parts of the foundation and frame of a house.
- list the advantages and disadvantages of different types of materials used for exterior construction.
- list basic types of windows used in houses.
- distinguish between different types of doors.
- explain how computer applications can assist the house construction process.

## Bulletin Boards

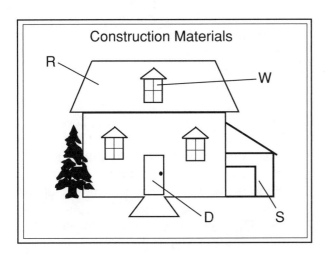

### Title: *Construction Materials*

Draw or collect pictures of construction materials you might use on the exterior of a house. Place an illustration of appropriate materials over each label as follows: *roofing* (R), *windows* (W), *siding* (S), and *doors* (D).

### Title: *Using Architectural Drawings in Construction*

Find prints of architectural drawings and mount the sections that show the following construction steps: foundation, floor frame, wall frame, and roof frame. Label each section.

### Title: *House Construction from the Bottom Up*

Draw a pyramid and divide it into three horizontal sections. Label the bottom section *Foundation and Frame*; the middle section *Exterior Construction*; and the top section *Windows and Doors*. Place pictures illustrating each section in the appropriate part of the pyramid. You may want to cut the title from brown paper and give the letters a wood appearance by drawing on them grain lines and black dots for nails.

## Teaching Materials

**Text**, pages 196-214
*To Know*
*To Review*
*In Your Community*
*To Think About*
*Using Technology*

**Student Activity Guide**
A. *Construction Materials*
B. *Foundation and Framing*
C. *Choosing Windows and Doors*

**Teacher's Resources**
*Footing and Foundation*, transparency master 8-1
*Floor and Wall Frame*, transparency master 8-2
*Roof Frame*, transparency master 8-3
*Window Styles*, color transparencies CT-11A, CT-11B, and CT-11C
Chapter 8 Test

## Introductory Activities

1. Review with students the purpose of architectural drawings and detail views, which were both described in Chapter 7.
2. Have students list the types of detail views they think would be required to construct a house's foundation, frame, and exterior.

3. Have students find and discuss the glossary and/or dictionary definitions of key terms listed in the *To Know* section of the text. Have them add these to their card files.

## Strategies to Reteach, Reinforce, Enrich, and Extend Text Concepts

### The Foundation and the Frame

4. **RF** *Footing and Foundation*, transparency master 8-1, TR. Use this transparency to show the details of the footing and foundation. Discuss why certain materials and procedures are used in constructing these sections. Point out the anchor bolts, sill sealer, sill plate, footing, and foundation wall.
5. **RF** *Floor and Wall Frame*, transparency master 8-2, TR. Use this transparency to show the details of floor and wall framing. Discuss why certain materials and procedures are used in constructing these sections. Point out the sill plate, joists, girder, studs, and headers.
6. **RF** *Foundation and Framing*, Activity B, SAG. Students are asked to label and define the various parts of the foundation and framing.
7. **RF** *Roof Frame*, transparency master 8-3, TR. Use this transparency to show the details of roof framing. Point out the rafters, ridge, and trusses. Explain the roof frame also forms the frame for the ceiling.

### Materials Used for Exterior Construction

8. **RF** *Construction Materials*, Activity A, SAG. Students are asked to identify the advantages and disadvantages of using various construction materials.
9. **ER** Have students collect and mount on Bulletin Board I pictures of materials or houses constructed of various materials. Have students list some advantages and disadvantages of each material. (Save the pictures for Item 10.)
10. **EX** Have students examine catalogs and determine the costs of materials shown in the pictures from Item 9. Have students determine the best buys and explain their choices.
11. **RF** Discuss the materials used in constructing a roof. Have students list the functions of roofing materials.
12. **EX** Arrange a visit to a house construction site. Students should look for the sections discussed in the chapter. Have the builder show the students the detail sections of the architectural drawings used to construct them.
13. **EX** Have students make gingerbread houses. Discuss the importance of exact measurements, level surfaces, and straight and square framework. Have students compare the sections of their gingerbread houses to real houses. (Students may wish to decorate the gingerbread houses and donate them to Head Start or a retirement home.)

### Windows and Doors

14. **RF** Have students study Figure 8-8 in the text and discuss the purpose of each part of a window. Using a school window for an example, ask volunteers to point out the important parts.
15. **RF** Have students find the meanings of the window terms *muntins* and *bars*. Discuss the purposes of these parts.
16. **ER** *Window Styles*, color transparencies CT-11A, CT-11B, and CT-11C, TR. Use these transparencies to introduce the various window styles. Point out the muntins and bars. Ask students which types they like and why.
17. **ER** Have students report to the class the styles of windows in their homes.
18. **RF** Have students discuss the types of doors available, their uses, advantages, and disadvantages.
19. **ER** Have students examine the doors in school and in their homes. Have students list the various types they find and briefly report them to the class.
20. **EX** Arrange a visit to a building supply store. Have students look for the various types of windows and doors available. Discuss the various materials used to make them. Have students determine where each type of window and door would be

appropriately used. Have them justify their answers.
21. **ER** *Choosing Windows and Doors,* Activity C, SAG. Students are asked to help a family, based on the information provided, choose windows and doors.

## Computer Applications in Construction

22. **RF** Have students list advantages of using computers to assist with decisions in house construction.
23. **RT** Ask students to work in small groups to create posters illustrating uses for computers in the house construction process.
24. **ER** Have students search online for software programs that might be used in the construction of housing. Ask students to report their findings to the class.
25. **EX** Invite a housing professional to talk to the class about how designers use computers in their careers. If the speaker worked in a housing career before computers were widely used, what changes has he or she noted in the job as a result of technology?

## Chapter Review

26. **ER** Have teams of three students alternate talking for one minute apiece about what the chapter covered and continue until nothing is left to report. Ask team members to write individual summaries of what they learned from the chapter.

## Answer Key

### Text

*To Review,* page 212

1. so the house will settle evenly
2. (List two:) loose soil, footing placed above the frost line, uneven settling
3. joists, studs, rafters
4. (List three:) a common material, suitable for a variety of exterior styles, easy to cut and assemble, requires simple tools
5. aluminum: advantages—durable, needs no paint, weather- and corrosion-resistant; disadvantages—dents, conducts electricity

vinyl: advantages—durable, does not conduct electricity, needs no paint, expands and contracts with weather changes; disadvantages—will show dents

pressed wood and fiberboard: advantages—easy to paint, less expensive than plywood, have special surface treatments available; disadvantages—cannot be stained

fiber cement: advantages—very stable, will not burn, has a zero smoke-development rating, is less expensive than brick with all the benefits, holds paint two to three times longer than wood, resists moisture and pests; disadvantages—requires painting

6. (List five:) asphalt, fiberglass, vinyl, wood, tile, slate, concrete, metal
7. A. swinging
   B. sliding
   C. swinging
   D. fixed
   E. sliding
   F. swinging
   G. swinging
8. An interior door has a hollow core, while an exterior door has a solid core.
9. A solid-core door is heavier and has tightly fitted blocks of wood or particle board covered with veneer. A hollow-core door is lighter and has wood strips, stiff cardboard, or paper honeycomb covered with a stronger outside frame.
10. (List two:) speeds the process of designing housing, helps assure the accuracy of the designs, provides a realistic view of the final house for the client

## Student Activity Guide

*Foundation and Framing,* Activity B

1. I—vertical framing members that make up the wall frame
2. F—series of beams supporting the roof
3. G—horizontal line at which the two slopes of the roof meet
4. E—small, built-up beam that carries the load of the structure over door and window openings
5. B—lightweight horizontal support member
6. J—covering of plywood sheets that is nailed directly to the floor joists
7. C—the very bottom of the foundation

8. A—large horizontal member that takes the end load of joists
9. D—supports the load of the house between the footing and the floor
10. H—first piece of lumber bolted to the foundation wall

## *Choosing Windows and Doors,* Activity C

1. (List three:) provide natural light, air circulation, a view, and a pleasant appearance
2. vinyl, wood covered with vinyl or aluminum
3. awning, hopper, casement, or jalousie
4. casement
5. awning
6. hopper
7. bay window
8. add skylight or clerestory
9. sliding
10. solid-core
11. hollow-core
12. French doors
(Students may justify other answers.)

# Teacher's Resources

## Chapter 8 Test

| | | | | | |
|---|---|---|---|---|---|
| 1. | D | 12. | D | 23. | T |
| 2. | D | 13. | E | 24. | A |
| 3. | A | 14. | F | 25. | C |
| 4. | E | 15. | T | 26. | C |
| 5. | A | 16. | F | 27. | A |
| 6. | C | 17. | T | 28. | C |
| 7. | D | 18. | T | 29. | D |
| 8. | A, B | 19. | F | 30. | B |
| 9. | A | 20. | T | 31. | A |
| 10. | B | 21. | F | 32. | D |
| 11. | C | 22. | F | 33. | B |

34. The freezing and thawing that occurs at the frost line causes expansion and contraction. To keep foundation cracks to a minimum, the foundation's footings should be placed below the frost line.
35. aluminum: advantages—durable, needs no paint, weather- and corrosion-resistant; disadvantages—dents, conducts electricity

    vinyl: advantages—durable, does not conduct electricity, needs no paint, expands and contracts with weather changes; disadvantages—will show dents

    pressed wood and fiberboard: advantages—easy to paint, less expensive than plywood, have special surface treatments available; disadvantages—cannot be stained

    fiber cement: advantages—very stable, will not burn, has a zero smoke-development rating, is less expensive than brick with all the benefits, holds paint two to three times longer than wood, resists moisture, and pests; disadvantages—requires painting

Transparency Master 8-1

# Footing and Foundation

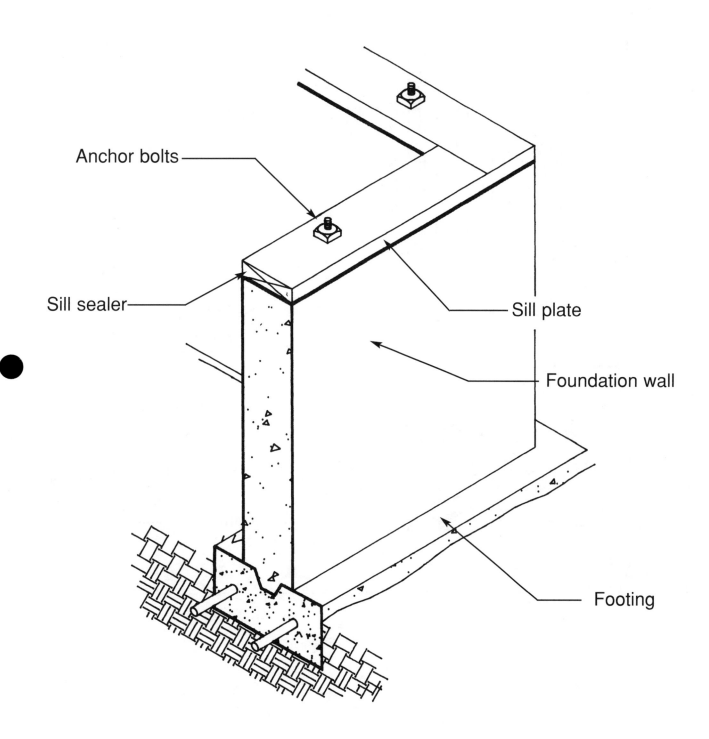

Chapter 8   House Construction   157

Transparency Master 8-2

# Floor and Wall Frame

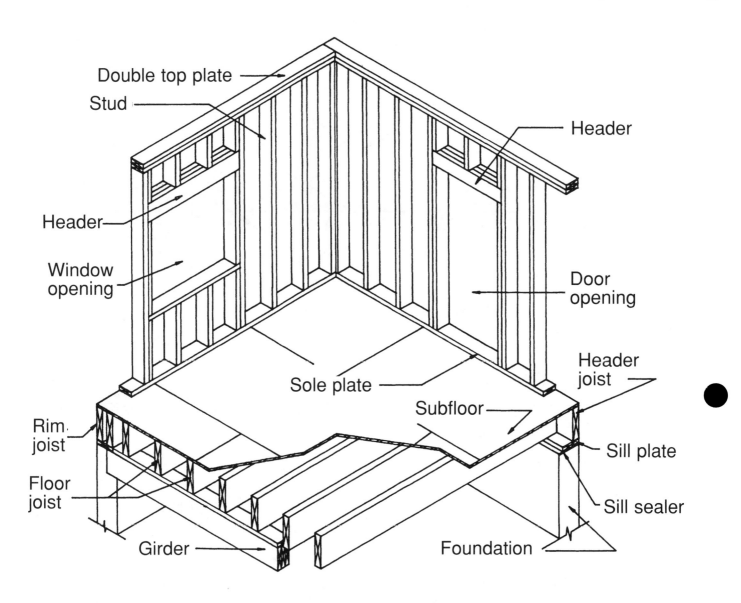

158 Chapter 8 House Construction

## Roof Frame

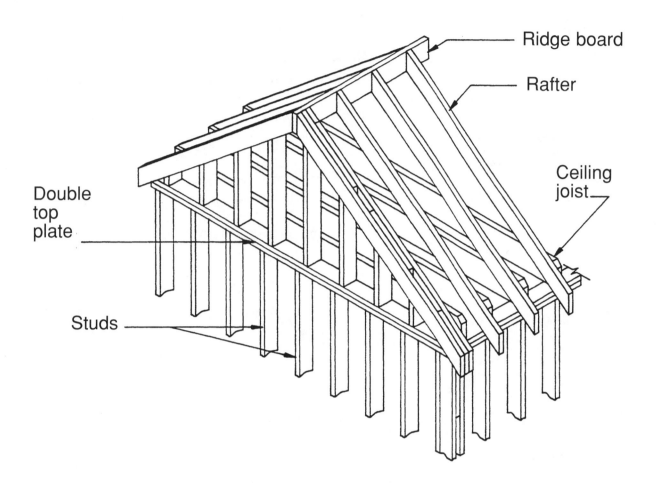

Reproducible Test Master

# House Construction

Name _____

Date _____ Period _____ Score _____

### Chapter 8 Test

❏ Matching: Match each of the following window styles with the appropriate window type. (Window types may be used more than once.)

**Window Styles**

_____ 1. Awning.

_____ 2. Casement.

_____ 3. Clerestory.

_____ 4. Double hung.

_____ 5. Half-round.

_____ 6. Hopper.

_____ 7. Jalousie.

_____ 8. Two-sash.

**Window Types**
A. fixed
B. horizontal sliding
C. swings in
D. swings out
E. vertical sliding

❏ Matching: Match each of the following door types with the construction method used.

**Door Construction**

_____ 9. Core framework covered with wood or metal.

_____ 10. Glass panels.

_____ 11. Lightweight core with heavy outside frame.

_____ 12. Tightly fitted blocks of covered veneer.

_____ 13. Vertical and horizontal members around panels.

**Door Types**
A. flush
B. framed glass
C. hollow-core
D. solid-core
E. stile and rail

❏ True/False: Circle *T* if the statement is true or *F* if the statement is false.

T  F  14. Understanding how a house is constructed *cannot* help a person make good decisions about buying a previously owned house.

T  F  15. The foundation and frame form the basic structure of a house.

T  F  16. The frost line causes cracks to appear in the foundation wall.

T  F  17. The first piece of lumber applied in house construction is the sill plate.

T  F  18. Joists are lightweight horizontal support members.

(Continued)

T  F  19. Walls are generally assembled upright on the subfloor.

T  F  20. The ridge is the horizontal line where the highest point of the roof frame meets.

T  F  21. Exterior wood siding can be left unfinished because it does *not* need special protection from the elements.

T  F  22. Masonry siding is expensive to maintain.

T  F  23. Looking for patches is important when inspecting a roof.

❏ Multiple Choice: Choose the best response. Write the letter in the space provided.

_____ 24. The very bottom part of the foundation is the _____.
A. footing
B. frost line
C. rebar
D. stress crack

_____ 25. _____ are the pieces of horizontal reinforcing steel in the footing.
A. Joists
B. Rafters
C. Rebars
D. Studs

_____ 26. Anchor bolts are set about _____ feet apart into the concrete of the foundation wall.
A. two
B. four
C. six
D. eight

_____ 27. A _____ supports the load of the floor joists in the middle of a wide room.
A. girder
B. header
C. rafter
D. stud

_____ 28. The disadvantage of wood siding is that it _____.
A. is difficult to assemble
B. is difficult to cut
C. must be protected against the elements
D. All of the above.

_____ 29. Manufactured siding is made from such materials as _____.
A. aluminum and vinyl
B. pressed wood
C. fiber cement
D. All of the above.

_____ 30. A veneer wall is a _____.
A. bond
B. nonsupporting wall
C. wall frame
D. All of the above.

(Continued)

_____ 31. The most common roofing material is _____.
   A. asphalt shingles
   B. metal
   C. shakes
   D. tile

_____ 32. Skylights are usually located _____.
   A. above a clerestory window
   B. high on a wall
   C. in a bay window
   D. in a ceiling or roof

_____ 33. An example of a framed-glass door is a _____.
   A. flush door
   B. French door
   C. hollow-core door
   D. solid-core door

❑ Essay Questions: Provide complete responses to the following questions or statements.

34. Describe the frost line and why it is important for home builders.

35. Give the advantages and disadvantages of the following types of siding:
   A. wood
   B. aluminum
   C. vinyl
   D. pressed wood and fiberboard
   E. fiber cement
   F. masonry

# CHAPTER 9
# The Systems Within

## Objectives

After studying this chapter, students will be able to

- describe the parts of the electrical system.
- tell how natural gas and propane gas reach gas-burning appliances.
- explain the functions of the two main parts of the plumbing system.
- list the different types of heating systems.
- explain how a cooling system works.
- determine ways to conserve energy in the house.

## Bulletin Boards

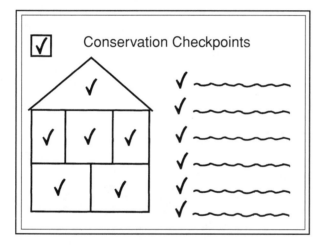

Title: *Conservation Checkpoints*

Under the title mount a drawing of a house on one side of the board, or use a house drawn for a previous bulletin board. Place check marks in each room. Develop a list of energy conservation recommendations from the "Conserving Energy" section of the text. Place check marks before each point as shown.

Title: *The Systems Within*

Cut shapes or find pictures of a lightbulb, propane tank, pipeline, fireplace, and fan. Mount the shapes on the board and label each with the appropriate term: *Electrical, Gas, Plumbing, Heating,* or *Cooling.*

## Teaching Materials

**Text**, pages 215-237
  *To Know*
  *To Review*
  *In Your Community*
  *To Think About*
  *Using Technology*

**Student Activity Guide**
  A. *Electricity in Your Home*
  B. *Household Plumbing*
  C. *Heating Systems*
  D. *Systems Savvy*

**Teacher's Resources**
  *Electricity in the House,* transparency master 9-1
  *Water Supply System,* transparency master 9-2
  *Water Disposal System,* transparency master 9-3
  *Solar Heating Systems,* color transparency CT-12
  *Insulation,* reproducible master 9-4
  Chapter 9 Test

## Introductory Activities

1. Have students study an architectural drawing showing the paths of the electrical and plumbing systems. Have them trace the paths with markers.
2. Have students find and discuss the glossary and/or dictionary definitions of key terms listed in the *To Know* section of the text. Have them add these to their card files.

# Strategies to Reteach, Reinforce, Enrich, and Extend Text Concepts

## Electrical Systems

3. **RT** Ask students to list all the uses of electricity in their homes.
4. **RT** Have students make a list of the electrical terms and give their meanings.
5. **ER** Bring in an electric bill for students to study. Have them find or determine the cost per watt, total watts used, billing period, and payment due date.
6. **RF** *Electricity in Your Home*, Activity A, SAG. Students are asked to list items in their homes that are powered by electricity. Then they are to write in the spaces provided how their lives would be without electricity.
7. **RF** *Electricity in the House*, transparency master 9-1, TR. Use this transparency to discuss with students electrical lines underground and above ground. Have them discuss the advantages and disadvantages of each.
8. **RF** Arrange for a school maintenance person to show students the school's service entrance panel and circuit breakers or fuses. Discuss what happens when a circuit is broken and how it can be restored.
9. **EX** Ask students to find out how many circuits are in their homes and how to restore the current if a circuit is broken.
10. **ER** Have students record their home meter readings at a certain time every day for a week. Then have each student calculate average electricity usage per day for the period.
11. **EX** Have students write reports about electricity and safety. Compile the reports into a master list of safety tips and distribute to students.
12. **EX** Have students write research papers on the history of electricity. Students could present a short play on how electricity was discovered.

## Gas as an Energy Source

13. **RF** Have students list the appliances in their homes that use gas.
14. **EX** Have students read a gas meter, study a gas bill, and list the terms on the bill. Have them find out the meanings of unfamiliar terms and discuss how they are used on the gas bill.
15. **RF** Compare natural and propane gas, indicating the appropriateness of each type as a household fuel.
16. **RF** Survey students to learn how many use propane gas in their homes.
17. **EX** Invite a spokesperson from your local gas company to speak on the history and use of natural gas. Have students write short reports on the speaker's comments.

## Plumbing Systems

18. **EX** Divide the class into groups and assign each group a particular plumbing problem (leaky kitchen faucet, broken pipeline, clogged drain). Have each group research how to solve the problem and estimate the cost of repair. Students may use their parents, books, and retail stores as resources. Have students give oral reports on how they would solve the problems, what materials would be required, and how much the repairs would cost.
19. **RF** *Water Supply System*, transparency master 9-2, TR. Use this transparency to introduce the plumbing system that brings water into a house.
20. **ER** Have students locate the shutoff valves to plumbing fixtures in their homes. With their parent's permission (and the permission of the building's owner, if applicable) have students open and close one of the valves. They should locate the shutoff valves to the water mains at their houses.
21. **RF** *Water Disposal System*, transparency master 9-3, TR. Use this transparency to show students a water disposal system. Discuss why incoming water is pressurized but wastewater is not.
22. **EX** Have groups of students research and write one-page reports on one of the following topics: recycling water, septic tanks and leach beds, or plumbing fixtures. Each group should report to the class.
23. **EX** Visit a house under construction and, with the permission of the builder, have students examine the plumbing. Have students determine which are gas lines,

incoming water lines, and wastewater lines. Also determine the type of pipe materials that are used.

24. **ER** *Household Plumbing*, Activity B, SAG. Students are asked to mount pictures of bathroom fixtures they like and answer related questions.

## Heating Systems

25. **RF** Compare the four conventional heating systems in terms of the type of fuel used and the methods of heating and moving the air.
26. **RF** *Solar Heating Systems*, color transparency CT-12, TR. Use the transparency to introduce the concept of using solar energy in homes for heat.
27. **RF** Have students compare the following: fireplaces with an insert versus those without; radiant stoves versus circulating stoves. Ask students why pellet stoves are sometimes chosen.
28. **ER** Survey students to learn the type of heat used in their homes. Tabulate the results.
29. **EX** Arrange for students to visit a house equipped for solar heating. Have someone point out the system's features while explaining how it works.
30. **ER** *Heating Systems*, Activity C, SAG. Students are asked to describe various heating systems, give advantages and disadvantages of each, and explain which they prefer.

## Cooling Systems

31. **RF** Compare a central air conditioner and room air conditioner. Have students describe the functions of the compressor and the condenser.
32. **RF** Have students describe how a heat pump can serve as an air conditioner.
33. **ER** Arrange for a maintenance person to show and explain the air conditioning system of the school.

## Conserving Energy

34. **ER** Have students determine the amount of the country's energy that will be used in housing if the stated goal of the U.S. Department of Energy is reached.
35. **RF** Have students explain what insulation does and what R-value means.
36. **RF** Have students compare the uses of blanket insulation, board insulation, and loose fill. Have students explain how the various forms of these insulating materials determine their use.
37. **RF** Have students find and name the various types of weather stripping used in their homes and school.
38. **ER** Arrange a visit to a building supply store and examine the various types of insulation and weather stripping. Have a salesperson explain the uses of each.
39. **ER** *Insulation*, reproducible master 9-4, TR. Have students provide the information requested.
40. **RF** Have students suggest tasks that a personal computer can monitor to conserve energy in housing.
41. **EX** Divide the class into groups and assign each group a certain room of a house. Have each group devise a list of energy conservation tips for the assigned room. Combine the lists into a pamphlet and make copies for each student to keep.

## Chapter Review

42. **RF** *Systems Savvy*, Activity D, SAG. Students are asked to match the terms from the chapter with the identifying phrases.

## Answer Key

### Text

*To Review,* pages 235-236

1. the movement of electrons along a conductor
2. large appliances such as a range, refrigerator, water heater, and furnace
3. for gas leaks
4. false
5. true
6. (Student response. See pages 223-225 of the text.)
7. has little air movement, no noise, and no ducts
8. A fireplace is an open chamber in which wood burns (or gas or electricity give the appearance of a wood fire) and smoke exits through the chimney. A wood-burning stove is a closed chamber that

produces heat by burning wood. A pellet stove is similar to a wood-burning stove, but it creates more heat by burning pellets of compressed organic material.
9. refrigerant
10. board
11. by managing the systems that use energy

# Student Activity Guide

## *Household Plumbing,* Activity B

1. (Student response.)
2. at the water heater
3. so separate parts of the system can be repaired without shutting off the water for the entire house
4. Waste disposal pipes are much larger than water supply lines and are not pressurized.
5. through a soil stack
6. to catch and hold a quantity of water that forms a seal, which prevents sewage gases from backing into the house

## *Systems Savvy,* Activity D

1. F or G
2. C
3. R
4. K
5. U
6. M
7. T
8. A
9. O
10. E
11. L
12. D
13. H
14. Q
15. V
16. P
17. S
18. B
19. N
20. J

# Teacher's Resources

## *Insulation,* reproducible master 9-4

1. resistance of a material to heat movement
2. board insulation
3. loose fill
4. (List three:) fibrous glass, rock wool, cellulose, urethane, polystyrene
5. safety factors, use considerations, shape and size requirements, proper R-value
6. A or C
7. B
8. C
9. A
10. B
11. B
12. A or C

13. B
14. A
15. A or C

## Chapter 9 Test

1. J
2. E
3. O
4. A
5. N
6. H
7. K
8. C
9. D
10. M
11. T
12. F
13. F
14. T
15. T
16. F
17. T
18. F
19. T
20. T
21. C
22. B
23. D
24. D
25. D
26. D
27. C
28. C
29. A
30. B

31. (Student response. See pages 227-228 of the text.)
32. amount of smoke produced per hour as well as the heat produced per unit of fuel used
33. In moderately cold weather, it transfers heat from the ground or outside air into the house. In warm weather it transfers heat from indoors outside.
34. R-value is the resistance of a material to the movement of heat. The higher the R-value is, the greater the resistance.
35. (List five:) turn lights on and off, roll shades up and down, adjust heating, adjust ventilation, adjust air conditioning, adjust interior temperature, report maintenance and equipment problems, monitor systems for dirty filters

Transparency Master 9-1

# Electricity in the House

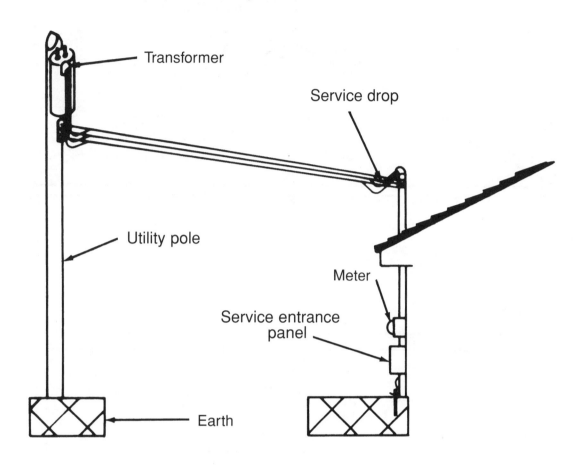

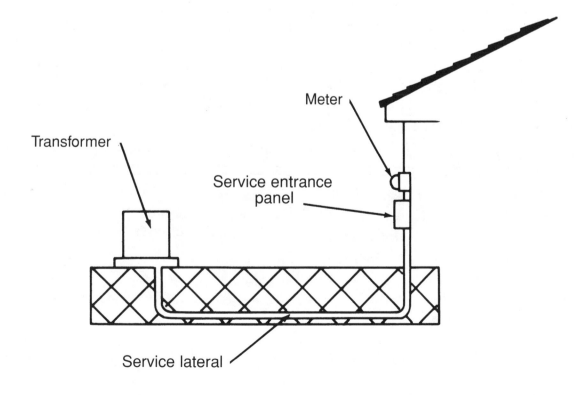

Transparency Master 9-2

# Water Supply System

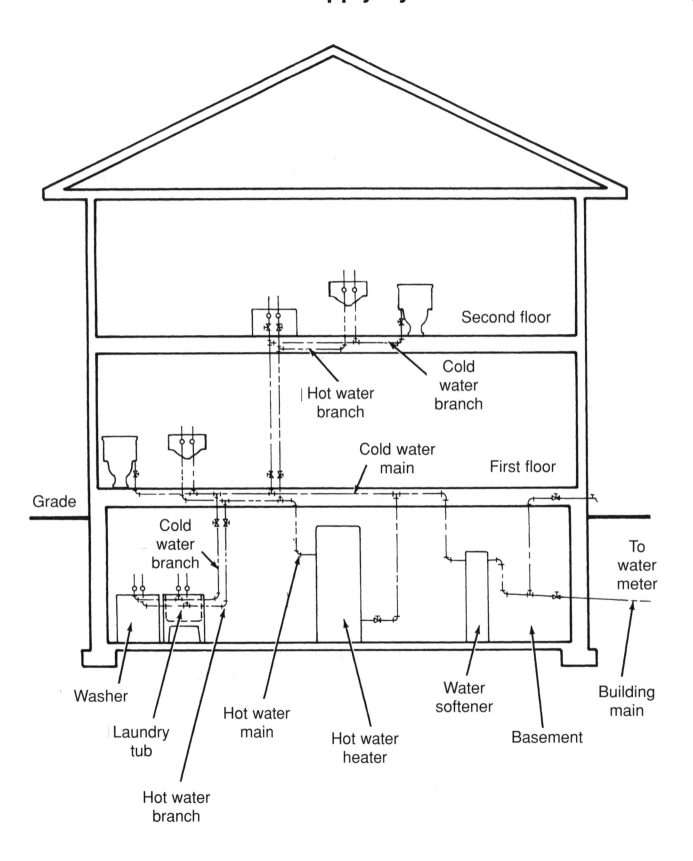

# Water Disposal System

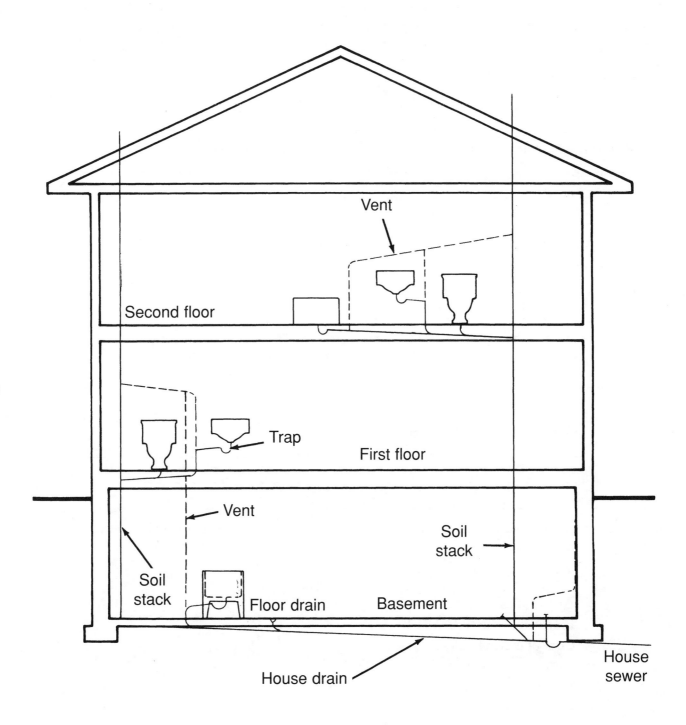

Reproducible Master 9-4

# Insulation

Name _____ Date _____ Period _____

Answer these questions and follow the directions below.

1. What is R-value?
   _____
   _____
   _____

2. Which type of insulation has the highest R-value per inch of thickness?
   _____
   _____
   _____

3. Which type of insulation is the easiest to use in hard-to-reach places?
   _____
   _____
   _____

4. What are three of the materials used to make insulation?
   _____
   _____
   _____

5. What determines the specific insulation material used in a job?
   _____
   _____
   _____

Match the form of insulation with the area where it is best used. (Answers may be used more than once.)

**Area of Use**

_____ 6. Attic.
_____ 7. Between concrete and earth.
_____ 8. Core of concrete block.
_____ 9. Floor.
_____ 10. Footing.
_____ 11. Foundation wall.
_____ 12. Frame wall.
_____ 13. Outside studs.
_____ 14. Pipes and ducts.
_____ 15. Wall.

**Form of Insulation**

A. blanket
B. board
C. loose fill

Reproducible Test Master

# The Systems Within

Name _____

Date _____ Period _____ Score _____

## Chapter 9 Test

❑ Matching: Match the following terms and identifying phrases.

_____ 1. Connecting wires from a pole transformer to the house entry.

_____ 2. Coal and petroleum.

_____ 3. Measure of electrical power the consumer uses.

_____ 4. Measure of electricity passing through a conductor.

_____ 5. Measure of pressure pushing an electrical current.

_____ 6. Measures electrical usage.

_____ 7. Metal box dividing electricity into circuits.

_____ 8. Overcurrent device.

_____ 9. Pipe that holds electrical wires.

_____ 10. Pipe that vents gas outside.

A. ampere
B. circuit
C. circuit breaker
D. conduit
E. fossil fuels
F. leach bed
G. leach line
H. meter
I. propane
J. service drop
K. service entrance panel
L. shutoff valve
M. soil stack
N. voltage
O. watts

❑ True/False: Circle *T* if the statement is true or *F* if the statement is false.

T  F  11. The mechanical systems in a house include the systems that provide electricity, gas, and water to the house.

T  F  12. The movement of electrons along an ampere is called an electric current.

T  F  13. The service lateral monitors electrical usage in a house.

T  F  14. Gas fuels include natural gas and propane gas.

T  F  15. Natural gas comes from under the ground.

T  F  16. Gas lines use copper tubing.

T  F  17. Water may pass through a water softener or filter inside a house.

T  F  18. Traps are installed to make it possible to repair leaks without shutting off all the water in a house.

T  F  19. Wastewater that goes through a sewer treatment system can be recycled.

T  F  20. A heat pump can be used to heat and cool a house.

(Continued)

Reproducible Test Master

❏ Multiple Choice: Choose the best response. Write the letter in the space provided.

_____ 21. When electrons follow a path from the source of electricity to a device and back to the source, an electric _____ is formed.
   A. ampere
   B. circuit
   C. current
   D. voltage

_____ 22. Large appliances such as the kitchen range may require _____ volts.
   A. 120
   B. 220
   C. 320
   D. 440

_____ 23. Consumers have their electrical power measured in _____.
   A. amperes
   B. meters
   C. volts
   D. watts

_____ 24. Electrical power comes from _____.
   A. atomic fission
   B. falling water
   C. fossil fuels
   D. All of the above.

_____ 25. Fuel that is delivered in pressurized cylinders or tanks is _____.
   A. atomic fission
   B. electricity
   C. natural gas
   D. propane gas

_____ 26. The plumbing system includes _____.
   A. gas lines
   B. hot and cold water lines
   C. wastewater lines
   D. All of the above.

_____ 27. Each plumbing fixture is equipped with a _____ to form a water seal.
   A. septic tank
   B. soil stack
   C. trap
   D. water closet

_____ 28. Plumbing fixtures are made of materials that are _____.
   A. absorbent and easy to clean
   B. absorbent and smooth
   C. durable and easy to clean
   D. All of the above.

(Continued)

_____ 29. In _____ heating and cooling systems, ducts are required.
   A. forced-air
   B. hydronic
   C. radiant
   D. solar

_____ 30. About _____ of all the energy used in this country is used in housing.
   A. one-tenth
   B. one-fifth
   C. one-third
   D. one-half

❑ Essay Questions: Provide complete responses to the following questions or statements.

31. Describe the following stoves: radiant, circulating, and pellet.

32. What heating equipment standards are set by the U.S. Environmental Protection Agency?

33. Explain how a heat pump works.

34. Explain why the R-value of insulation is important.

35. List five tasks that a personal computer can monitor to conserve energy in housing.

PART 4

# The Inside Story

Goal: Students will learn how to create interior environments that are pleasing and functional.

## Bulletin Board

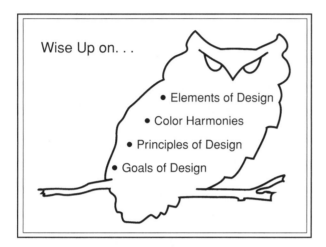

Title: *Wise Up on...*

Under the title, place a drawing of a large owl on the board. Use the board to introduce the topics in Part Four. As each chapter or group of chapters is studied, the topics inside the owl can be changed to reflect the subject matter. For instance, the topics listed in the drawing above are the key subjects the class will study in Chapters 10-12.

## Teaching Materials

**Text**
Chapters 10-18, pages 238-427
*To Know*
*To Review*
*In Your Community*
*To Think About*
*Using Technology*

**Teacher's Resources**
*The Inside Story*, transparency master IV-A
*The Inside Story*, transparency master overlays IV-B and IV-C

## Introductory Activities

1. *The Inside Story*, transparency master IV-A, TR. Use this transparency to introduce students to the concepts in Chapters 10-13. Explain that Chapters 1 to 9 provided background information to help students make wise decisions when choosing a home. Part Four will help them make wise decisions about the interior environment of a house. Have students suggest reasons it is important to understand the design elements and principles in Chapters 10-12 as well as textile facts described in Chapter 13.

2. *The Inside Story*, transparency master overlay IV-B, TR. Superimpose this transparency on *The Inside Story*, transparency master IV-A. Use the combined image to introduce concepts in Chapters 14-16. Have students suggest what is meant by the term *backgrounds*. Explain that backgrounds are more satisfying when the concepts learned in Chapters 10-13 are used. Ask students how knowledge of the design, construction, and arrangement of furniture can help them improve their living space. (This transparency overlay is also used in Item 3.)

3. *The Inside Story*, transparency master overlay IV-C, TR. Superimpose this transparency on two others—*The Inside Story*, transparency master IV-A and transparency master overlay IV-B. Use the combined image to introduce the concepts in Chapters 17 and 18. Ask students what is meant by finishing touches and why knowledge of equipment can help with decisions about inside space.

4. Have students write a descriptive story of a room interior they like. (Encourage the use of detailed descriptions to help others visualize the space.) Ask students to identify areas or spaces within the room and describe the functions that occur in each.

5. Have students work in groups to make a collage of pictures and captions that describe the inside of a home. For each collage, ask students outside the group to determine the various functions and features it depicts.

Transparency Master IV-A

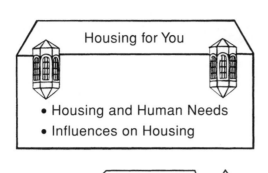

Housing for You
- Housing and Human Needs
- Influences on Housing

Making Housing Choices
- Using Decision-Making Skills
- Choosing a Place to Live
- Acquiring Housing

From the Ground Up
- The Evolution of Exteriors
- Understanding House Plans
- House Construction
- The Systems Within

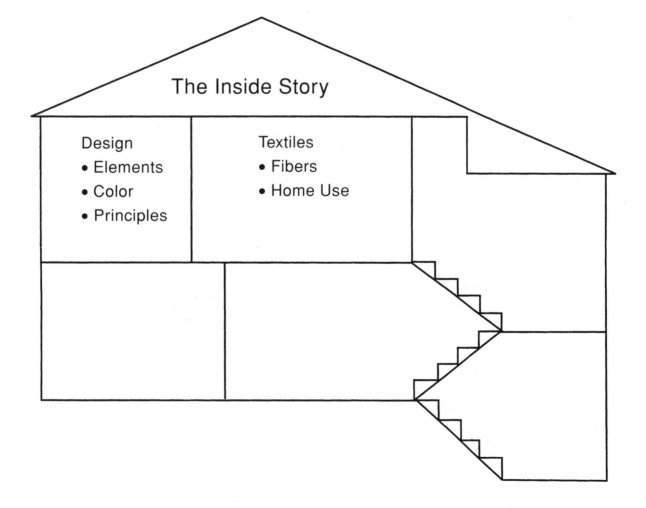

The Inside Story

Design
- Elements
- Color
- Principles

Textiles
- Fibers
- Home Use

Transparency Master Overlay IV-B

**Interior Backgrounds**
- Floor
- Walls
- Ceiling

**Furniture**
- Styles and Construction
- Arrangement and Selection

Transparency Master Overlay IV-C

**Finishing Touches**
- Window Treatments
- Light Accessories

**Appliances**
- Consumer Satisfaction
- Kitchen
- Laundry

# CHAPTER 10
# Elements of Design

## Objectives

After studying this chapter, students will be able to

- list the three characteristics of design.
- describe the different types of lines and explain their effects.
- demonstrate the different types of form.
- explain how space is used in design.
- identify high mass and low mass.
- describe tactile texture and visual texture.

## Bulletin Boards

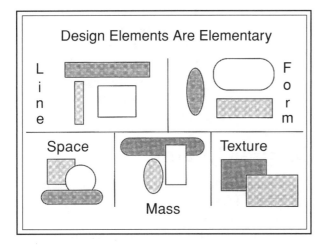

Title: *Design Elements Are Elementary*

Under the title, divide the board into five squares. In each square place the name of one element of design: *Line, Form, Space, Mass,* and *Texture*. Mount examples of each element.

Title: *Size Them Up*

Mount pictures of three rooms of different sizes. Write these questions on the board: How would you describe these rooms? How do they make you feel?

## Teaching Materials

Text, pages 240-252
  *To Know*
  *To Review*
  *In Your Community*
  *To Think About*
  *Using Technology*
Student Activity Guide
  A. *Design Characteristics*
  B. *Lines*
  C. *Form*
  D. *Space and Mass*
Teacher's Resources
  *Characteristics of Design*, transparency master 10-1
  *Using Line in Housing*, transparency master 10-2
  *Elements of Design*, color transparency CT-13
  Chapter 10 Test

## Introductory Activities

1. Use Bulletin Board I to introduce the concepts in Chapter 10. Discuss the importance of learning basic facts about design.
2. Have students find and discuss the glossary and/or dictionary definitions of key terms listed in the *To Know* section of the text. Have them add these to their card files.

## Strategies to Reteach, Reinforce, Enrich, and Extend Text Concepts

### Design Characteristics

3. **RF** Have students explain the term *visual imagery*. Then have them list the messages they receive from their classroom through visual imagery.
4. **RT** *Characteristics of Design*, transparency master 10-1, TR. Use this transparency to

introduce the concepts of function, construction, and aesthetics as characteristics of design. Have students list terms that relate to each topic. Write these on the transparency. Have students discuss which factors on the list are important in designing housing.

5. **RF**  *Design Characteristics*, Activity A, SAG. Students are asked to create a new product, sketch it, and answer the questions that follow.
6. **ER**  Have students work in small groups to rank the three design characteristics in order of importance. Dissolve the groups and take a student vote on the rank order of the three characteristics. Have students discuss reasons for their different votes.

## Elements of Design

7. **RF**  *Lines*, Activity B, SAG. Students are asked to follow the instructions and answer the questions about lines.
8. **RF**  *Using Line in Housing*, transparency master 10-2, TR. Use this transparency to discuss how lines show direction and convey feelings.
9. **RF**  Have students find illustrations of rooms that contain the various lines in housing. Have them label the predominant lines used and describe the feelings they convey.
10. **EX**  Have students bring in cartoons and discuss the types of lines used to convey meanings. (For instance, straight lines are used in more serious cartoons; rounded lines are used for funny, friendly characters.) Have students discuss how lines can be used to convey meanings in rooms.
11. **ER**  Divide the class into four groups and assign each group one of the following: realistic form, abstract form, geometric form, and free form. The groups are to find and mount pictures of their assigned forms. Have each group present its results to the class.
12. **RF**  *Form*, Activity C, SAG. Students are asked to find or draw pictures illustrating four types of form and list the guidelines for using form in design.
13. **RF**  Have students explain what *form follows function* means.
14. **RF**  Have students discuss the three guidelines for using form in housing decisions.
15. **RT**  Have students explain the term *space* as a design element.
16. **RF**  Have students discuss the feelings different amounts of space convey to them.
17. **RF**  Have students brainstorm ways to make a space seem larger or smaller.
18. **RF**  Have students discuss the relationship between space and mass.
19. **RF**  Have students find examples in their classroom of high mass and low mass.
20. **ER**  *Space and Mass*, Activity D, SAG. Students are to answer questions about space and mass as the elements of design.
21. **RF**  Have students explain how texture affects the senses of touch and sight.
22. **ER**  Have students make a collage focusing on texture. They may use objects, pictures, and words. Have students describe the textures and discuss their reactions to them.
23. **ER**  Have students look at pictures of different styles of home furnishings, such as chairs, beds, and lamps. Students should discuss how the elements of design—line, form, space, mass, and texture—are used in the objects. Ask students to discuss how the elements of design are used differently in formal and informal settings.

## Chapter Review

24. **EX**  *Elements of Design*, color transparency CT-13, TR. This transparency can be used to discuss the five elements of design discussed in this chapter. Point out how adding each element of design transforms the figure from a one-dimensional line to a three-dimensional form with mass and texture. Have students compare this with the way elements of design are used to transform rooms in a house.
25. **EX**  Have each student clip and mount a picture of a room or area within a home. Students should write a critique of the room in terms of its design elements. Students should also discuss the characteristics of the designs used.
26. **RF**  Have students work in small groups to devise a chapter test. Then have groups exchange tests, complete their new tests, and return them to their originators for correcting.

# Answer Key

## Text

### *To Review*, page 250
1. the language of sight
2. function
3. Horizontal lines communicate relaxation, calmness, and restfulness. Vertical lines communicate height, strength, dignity, and stability. Diagonal lines communicate activity ranging from little energy to chaos.
4. A. realistic
   B. free form
   C. geometric
   D. abstract
5. Form follows function; related forms are more agreeable than unrelated forms; and gradual change in form can direct the eyes smoothly.
6. It is more comfortable and less confusing to the eyes.
7. area rugs, furniture arrangement, kitchen island
8. Form contains both.
9. high
10. Tactile texture is how a surface actually feels, and visual texture is how it appears to feel by the way it looks.

## Student Activity Guide

### *Lines*, Activity B
1. horizontal
2. diagonal
3. vertical
4. curved
5. Line is the joining of two dots.
6. relaxation, calmness, restfulness
7. height, strength, dignity, stability
8. action, excitement, jolting
9. organization, eternity, conformity
10. (Student response.)

### *Space and Mass*, Activity D
1. the area inside or around a form
2. (Student response.)
3. (Student response.)
4. (Student response.)
5. (Student response.)
6. with large open spaces
7. with space divided into smaller areas
8. the amount of pattern or number of objects in a space
9. Form contains both.
10. (Student response.)

## Teacher's Resources

### Chapter 10 Test

| | | |
|---|---|---|
| 1. K | 11. A | 21. T |
| 2. C | 12. T | 22. D |
| 3. F | 13. T | 23. B |
| 4. L | 14. F | 24. C |
| 5. I | 15. F | 25. D |
| 6. G | 16. T | 26. A |
| 7. B | 17. F | 27. D |
| 8. M | 18. T | 28. C |
| 9. D | 19. T | 29. B |
| 10. E | 20. F | 30. D |

31. (Student response.)
32. Function is how a design works and how it is used. Construction is the materials and structure of a design. Aesthetics is the effect or appearance of the design.
33. The function of a design is determined before its appearance is developed.
34. Form contains space and mass.
35. Large space gives a feeling of freedom and can make you feel small, lost, and overwhelmed. Small space gives feelings of coziness, intimacy, and comfort, but can make you feel crowded and uncomfortable.

# Characteristics of Design

- Function

- Construction

- Aesthetics

- 

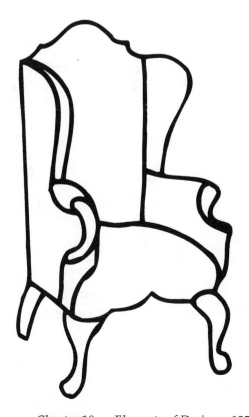

Transparency Master 10-2

# Using Line in Housing

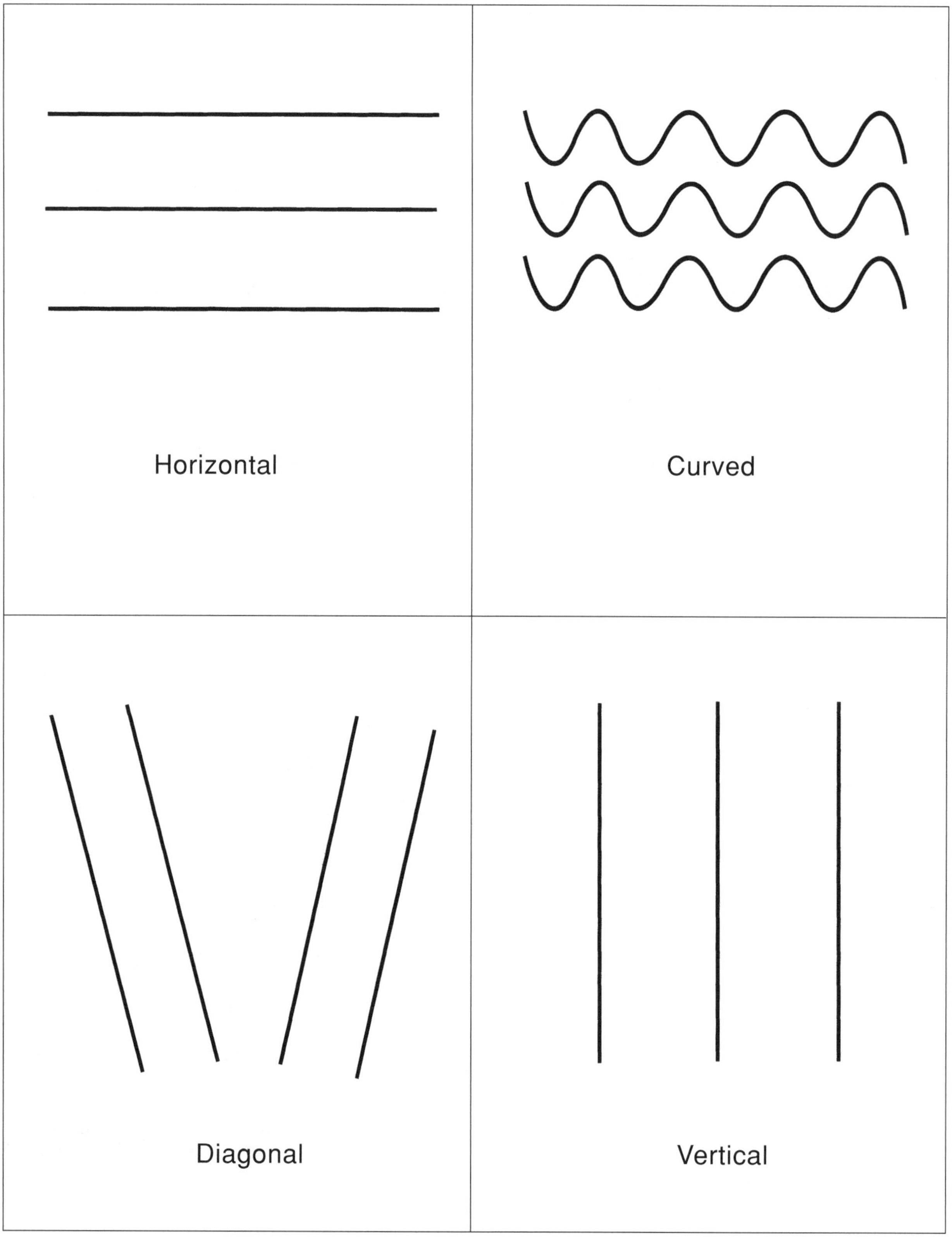

Horizontal

Curved

Diagonal

Vertical

Reproducible Test Master

# Elements of Design

Name _____

Date _____ Period _____ Score _____

### Chapter 10 Test

❑ Match each description with its most closely related element of design.

**Descriptions**

_____ 1. Area around a form.

_____ 2. Line between parallel and perpendicular.

_____ 3. Crowded space.

_____ 4. Feel of a surface.

_____ 5. Lifelike and normal appearance.

_____ 6. Line parallel to the ground.

_____ 7. Part of a circle.

_____ 8. Line perpendicular to the ground.

_____ 9. Random or flowing shape.

_____ 10. Squares, rectangles, and circles.

_____ 11. Stylized or rearranged appearance.

**Elements of Design**

A. abstract form
B. curved line
C. diagonal line
D. free form
E. geometric forms
F. high mass
G. horizontal line
H. low mass
I. realistic form
J. shape
K. space
L. tactile texture
M. vertical line
N. visual texture

❑ True/False: Circle *T* if the statement is true or *F* if the statement is false.

T   F   12. *Beauty* is another term for *aesthetics*.

T   F   13. The elements of design are color, line, form, space, mass, and texture.

T   F   14. Horizontal lines are perpendicular to the ground.

T   F   15. Diagonal lines angle between vertical and curved lines.

T   F   16. Geometric shapes do *not* appear in free form.

T   F   17. A guideline for using form in design is *form follows shape*.

T   F   18. Mass is the amount of patterns or objects in an area.

T   F   19. High mass means a space is visually crowded.

T   F   20. Tactile texture refers to the way a surface appears.

T   F   21. A rough texture creates a casual atmosphere.

(Continued)

Reproducible Test Master

❑ Multiple Choice: Choose the best response. Write the letter in the space provided.

_____ 22. The function of a design refers to its _____.
   A. convenience
   B. organization
   C. usefulness
   D. All of the above.

_____ 23. _____ is *not* an element of design.
   A. Color
   B. Function
   C. Line
   D. Texture

_____ 24. _____ lines communicate feelings of relaxation and calmness.
   A. Curved
   B. Diagonal
   C. Horizontal
   D. Vertical

_____ 25. _____ lines communicate strength and dignity.
   A. Curved
   B. Diagonal
   C. Horizontal
   D. Vertical

_____ 26. _____ lines reflect organization, uniformity, and eternity.
   A. Circular
   B. Diagonal
   C. Horizontal
   D. Vertical

_____ 27. _____ is *not* a guideline to consider when using form in housing design.
   A. Form follows function
   B. Gradual change smoothly directs the eyes
   C. Related forms are more agreeable than unrelated forms
   D. Structure is materials and methods

_____ 28. Space described as cozy and comfortable is _____.
   A. tall
   B. large
   C. small
   D. All of the above.

_____ 29. _____ refers to the amount of pattern or number of objects in a space.
   A. Form
   B. Mass
   C. Shape
   D. Texture

_____ 30. The texture a surface appears to have is called _____.
   A. abstract form
   B. free form
   C. tactile texture
   D. visual texture

(Continued)

❑ Essay Questions: Provide complete responses to the following questions or statements.

31. Give an example of visual imagery.

32. Name and explain the three characteristics of design.

33. Explain *form follows function*.

34. Explain how space and mass are related to form.

35. List the different feelings that large spaces and small spaces communicate.

# CHAPTER 11
# Using Color Effectively

## Objectives

After studying this chapter, students will be able to

- explain the meaning of different colors.
- understand how color influences human behavior.
- describe the relationships between colors on the color wheel.
- give examples of color harmonies.
- plan pleasing color harmonies.

## Bulletin Boards

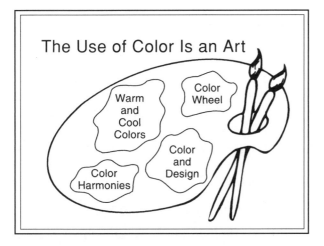

Title: *The Use of Color Is an Art*

Make a large paint palette from lightweight cardboard. Add four large spots in different colors on the palette and label them as follows: *Warm and Cool Colors, Color Wheel, Color and Design,* and *Color Harmonies.* Place two large paintbrushes through the end of the palette as shown. Tape the back of the brushes to the palette.

Title: *Color Affects the Whole Design*

Divide the board into five sections with the following labels at the bottom of each: *Line, Space, Mass, Texture* and *Form.* In each section, mount pictures that are good examples of color used with the other elements of design.

## Teaching Materials

**Text**, pages 253-272
 *To Know*
 *To Review*
 *In Your Community*
 *To Think About*
 *Using Technology*
**Student Activity Guide**
 A. *Psychological Effects of Color*
 B. *The Color Wheel*
 C. *Tints and Shades*
 D. *Color Quiz*
 E. *Color Harmonies*
 F. *Designing with Color*
**Teacher's Resources**
 *Primary Colors*, color transparency CT-14
 *Secondary Colors*, color transparency CT-15
 *Intermediate Colors*, color transparency CT-16
 *Value Grid*, reproducible master 11-1
 *Creating Color Harmonies*, reproducible master 11-2
 Chapter 11 Test

## Introductory Activities

1. Write a list of colors. Read each color aloud, having students write the first word or feeling that comes to mind. Have students discuss and compare their responses.
2. Demonstrate (or have a student demonstrate) with tempera paint how to combine primary colors to make secondary colors. Use black and white with the colors to demonstrate shades and tints. (Save some of the primary and secondary colors for Item 3.)
3. Demonstrate (or have a student demonstrate) with colors from Item 2 how to combine primary colors and secondary colors to make the intermediate colors.

Combine equal amounts of the three primary colors and three secondary colors to make a neutral color. Compare the results of the primary color combination and the secondary color combination.

## Strategies to Reteach, Reinforce, Enrich, and Extend Text Concepts

### Understanding Color

4. **RF** Have students discuss how color is used in commercial settings such as fast-food restaurants, family restaurants, clothing stores, hotel rooms, and hotel lobbies. Students should try to determine what effect is desired by using the colors.
5. **ER** *Psychological Effects of Color*, Activity A, SAG. Students are asked to describe how the colors listed make them feel. Then they are to evaluate their choices for colors in rooms by answering the questions that follow.

### The Color Wheel

6. **RF** *Primary Colors*, color transparency CT-14, TR. Use this transparency to introduce students to the primary colors. (This transparency is also used in Item 7.)
7. **RF** *Secondary Colors*, color transparency CT-15, TR. Use this transparency to introduce students to the secondary colors. Also use it as an overlay on *Primary Colors*, color transparency CT-14, to show the relationship between primary and secondary colors. (This transparency overlay is also used in Item 8.)
8. **RF** *Intermediate Colors*, color transparency CT-16, TR. Superimpose this on *Primary Colors* transparency CT-14 and *Secondary Colors* transparency CT-15. Use the combined image to discuss how intermediate colors are formed. Explain that the primary color is listed first in the name of an intermediate color.
9. **RT** Have students identify the primary, secondary, and intermediate colors on the color wheel.
10. **ER** *The Color Wheel*, Activity B, SAG. Students are asked to complete the color wheel and statements about it.
11. **EX** *Tints and Shades*, Activity C, SAG. Using two colors from the color wheel, students are asked to create a value scale of tints and shades for each.
12. **RF** Have students place a piece of green paper next to a piece of red paper. Then have them place another piece of green paper next to a gray paper. Which green looks brighter? Discuss observations as a class.
13. **EX** *Value Grid*, reproducible master 11-1, TR. Have students select three primary or secondary colors and fill the squares with the proper hues and intensities to complete the grid. Students may use paint samples, fabric swatches, or carpet samples. All samples on the grid should be in the same medium.
14. **ER** Demonstrate how black and white are related to other colors. To show how black is created, mix pigments of the primary colors together. Explain that primary colors can be used to make all the colors on the color wheel, so black is a combination of all colors. To show how white is created, mount a color wheel on a cardboard circle of the same size. Place two small holes on opposite sides of the center of the wheel so the holes are one-half to one inch apart. Run strings about two feet long through the holes. Hold the strings out and center the wheel on the strings. Wind the strings and pull them out so the wheel spins. As the wheel spins, it will appear white. Explain that all the colors are being reflected off the wheel to create the appearance of the absence of color, or white.
15. **RF** Have students review the results of combining the primary colors, and in a separate test, the secondary colors. Explain how neutrals are produced.
16. **RF** Have students discuss how warm and cool colors can affect the appearance of an object.
17. **RF** *Color Quiz*, Activity D, SAG. Students are asked to complete the statements about color by filling in the blanks.

### Color Harmonies

18. **ER** Have students work in small groups to find pictures from magazines or catalogs representing various color harmonies.

Assign each group one or two color harmonies. Have students discuss what they like and dislike about their assigned harmonies. (Save pictures for Item 21.)

19. **ER** *Creating Color Harmonies*, reproducible master 11-2, TR. Have students use the worksheet to select a color harmony of their choice and provide samples or pictures of items that coordinate with it. Students are asked to fill in the color wheel to reflect the color harmony chosen. Samples or pictures of coordinating items are then attached to the worksheet.

20. **ER** *Color Harmonies*, Activity E, SAG. Students are asked to match the harmonies and color combinations with the descriptions provided. Then they are to mount pictures or fabric swatches for two color harmonies.

## Using Color Harmonies

21. **EX** Have students study the pictures collected in Item 18. Have them discuss the moods and styles of each room, the lifestyles of the people living there, and the item(s) pulling the colors together. Ask them which direction each room should face—a sunny or shady exposure.

22. **ER** Ask an interior designer or decorator to show the class a decorated model home or showroom. Ask the designer to discuss the use of color values, color intensities, warm and cool colors, and color harmonies.

23. **RF** Have students make a list of guidelines for using color.

24. **RF** *Designing with Color*, Activity F, SAG. Students are asked to imagine redecorating rooms in their houses and answer questions to help choose an appropriate color harmony.

## Chapter Review

25. **RF** Make flash cards with definitions and pictures of various color harmonies. At the beginning of class, give each student a card. Have each student stand and report the color harmony shown and defined on his or her card.

26. **RF** Have students make scrapbooks using the *To Know* terms listed in the text at the beginning of the chapter. Each page should have a picture representing one of the terms with the appropriate label. Students can use the pictures they have already gathered for previous activities.

# Answer Key

## Text

### *To Review*, page 271

1. Red conveys power, danger, strength, excitement, and boldness. Green conveys nature, peace, friendliness, and coolness. Violet conveys royalty, dignity, and drama.
2. orange—yellow and red; green—yellow and blue; violet—red and blue
3. primary color
4. Value is the lightness or darkness. Intensity is the brightness or dullness.
5. by adding white, gray, or black
6. warm; cool
7. (Student response. See pages 259-264 of the text.)
8. true
9. low

## Student Activity Guide

### *The Color Wheel*, Activity B

1. primary
2. secondary
3. intermediate
4. intermediate
5. primary
6. secondary

(Color wheel should resemble Figure 11-4 of the text.)

### *Color Quiz*, Activity D

1. color wheel
2. hue
3. value
4. tint
5. shade
6. intensity
7. complement
8. neutrals
9. warm
10. cool

## *Color Harmonies,* Activity E

1. C-I
2. A-K
3. E-H
4. B-L
5. F-G
6. D-J

(Color harmony examples are student response.)

# Teacher's Resources

## Chapter 11 Test

1. E
2. D
3. H
4. I
5. B
6. C
7. G
8. J
9. F
10. A
11. F
12. T
13. F
14. T
15. T
16. F
17. T
18. T
19. T
20. T
21. A
22. D
23. B
24. C
25. D
26. B
27. A
28. C
29. A
30. D
31. (Student response. See pages 259-264 of the text.)
32. Neutrals are black, gray, and white. They can be used together as a color harmony or with other color harmonies.
33. Colors may be split or separated by another color on one or both sides of a complementary color.
34. (Student response. See pages 265-266 of the text.)
35. (Student response. See pages 269-270 of the text.)

Reproducible Master 11-1

# Value Grid

**Name** _____ **Date** _____ **Period** _____

Select three primary or secondary hues and write their names in the chart below. Then complete the following grid by placing the appropriate color samples in the squares. You may use magazine pictures, fabric or paint samples, colored pencils, or watercolors.

| Value | Hue | | |
|---|---|---|---|
| | 1. | 2. | 3. |
| Light Tint | | | |
| Dark Tint | | | |
| Hue | | | |
| Light Shade | | | |
| Dark Shade | | | |

Chapter 11  *Using Color Effectively*  195

Reproducible Master 11-2

# Creating Color Harmonies

**Name** _____ **Date** _____ **Period** _____

Choose a color harmony and fill in the color wheel below to depict it. Select a main color and accent colors from the color harmony. Then mount fabric, paint, and other samples as well as pictures of complementary furniture and accessories. Attach additional pages if necessary.

Color harmony: _____

Main color: _____

Accent colors: _____

Reproducible Test Master

# Using Color Effectively

Name _____

Date _____ Period _____ Score _____

### Chapter 11 Test

❏ Matching: Match the following color groupings and identifying phrases.

_____ 1. Black, white, and gray.

_____ 2. Blue-green, forest green, and pale green.

_____ 3. Colors mixed with black.

_____ 4. Colors mixed with white.

_____ 5. Green and blue.

_____ 6. Orange and blue.

_____ 7. Orange, green, and violet.

_____ 8. Red and orange.

_____ 9. Red, yellow, and blue.

_____ 10. Yellow, yellow-green, and green.

A. analogous colors
B. cool colors
C. complementary colors
D. monochromatic colors
E. neutrals
F. primary colors
G. secondary colors
H. shades
I. tints
J. warm colors

❏ True/False: Circle *T* if the statement is true or *F* if the statement is false.

T  F  11. Color is usually the last thing others notice about your home.

T  F  12. Color is an element of design.

T  F  13. The three basic colors are called harmony colors.

T  F  14. Secondary colors are made by mixing two primary colors.

T  F  15. The name of a color is called a hue.

T  F  16. Tints are colors mixed with black.

T  F  17. Intensity refers to the brightness or dullness of a color.

T  F  18. When a neutral is added to a hue, the value is changed.

T  F  19. Green is considered a cool color.

T  F  20. A monochromatic color harmony is based on a single color.

❏ Multiple Choice: Choose the best response. Write the letter in the space provided.

_____ 21. The color wheel has _____.
   A. primary, secondary, and intermediate colors
   B. primary and secondary colors
   C. primary colors only
   D. secondary colors only

(Continued)

_____ 22. A primary color is _____.
   A. green
   B. orange
   C. pink
   D. red

_____ 23. A secondary color is _____.
   A. black
   B. violet
   C. white
   D. yellow

_____ 24. Adding white to a color makes it _____.
   A. a different hue
   B. a shade
   C. a tint
   D. more intense

_____ 25. The lightness or darkness of a color is called _____.
   A. harmony
   B. intensity
   C. neutral
   D. value

_____ 26. The brightness or dullness of a hue is called _____.
   A. harmony
   B. intensity
   C. neutral
   D. value

_____ 27. The warmest colors are _____.
   A. red, orange, and yellow
   B. blue and orange
   C. white and red
   D. yellow, green, and orange

_____ 28. The color harmony that is based on a single hue is called _____.
   A. analogous
   B. double-complementary
   C. monochromatic
   D. triadic

_____ 29. Combinations of three to five colors adjacent to each other on the color wheel describe the _____ color harmony.
   A. analogous
   B. double-complementary
   C. monochromatic
   D. triadic

_____ 30. A color harmony using red, blue, and yellow is a(n) _____ color harmony.
   A. analogous
   B. double-complementary
   C. monochromatic
   D. triadic

(Continued)

❏ Essay Questions: Provide complete responses to the following questions or statements.
31. Describe and give an example of two different types of color harmonies.
32. What are neutrals and how are they used in color harmonies?
33. Explain how variations of the complementary color harmony can be made.
34. Explain how color and lifestyles are related.
35. Give five guidelines for using color correctly.

# CHAPTER 12
# Using the Principles of Design

## Objectives

After studying this chapter, students will be able to

- determine how proportion and scale are related to objects.
- give examples of formal and informal balance.
- explain how emphasis creates a focal point.
- list the different types of rhythm.
- describe the goals of design.
- give examples of sensory design.

## Bulletin Boards

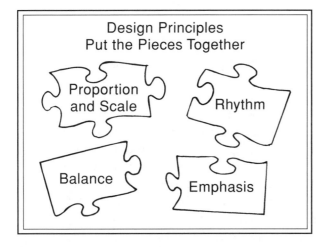

Title: *Design Principles Put the Pieces Together*

Cut out shapes resembling puzzle pieces. Label each piece with one of the following design principles: *Proportion and Scale, Rhythm, Balance,* and *Emphasis.*

Title: *Applying the Principles of Design*

Have students make a collage of pictures illustrating the principles of design. Label the features according to the design principle used.

## Teaching Materials

**Text**, pages 273-287
*To Know*
*To Review*
*In Your Community*
*To Think About*
*Using Technology*

**Student Activity Guide**
A. *Golden Guidelines*
B. *The Principle of Rhythm*
C. *Using the Principles of Design*
D. *Design in Reverse*

**Teacher's Resources**
*Rhythm in Design*, color transparency CT-17
*Current Design Trends*, reproducible master 12-1
Chapter 12 Test

## Introductory Activities

1. Have students discuss the topics listed on Bulletin Board I.
2. Have students find and discuss the glossary and/or dictionary definitions of key terms listed in the *To Know* section of the text. Have them add these to their card files.

## Strategies to Reteach, Reinforce, Enrich, and Extend Text Concepts

### The Principles of Design

3. **RF** Have students compare the terms *proportion* and *scale*. Have them find objects in the classroom that are examples.
4. **ER** *Golden Guidelines,* Activity A, SAG. Students are asked to answer the questions regarding the Greek guidelines for using proportion.
5. **RF** Have students describe visual weight. Have them choose two objects in the classroom that appear to be the same weight.

Chapter 12   Using the Principles of Design   201

Have students place each object on scales to see the difference in the weights.
6. **RF** Have each student find and discuss a picture of a room that has good proportion.
7. **RF** Have students compare formal and informal balance. Then have them identify examples of the two types of balance in the classroom.
8. **RF** Discuss emphasis and have students find the point of emphasis in pictures from the text.
9. **RF** *Rhythm in Design*, color transparency CT-17, TR. Use this transparency to introduce the types of rhythm in design. Have students find examples of rhythm in the classroom.
10. **RF** *The Principle of Rhythm*, Activity B, SAG. Students are asked to label and write a brief explanation of the type of rhythm used in each window.

## Goals of Design

11. **RT** Have students discuss the goals of design and how they can be achieved.
12. **RF** Ask students to compare the terms *harmony* and *unity*. Have them discuss how variety adds interest to design.
13. **RF** Have students list ways to achieve harmony and unity in a room.
14. **ER** Have students describe their ideas of beautiful home decorating in a one-page paper. Students should compare their tastes with the concepts discussed in the chapter.
15. **ER** Show slides or pictures of various rooms. As you display each one, have the class discuss the activities and lifestyles appropriate for the room's furnishings. Discuss the use and convenience of the room arrangements. Relate these to the goals of design.
16. **ER** *Current Design Trends*, reproducible master 12-1, TR. Have students interview an interior decorator or design specialist to learn about current trends in interior design.
17. **EX** Make arrangements with an interior decorator or design specialist to visit a decorated model home. Ask the designer to discuss the use of design elements and principles in the model. Have students determine which goals of design were evident.

## Sensory Design

18. **ER** Have students conduct a sensory analysis of objects in the classroom by recording their observations to the following questions on notebook paper: What surfaces or objects make noise or absorb it? What aspects of the classroom evoke the sense of smell? Other than hard, flat surfaces, what items affect the sense of touch? Have students discuss sensory design and why it is important.
19. **EX** Have students talk to someone who provides housing or housing assistance to people who have lost the sense of hearing or sight. Ask students to find out what special measures are taken to help these individuals live full lives and avoid safety and security problems.

## Chapter Review

20. **ER** *Using the Principles of Design*, Activity C, SAG. Students are asked to describe how the principles of design are used in the room illustrated.
21. **RF** Use a short video titled *American Elegance* to help students identify design elements and principles and determine if design goals have been met. The video is available for purchase from Winterthur Museum and Gardens in Winterthur, Delaware, by phoning 302-888-4600.
22. **RF** *Design in Reverse*, Activity D, SAG. Students are asked to write questions for the answers given. Then, working in small groups, students are to ask group members their questions.

## Answer Key

### Text

*To Review*, page 285
1. false
2. large
3. Formal balance is the symmetrical arrangement of identical objects on both sides of a center point, while informal balance is the arrangement of different but equivalent

objects on both sides. (The sketch is student response.)
4. by using color, size, proportion, scale, or theme (The example is student response.)
5. repetition, gradation, radiation, opposition, transition
6. Function is purpose, whereas appropriateness is suitability. If an object fits its function, it will be appropriate.
7. using variety
8. The elements and principles of design have been developed as a result of studying what people consider beautiful.
9. (Student response.)

## Student Activity Guide

### *Golden Guidelines*, Activity A

1. Greece
2. (Student response.)
3. golden rectangle
4. (Student response.)
5. golden section
6. (Student response.)
7. golden mean

### *The Principle of Rhythm*, Activity B

1. radiation
2. repetition
3. opposition
4. transition
5. gradation

### *Design in Reverse*, Activity D

1. What are the principles of design?
2. What is proportion?
3. What are the three guidelines for using proportion that were developed by the Greeks and have been used for centuries?
4. What is scale?
5. What features add visual weight to objects?
6. What type of balance is created by arranging different, but equivalent, objects on both sides of a center point?
7. What can be used to create focal points?
8. What is repetition?
9. What is gradation?
10. What are the goals of design?
11. What is unity?
12. What is sensory design?

(Students may justify other responses.)

# Teacher's Resources

## Chapter 12 Test

1. I
2. M
3. C
4. A
5. G
6. F
7. N
8. K
9. H
10. L
11. T
12. T
13. T
14. T
15. F
16. F
17. T
18. F
19. F
20. T
21. C
22. A
23. D
24. C
25. B
26. C
27. B
28. D
29. D
30. D

31. proportion, scale, balance, emphasis, rhythm
32. (Student response.)
33. Formal balance is the symmetrical arrangement of identical objects on both sides of a center point. Informal balance is the asymmetrical arrangement of unlike objects.
34. (List three:) letting only one of each element dominate, using mostly formal or informal balance, having mostly large or small proportion, having one point of emphasis
35. Sensory design is applying design with regard to the senses of sight, hearing, smell, and touch. (The example is student response.)

Reproducible Master 12-1

# Current Design Trends

Name _____ Date _____ Period _____

Interview an interior decorator or design specialist to learn about current trends in interior design.

I. Find local department stores or businesses that provide interior design service. List the information below:

Company Name                                           Phone Number

1. _____
2. _____
3. _____
4. _____

II. Call one of the businesses listed above and make arrangements for a 20-minute interview with an interior decorator or design specialist. Introduce yourself. Explain the course content and your interview assignment. Record the following information:

Interview date: _____ Time: _____

Person's name: _____ Title: _____

Address: _____

(Circle the business above to which you will be going.)

III. Plan for the interview. List interview questions about current trends in interior design below.

_____
_____
_____
_____
_____
_____
_____

IV. Notes from interview to share in class:

_____
_____
_____
_____
_____
_____
_____
_____
_____

V. Send a letter of appreciation to the person you interviewed.

Reproducible Test Master

# Using the Principles of Design

Name _____

Date _____ Period _____ Score _____

**Chapter 12 Test**

❑ Matching: Match the following terms and examples.

_____ 1. An example is a sunburst.
_____ 2. Curved lines.
_____ 3. Division between one-half and one-third.
_____ 4. Focal point.
_____ 5. Lines forming a right angle.
_____ 6. Different objects arranged asymmetrically.
_____ 7. Perception of an object's weight.
_____ 8. Organized pattern of a design element.
_____ 9. Relation of the parts to the whole.
_____ 10. Relative size of one part to the others.

A. emphasis
B. formal balance
C. golden mean
D. gradation
E. harmony
F. informal balance
G. opposition
H. proportion
I. radiation
J. repetition
K. rhythm
L. scale
M. transition
N. visual weight

❑ True/False: Circle *T* if the statement is true or *F* if the statement is false.

T F 11. The Greeks developed guidelines for the use of proportion.

T F 12. The golden rectangle has sides in a ratio of 2:3.

T F 13. Emphasis is the center of interest in a design.

T F 14. Furnishings need to be in scale with the people using them.

T F 15. Visual weight can be achieved by using light colors and textures.

T F 16. Architectural features are always the focal point in a room.

T F 17. All types of rhythm are based on some repetition.

T F 18. Diagonal lines are used to create rhythm by transition.

T F 19. Beauty is a principle of design.

T F 20. Sensory design is used to make housing more accessible.

(Continued)

Reproducible Test Master

❏ Multiple Choice: Choose the best response. Write the letter in the space provided.

_____ 21. _____ is a principle of design.
A. Color
B. Line
C. Rhythm
D. Texture

_____ 22. _____ is *not* a principle of design.
A. Form
B. Proportion
C. Scale
D. Transition

_____ 23. The ratio of size and weight of parts to the whole is _____.
A. balance
B. emphasis
C. harmony
D. proportion

_____ 24. The _____ is the division of a form or line in which the smaller portion is the same ratio to the larger portion as the larger portion is to the whole.
A. golden mean
B. golden rectangle
C. golden section
D. All of the above.

_____ 25. In a small room it is wise to have furnishings that appear _____ in visual weight.
A. heavy
B. light
C. mixed
D. patterned

_____ 26. Lines flowing outward from a central point is rhythm by _____.
A. gradation
B. opposition
C. radiation
D. repetition

_____ 27. Lines meeting at right angles is rhythm by _____.
A. gradation
B. opposition
C. radiation
D. repetition

_____ 28. When _____ is present in a design, you see the room as a whole instead of separate parts.
A. beauty
B. function
C. rhythm
D. unity

(Continued)

_____ 29. Variety _____.
   A. adds interest to a design
   B. can cause confusion
   C. is change or contrast
   D. All of the above.

_____ 30. Generally, the word *beauty* is used to describe _____.
   A. elements and principles of design
   B. furnishings and their surroundings
   C. unity with variation
   D. well-designed and pleasing objects

❑ Essay Questions: Provide complete responses to the following questions or statements.

31. List the principles of design.

32. Describe a room that has good proportion.

33. Compare formal and informal balance.

34. List three ways to achieve unity with variety.

35. Explain what is meant by sensory design. Give an example.

# CHAPTER 13
# Textiles in Today's Homes

## Objectives

After studying this chapter, students will be able to

- distinguish between natural fibers and manufactured fibers.
- list characteristics of various fibers.
- describe the fabric construction processes.
- identify appropriate textiles for various household uses.
- explain the benefits of textile laws.

## Bulletin Boards

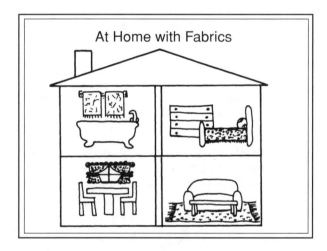

Title: *At Home with Fabrics*

Under the title, draw a house with rooms. Draw or collect pictures that depict the use of fabrics in the home and place these inside the rooms.

Title: *The Label Counts*

Collect labels or illustrations of labels from household textiles. Mount them inside the outline of a house. Draw arrows pointing to the various types of information on the labels.

## Teaching Materials

*Text*, pages 288-308
   *To Know*
   *To Review*
   *In Your Community*
   *To Think About*
   *Using Technology*
**Student Activity Guide**
   A. *Facts About Fibers*
   B. *Understanding Household Textiles*
   C. *Choosing Textiles for the Home*
   D. *Fabrics for Window Treatments*
   E. *Textile Review*
**Teacher's Resources**
   *Fabric Weaves*, color transparency CT-18
   *Construction Methods for Carpets and Rugs*, reproducible master 13-1
   *Textiles for Upholstered Furniture*, reproducible master 13-2
   Chapter 13 Test

## Introductory Activities

1. Have students study the bulletin board *At Home with Fabrics* and brainstorm the fabrics used in their homes. Have them make a master list. Discuss how fabrics begin with plants, animals, and test tubes.
2. Have students find and discuss the glossary and/or dictionary definitions of key terms listed in the *To Know* section of the text. Have them add these to their card files.

## Strategies to Reteach, Reinforce, Enrich, and Extend Text Concepts

### Understanding Fibers, Yarns, and Fabrics

3. **RF** Have students find magazine advertisements of household textiles and catalog

descriptions. Based on the information provided, have students clip and sort the ads into three categories: natural fibers, manufactured fibers, and blends. (Save ads for Items 4, 5, 6, and 16.)
4. **RF** Have students use ads for natural and manufactured fabrics to identify the various fiber types within the two major groups. (Reuse the appropriate ads saved from Item 3.) Have students mount the ads on cards and label them.
5. **ER** Have students distinguish between generic names and trade names in the ads collected in Item 3. Have students add the information to the cards they prepared in Item 4.
6. **ER** Using Figures 13-1, 13-2, and 13-3, have students identify the characteristics of the various fibers shown in the advertisements collected in Item 3. Have students add the information to the cards they prepared in Item 4.
7. **RF** *Facts About Fibers*, Activity A, SAG. Students are asked to list the strengths and weaknesses of three natural and seven manufactured fibers.
8. **RF** *Fabric Weaves*, color transparency CT-18, TR. Use this transparency to show the variations of the plain weave.
9. **RF** Have students identify the types of weaves in the garments they are wearing.
10. **RF** Discuss with students types of fabrics such as felted, tanned, and bonded.
11. **ER** Provide students with fabric swatches. Have them examine the swatches and determine if they are woven, knitted, or bonded. Then identify the various methods of construction. (Save the swatches for Items 14 and 15.)
12. **RF** *Understanding Household Textiles*, Activity B, SAG. Students are asked to mount examples of woven, knitted, and nonwoven fabrics and answer related questions.
13. **RF** Discuss with students fabric modifications such as designs, dyes, and finishes.
14. **ER** Gather the swatches with designs from those used in Item 11. Have students identify those with structural designs versus applied designs.
15. **ER** Collect the dyed swatches from those used in Item 11. Have students try to determine which swatches are stock dyed versus piece dyed.
16. **ER** Have students examine the ads collected in Item 3 for any textile finishes mentioned. Ask students to list the finishes and identify what each does.
17. **RF** With textbooks closed, have students list as many fabrics with trade names as possible.

## Textiles for Home Use

18. **EX** *Choosing Textiles for the Home*, Activity C, SAG. Students are asked to describe factors to consider when choosing household textiles.
19. **ER** Discuss with students the following factors to consider when selecting textiles for home use: appearance, durability, maintenance, comfort, ease of construction, and cost. Have students rank the factors in order of importance to them and explain their decisions.

## Textiles for Floor Treatments

20. **ER** Collect a variety of household fabric samples and mount them on poster board. Underneath each sample, list the sample's fiber content and its household use.
21. **RF** Have students study the construction methods for carpets in Figure 13-13 and discuss the differences in the results of each method.
22. **RF** *Construction Methods for Carpets and Rugs*, reproducible master 13-1, TR. Students are asked to label the methods of carpet construction and answer related questions.
23. **ER** Provide samples of carpeting. Have students examine the samples to determine the construction methods. Discuss the various textures and how they were created. Have students read the labels to determine fiber content.

## Textiles for Upholstered Furniture

24. **RF** Have students collect pictures of upholstered furniture and determine if the furnishings are for formal or informal settings.

25. **RF** Have students make a list of characteristics desirable in upholstery fabrics. Have students identify fabrics that have the desired characteristics.
26. **ER** *Textiles for Upholstered Furniture*, reproducible master 13-2, TR. Students are asked to mount a picture of upholstered furniture and answer related questions.

## Textiles for Window Treatments

27. **RF** Discuss with students the various types of window treatments. Brainstorm the types of fabrics suitable for the treatments.
28. **ER** Have students evaluate the fabric used in two types of window treatments. Students should record the fiber content, method of construction, fabric modifications, and recommended care for each. Have students list the advantages and disadvantages of each window treatment.
29. **ER** *Fabrics for Window Treatments*, Activity D, SAG. Students are asked to mount a fabric swatch, sketch a window treatment appropriate for it, and answer related questions.
30. **EX** Visit a home furnishing store. Have someone discuss the fabrics used for floor coverings, upholstered furniture, and window treatments. Before the trip, have students make a list of related questions.

## Textiles for Kitchen, Bath, and Bed

31. **RF** Have students list the basic types of kitchen, bath, and bed linens needed in their first apartment or home. Save the list for Item 32.
32. **ER** Have students use their lists from Item 31 to identify the fabrics they think are best for each type of linen. Have students give reasons for their choices.

## Textile Laws

33. **RF** Discuss with students the laws summarized in the text and explain why the laws were enacted.
34. **RF** Have students look at the labels on various household fabrics. Have students determine what part of the information is required by law and identify the specific laws that apply.
35. **ER** Have each student select a textile law discussed in the text and write a one-page report.

## Chapter Review

36. **ER** Have each student choose a room in his or her house and list all the fabrics used there. Have them give information about the fiber contents, construction methods, and modifications to the fabrics listed. Have students list any textile laws that apply to the fabrics they have identified. Discuss the results with the class.
37. **RF** *Textile Review*, Activity E, SAG. Students are asked to use the clues to fill in the crossword puzzle.

## Answer Key

### Text

*To Review*, page 306

1. (Student response. See Figures 13-1 and 13-2 of the text.)
2. (Student response. See Figure 13-3 of the text.)
3. Natural fibers come from plant and animal sources whereas manufactured products come from wood cellulose, oil products, and other chemicals.
4. Fibers (staple and filament) are the beginning of fabrics. They are made into yarns that are woven or knitted to make fabrics.
5. Weaving is the interlacing of two sets of yarns at right angles. Knitting is the looping of yarns together with the use of needles.
6. by joining two layers of fabric together with an adhesive
7. installation, maintenance, replacement
8. Woven carpets are made with a loom on which the pile yarns and backing are interwoven. Tufted carpets are made by looping the yarns into the backing material and securing them with an adhesive and second backing.
9. (List three:) wool, nylon, and acrylic—indoor carpeting; rayon and cotton—scatter rugs; olefin—outdoor and kitchen carpeting
10. (List three:) where and how the furniture will be used, cleanability, maintenance

requirements, cost, appearance, fiber content, types of finishes
11. curtains, drapes
12. false
13. terry cloth, because of its absorbent quality
14. (Student response. See pages 304-305 of the text.)

## Student Activity Guide

### Understanding Household Textiles, Activity B

1. by interlacing two sets of yarns at right angles
2. lengthwise yarns
3. crosswise or filling yarns
4. plain, twill, satin
5. basket and rib
6. less durable
7. pile
8. nap
9. (Student response.)
10. (Student response.)
11. (Student response.)
12. by looping yarns together
13. They lack the stability and body needed for most home uses.
14. as backing for other fabrics
15. felted, tanned, or bonded fabrics
16. (Student response.)
17. (Student response.)
18. (Student response.)

### Textile Review, Activity E

Crossword answers:
1. OPAQUE
4. STRUCTURAL
6. PERCALE
7. FINISHES
8. LINEN
9. RECYCLED
10. BATHSHEET
11. BONDED
12. WATERPROOF
14. COMFORTER
15. SIZING
16. FITTEDSHEET
(also: SEAM, THREAD, PLEAT, DOWN, CUFF, TEES)

## Teacher's Resources

### Construction Methods for Carpets and Rugs, reproducible master 13-1

1. A. needlepunched
   B. interlocks fibers by using felting needles, producing a flat carpet that resembles felt
   C. indoor/outdoor carpets and rugs
2. A. woven
   B. made on a loom where the pile yarns and the backing are interwoven
   C. Axminster, velvet, Wilton
3. A. tufted
   B. loops yarn into the backing material and secures it with an adhesive to the backing and a second backing
   C. easy to do, less expensive than weaving

### Chapter 13 Test

1. N
2. F
3. G
4. A
5. C
6. L
7. I
8. M
9. J
10. K
11. T
12. F
13. F
14. T
15. F
16. F
17. F
18. T
19. T
20. T
21. C
22. B
23. D
24. A
25. D
26. B
27. B
28. C
29. C
30. A

31. Fibers are listed in order of predominance by weight. Natural and manufactured fibers are listed by generic names. Trade names can be given.
32. wool—wool fiber that has not been made into a product or used by a consumer; recycled wool—wool fiber from a woven or felted wool product that may have been used by a consumer
33. It prohibits the sale of fabrics that burn quickly.
34. (List three:) fiber content, fabric type, design, color, finish
35. A. satin
    B. basket
    C. plain

Reproducible Master 13-1

# Construction Methods for Carpets and Rugs

Name _____ Date _____ Period _____

Review the carpeting illustrations and answer the following questions.

1.

   A. What method of construction is used?
   B. How is this product produced?
   C. How is this carpet primarily used?

2. 

   A. What method of construction is used?
   B. How is this product produced?
   C. What are the three main types of this product?

3. 

   A. What method of construction is used?
   B. How is this product produced?
   C. How does this method compare with the other two?

Chapter 13   *Textiles in Today's Homes*   213

Reproducible Master 13-2

# Textiles for Upholstered Furniture

**Name** _____ **Date** _____ **Period** _____

Mount a picture of an upholstered furniture piece. Under the illustration, describe a suitable fabric and fiber. Describe the characteristics of the recommended fabric, explaining why it is suitable for the furniture piece.

[                                                                                              ]

What fabric is suitable for this furniture? what fiber?

_____

_____

_____

In what informal settings would this be fabric suitable?

_____

_____

_____

In what formal settings would this fabric be suitable?

_____

_____

_____

What type of finishes would you recommend for this fabric?

_____

_____

_____

Reproducible Test Master

# Textiles in Today's Homes

Name _____

Date _____ Period _____ Score _____

### Chapter 13 Test

❑ Matching: Match the following descriptions and terms.

_____ 1. A diagonal rib or cord pattern.

_____ 2. Another name for bedroom, bathroom, and kitchen textiles.

_____ 3. Classified as cellulosic and noncellulosic.

_____ 4. Extra large towel.

_____ 5. Filled bed cover.

_____ 6. Has loops that absorb moisture.

_____ 7. High quality sheet.

_____ 8. Made with leno weave.

_____ 9. Includes silk and wool.

_____ 10. Tablecloths, place mats, and napkins.

A. bath sheet
B. bedspread
C. comforter
D. fingertip towel
E. fitted sheet
F. linens
G. manufactured fibers
H. muslin
I. percale
J. protein natural fibers
K. table coverings
L. terry cloth
M. thermal blanket
N. wale

❑ True/False: Circle *T* if the statement is true or *F* if the statement is false.

T  F  11. Fibers are the raw materials from which fabric is made.

T  F  12. Cellulose natural fibers come from wood.

T  F  13. Protein natural fibers burn easily.

T  F  14. If a fiber is nonallergenic, it means you are not likely to develop an allergy from it.

T  F  15. Each fiber has a trade name.

T  F  16. Yarns are made from filaments and continuous fibers.

T  F  17. Warp yarns form the crosswise grain.

T  F  18. Grain is the direction thread runs in a woven fabric.

T  F  19. The rib weave is a variation of the plain weave.

T  F  20. The pile weave produces a nap.

(Continued)

Multiple Choice: Choose the best answer and write the corresponding letter in the blank.

_____ 21. _____ are some examples of fabrics produced by the pile weave.
   A. Damask, tapestry, and brocade
   B. Frieze, brocade, and satin
   C. Velvet, corduroy, and terry cloth
   D. Velveteen, tapestry, and brocade

_____ 22. A wale is characteristic of a _____ weave.
   A. rib
   B. twill
   C. basket
   D. plain

_____ 23. Structural designs are made by _____.
   A. piece dyeing
   B. printing on the surface
   C. stock dyeing
   D. varying the yarns

_____ 24. A finish can be applied to the _____.
   A. fabric
   B. fiber
   C. yarn
   D. All of the above.

_____ 25. When selecting fabrics for home use, you must make decisions about _____.
   A. appearance
   B. comfort
   C. cost
   D. All of the above.

_____ 26. The most common method of carpet construction is _____.
   A. needlepunching
   B. tufting
   C. weaving
   D. None of the above.

_____ 27. The most durable carpet is _____.
   A. cut pile
   B. level loop pile
   C. multilevel pile
   D. shag pile

_____ 28. The most-used fiber for carpets and rugs today is _____.
   A. acrylic
   B. cotton
   C. nylon
   D. wool

_____ 29. Upholstery fabric for informal settings is usually _____.
   A. elegant
   B. exposed to little wear
   C. a small or scenic print
   D. silk

(Continued)

Reproducible Test Master

_____ 30. Opaque window treatments _____.
  A. provide privacy both day and night
  B. allow a person to see outside when closed
  C. are always made of heavy, thick fabrics
  D. let light in

❏ Essay Questions: Provide complete responses to the following questions or statements.

31. Describe the contents of the Textile Fiber Products Identification Act.

32. Name and describe the two types of wool identified by the Wool Products Labeling Act.

33. Tell how the Flammable Fabrics Act protects consumers.

34. List three factors to consider when selecting household textiles.

35. Identify the following three types of weaves:

A.

B.

C.

Chapter 13   Textiles in Today's Homes   217

# CHAPTER 14
# Creating Interior Backgrounds

## Objectives

After studying this chapter, students will be able to

- compare floor treatments.
- describe several wall materials and wall treatments.
- explain how ceiling treatments serve as interior backgrounds.
- recognize the choices available for countertops.
- demonstrate how to plan satisfying interior backgrounds.

## Bulletin Boards

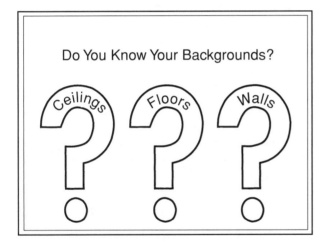

Title: *Do You Know Your Backgrounds?*

Under the title, draw three large question marks. Label the question marks *Floors*, *Walls*, and *Ceilings*. As students learn concepts about each topic, have them add answers around the appropriate question mark.

Title: *Paints and Painting*

Divide the board into three sections and label them as follows: *Paint Types and Uses*, *Paint Applicators and Cleanup*, and *Other Painting Tips*. Have students collect pictures, brochures, and articles about painting and display them in the appropriate section.

## Teaching Materials

**Text**, pages 309-330
  *To Know*
  *To Review*
  *In Your Community*
  *To Think About*
  *Using Technology*

**Student Activity Guide**
  A. *Floor Treatments*
  B. *Wallpaper*
  C. *Backgrounds Crossword*
  D. *Backgrounds*

**Teacher's Resources**
  *Illusions in Backgrounds*, color transparencies CT-19A, CT-19B, CT-19C, CT-19D, and CT-19E
  *Background Treatments*, reproducible master 14-1
  Chapter 14 Test

## Introductory Activities

1. Have students share stories of unusual backgrounds they have seen and bring in pictures of unusual background treatments found in famous homes and buildings.
2. Have students imagine walking into an empty room and deciding the background treatments. How would they make selections? Have students explain the process they would use.
3. Have students find and discuss the glossary and/or dictionary definitions of key terms listed in the *To Know* section of the text. Have them add these to their card files.
4. Show slides or magazine pictures of a variety of interiors. As students view each, have them discuss the moods the backgrounds create.

# Strategies to Reteach, Reinforce, Enrich, and Extend Text Concepts

## Floor Treatments

5. **ER** Have students make lists of the flooring materials used in their homes and school. Have them make a second list of the floor coverings used.
6. **ER** Assemble samples of hardwoods and softwoods. Have students examine the samples and discuss advantages and disadvantages of each.
7. **RF** Have students make a list of flooring materials that do not need floor coverings. List the advantages and disadvantages of each flooring material.
8. **ER** Have students collect and mount pictures of various types of floor coverings. Have students label them *soft* or *resilient*, list where each type would be appropriately used, and identify one advantage and disadvantage of each.
9. **RF** Have students work in small groups to make floor treatment charts with the following headings: *Type (soft or resilient); Cost (low, moderate, or high); Installation (easy to difficult); Maintenance and Care (easy to difficult);* and *Appropriate Use.*
10. **RF** Have students list where various types of carpets and rugs are appropriate.
11. **ER** *Floor Treatments,* Activity A, SAG. Students are asked to determine the best floor coverings for the situations listed. They are to mount pictures and complete the information on the form. (Save the worksheet for Item 20.)

## Walls

12. **RF** Have students discuss the functions of walls.
13. **RF** Have students examine the walls in the classroom and identify the materials used in their construction and treatment.
14. **ER** Have students examine the walls in their homes and make a list of the types of materials used in the construction and treatment.
15. **RF** Have students separate wall construction materials into those that need treatment and those that do not. Have them identify treatments appropriate for the materials.
16. **RF** Have students discuss the basic types of paint and their uses. Have them read labels on paint cans to find out suggested uses for each type of paint. Have them find where the various types have been used in the school.
17. **ER** Visit a paint and wallpaper store. Arrange for a sales associate to discuss with students the various types of paint, wallpaper, and fabric and the appropriate locations for their use. Before the trip, have students make a list of questions to ask.
18. **RF** Have students discuss the advantages and disadvantages of using mirrors and glass as wall treatments.
19. **EX** Have students research wall coverings of another period in history. Have them indicate the mood they conveyed, whether formal or informal.
20. **ER** Have students reuse the worksheet saved from Item 11 and determine the best wall treatments for the situations listed. Have them justify their choices.
21. **RF** *Illusions in Backgrounds,* color transparencies CT-19A, CT-19B, CT-19C, CT-19D, and CT-19E, TR. Use transparency CT-19A to show a wall treatment with bold color. Use transparency CT-19B to show contrasting floor/ceiling and wall treatments. To illustrate how the illusions of the height of the wall can be changed to appear higher or lower, use CT-19C, CT-19D, and CT-19E. Point out how the use of color as well as line affects the illusion of height. Remind students that all the walls in the set have the same dimensions. CT-19A can be used as an overlay to demonstrate this point.
22. **EX** *Wallpaper,* Activity B, SAG. Students are asked to mount or create wallpaper samples and provide the information requested.

## Ceiling Treatments

23. **RF** Have students discuss the purposes of ceilings and how they affect the appearance of rooms.
24. **ER** Have students find and mount pictures of unusual ceilings. Discuss the moods created by the various ceilings.

25. **RF** Have students find examples of ceilings that are plaster, acoustical plaster, and acoustical tile. Have students check the conditions of the ceilings to determine the ease of maintenance.

## Planning Your Background Treatments

26. **EX** Divide the class into three groups and assign one of the following categories to each: walls, floors, and countertops. Have students research the various types of backgrounds possible with their respective category. Ask them to determine which is the least expensive, most expensive, easiest to maintain, and most difficult to maintain. Discuss the findings.
27. **EX** Have students work in groups to make a list of guidelines to follow when planning backgrounds. Combine the lists to make a master list for each member of the class.
28. **ER** *Background Treatments*, reproducible master 14-1, TR. Use the master to make worksheets for students to use on a field trip. Arrange for the class to visit two or more model homes. Have students examine the floor, wall, ceiling, and countertop backgrounds in the model homes using the worksheet provided.

## Chapter Review

29. **RF** *Backgrounds Crossword*, Activity C, SAG. Students are asked to use the clues to fill in the crossword puzzle.
30. **EX** *Backgrounds*, Activity D, SAG. Students are asked to mount a picture of a room having backgrounds that dictated the room's furnishings. Students then evaluate the backgrounds by answering the questions provided.

## Answer Key

### Text

*To Review,* page 328

1. They help determine the total look of the room, show off furnishings, and create the desired mood.
2. Flooring materials are structurally part of the floor, while floor coverings are placed over the constructed floor and can be changed often.
3. (List two of each:) soft-floor coverings: wall-to-wall carpeting, room-size rugs, area rugs; resilient floor coverings: vinyl, laminate, cork tile
4. walls
5. (Student response. See pages 317-321 of the text.)
6. Use horizontal lines on the walls, extend the ceiling treatment down a short distance onto the walls, or use dark or patterned materials.
7. It absorbs and reduces the sound.
8. They coordinate well with a great variety of colors and designs.
9. It provides a dramatic look, but also makes the room look smaller.
10. (List six:) laminate, solid surface, ceramic tile, porcelain tile, natural stone, engineered quartz, metal, butcher block

## Student Activity Guide

*Backgrounds Crossword,* Activity C

# Teacher's Resources

## Chapter 14 Test

1. A, D
2. A
3. B
4. C, D
5. C, D
6. B, C, D
7. C, D
8. C, D
9. A, C, D
10. B, C, D
11. D
12. A, D
13. B, C
14. C, D
15. C
16. T
17. F
18. T
19. F
20. F
21. T
22. F
23. T
24. T
25. T
26. C
27. D
28. B
29. D
30. D
31. A
32. B
33. C
34. B
35. B

36. Enamel paints have the most gloss. Satin, or semigloss, paints have less gloss. Flat wall paints have no gloss.

37. (List three:) The same floor covering throughout makes the house seem larger and more unified. Choose color schemes and styles that allow changes in decorating scheme. Classic wall treatments can be mixed with various accessories and decorating plans. High gloss enamel paints are easier to clean than flat or semigloss. Bold patterns produce a dramatic look and make rooms look smaller. Fabrics for curtains and accessories may be coordinated with those on backgrounds. (Students may list others.)

38. (List three:) Use same floor covering throughout; separate areas with area rugs; use vertical or horizontal lines; use mirrors or glass; use lighter or darker colors; use bold or patterned materials. (Students may list others.)

Reproducible Master 14-1

# Background Treatments

**Name** _____ **Date** _____ **Period** _____

Visit a model home. Complete the following information about the backgrounds in the house.

1. Which background caught your eye first? Give the reason.

2. Which background treatment covers the largest area?

3. Describe the floor treatment in each of the following rooms:

    A. Kitchen:

    B. Living area:

    C. Master bedroom:

4. Describe the wall treatment in each of the following rooms:

    A. Kitchen:

    B. Living area:

    C. Master bedroom:

5. Describe the ceiling treatment used throughout the house. Did any of the rooms have a unique ceiling treatment?

6. Identify the treatments used in the countertops throughout the house.

    A. Kitchen:

    B. Master bathroom:

    C. Work area:

7. Describe a living unit for whom you think the home would be well-suited, based on the background treatments.

Chapter 14   *Creating Interior Backgrounds*   **223**

Reproducible Test Master

# Creating Interior Backgrounds

Name _____

Date _____ Period _____ Score _____

**Chapter 14 Test**

☐ Matching: Match the following terms and background treatments. (Each background treatment may match more than one term. List all possibilities.)

_____ 1. Acoustical plaster.
_____ 2. Acoustical tile.
_____ 3. Brick.
_____ 4. Carpeting.
_____ 5. Ceramic tile.
_____ 6. Cork.
_____ 7. Enamel paint.
_____ 8. Flat paint.
_____ 9. Hardwood.
_____ 10. Laminate.
_____ 11. Paneling.
_____ 12. Plaster.
_____ 13. Solid surface material.
_____ 14. Softwood.
_____ 15. Vinyl.

A. ceiling
B. countertop
C. floor
D. wall

☐ True/False: Circle *T* if the statement is true or *F* if the statement is false.

T F 16. Backgrounds help determine the total look of a room.
T F 17. The largest background area is the floor.
T F 18. Cork tile and laminate floor coverings are examples of resilient surfaces.
T F 19. Vinyl is the least expensive floor tile.
T F 20. Oak and larch are hardwoods used for floors.
T F 21. Finishes are used on wood floors to protect them.
T F 22. Wall-to-wall carpeting is best used to set off a conversational area.
T F 23. Gypsum wallboard is the most common material used for interior walls.
T F 24. Enamel paint is the most durable type of paint.
T F 25. Classic wall treatments are in style year after year.

(Continued)

Reproducible Test Master

❏ Multiple Choice: Choose the best answer and write the corresponding letter in the blank.

_____ 26. Examples of hardwood are _____.
    A. beech, cherry, and hemlock
    B. birch, hickory, and larch
    C. cherry, oak, and mahogany
    D. maple, yellow pine, and Douglas fir

_____ 27. An example of a resilient floor covering is _____.
    A. ceramic
    B. concrete
    C. stone
    D. vinyl

_____ 28. An example of a wall material that does *not* need treatment is _____.
    A. cement blocks
    B. paneling
    C. plaster
    D. All of the above.

_____ 29. _____ paints leave a rough surface.
    A. Enamel
    B. Flat
    C. Satin
    D. Textured

_____ 30. Wallpaper coated with vinyl _____.
    A. is easy to clean
    B. is durable
    C. resists stains
    D. All of the above.

_____ 31. The main purpose of acoustical plaster or tile is to _____.
    A. absorb sound
    B. be attractive
    C. clean easily
    D. insulate

_____ 32. The background treatment receiving the least amount of wear is the _____.
    A. floor
    B. ceiling
    C. wall
    D. countertop

_____ 33. _____ does *not* make a room appear larger.
    A. A high ceiling
    B. A wall of mirrors
    C. Patterned wallpaper
    D. Wall-to-wall carpeting

(Continued)

_____ 34. If a room is small, it can be made to look larger by _____.
  A. using bright colors
  B. using off-white paint
  C. painting one wall dark
  D. using rough textures

_____ 35. Average ceilings are _____ feet high.
  A. six
  B. eight
  C. ten
  D. None of the above.

❏ Essay Questions: Provide complete responses to the following questions or statements.

36. Name the three types of latex paints and describe the amount of gloss in each.

37. Give three suggestions to use when planning your background treatments.

38. List three ways to change the appearance of the size of a room.

# CHAPTER 15
# Furniture Styles and Construction

## Objectives

After studying this chapter, students will be able to

- describe various furniture styles.
- identify ways to evaluate quality furniture construction.
- tell how consumers are protected when buying furniture.

## Bulletin Boards

Title: *Don't Let Furniture Puzzle You*

Cut cardboard into large puzzle pieces. Place pictures of period furniture and labels on the appropriate pieces. Arrange the puzzle as shown.

Title: *Consumer Protection*

Collect hangtags and labels from furniture and furniture advertisements. Make a display of those that provide some type of consumer protection.

## Teaching Materials

**Text**, pages 331-357
    *To Know*
    *To Review*
    *In Your Community*
    *To Think About*
    *Using Technology*
**Student Activity Guide**
    A. *Furniture Styles*
    B. *Materials Make the Furniture*
    C. *Wood Joints*
    D. *Shopping for Upholstered Furniture*
    E. *Furniture Advertisements*
**Teacher's Resources**
    *Judging Furniture Quality*, color transparencies CT-20A and CT-20B
    *Wood Furniture Joints*, reproducible master 15-1
    *Upholstered Furniture Construction*, transparency master 15-2
    Chapter 15 Test

## Introductory Activities

1. Have students choose a room or area within a home and list the furniture in it. Have them identify the styles they know and the materials used in each piece.
2. Have students find and discuss the glossary and/or dictionary definitions of key terms listed in the *To Know* section of the text. Have them add these to their card files.

## Strategies to Reteach, Reinforce, Enrich, and Extend Text Concepts

### Choosing Furniture Styles

3. **RF** Discuss with students the terms *Traditional*, *Contemporary*, and *Modern* as they relate to periods of history and furniture styles influenced in various countries. Have students study the examples in Figure 15-1.

4. **ER** Have students research one period of history discussed in the chapter. Have them write papers about the culture and important events of the period as well as the preferences in furniture styles. Have students share their reports with the class.
5. **ER** Bring in pictures from magazines of various types of furniture and have students identify the traditional styles.
6. **RF** *Furniture Styles*, Activity A, SAG. Students are asked to identify the styles of furniture illustrated and match each with its description.
7. **RF** Have students compare the terms *antiques*, *collectibles*, and *reproductions*.
8. **ER** Provide catalogs or brochures showing antiques, collectibles, and reproductions. Have students compare the furniture pieces shown, identifying styles and prices.
9. **RF** Have students discuss the differences between modern and contemporary furniture styles.
10. **RF** Divide the class into three groups and assign one of the following furniture styles to each: Traditional, Contemporary, and Modern. Have the groups make displays showing examples.

## Evaluating Furniture Construction

11. **RF** *Materials Make the Furniture*, Activity B, SAG. Students are asked to list as many home furnishings as they can that fit the categories listed.
12. **ER** Have students discuss hardwoods and softwoods in terms of their uses in furniture construction. Students may browse through furniture catalogs to get ideas on how both types are used.
13. **RF** Have students discuss why veneered woods are used instead of solid woods in some furniture construction.
14. **RT** *Judging Furniture Quality*, color transparencies CT-20A and CT-20B, TR. Use these transparencies to introduce the most common types of wood joints. Discuss the use and strength of each type.
15. **RF** *Wood Joints*, Activity C, SAG. Students are asked to identify the wood joints shown and match each to its description.
16. **ER** *Wood Furniture Joints*, transparency master 15-1, TR. Have students examine various pieces of wood furniture to determine the types of joints used. Students should record their results on the worksheets.
17. **RF** Have students discuss how plastic, metal, and glass may be used in furniture. Discuss the most appropriate uses for each material. Have students name advantages and disadvantages of each.
18. **RF** Provide students with a variety of fabric samples to examine. Samples may be placed on cards and numbered. Have students review the information in Chapter 13 on upholstery fabrics. Have them identify whether each fabric is woven or nonwoven. For woven fabrics, have them identify the type of weave. Then discuss the fiber content and characteristics of each sample and the appropriateness of the fabrics for various types of furniture.
19. **RF** Have students work in small groups to make a list of guidelines to follow when choosing fabric for upholstery. Make a master list from the group lists.
20. **RF** *Upholstered Furniture Construction*, transparency master 15-2, TR. Use the transparency master to show the construction of upholstered furniture. Have students explain the function of each part.
21. **EX** Arrange a visit to a furniture or department store. Have students examine various types of furniture for style, construction materials, and construction methods. Have students examine the upholstered furniture for tailoring methods. Students should prepare lists of questions to ask the guide. (See Item 22 for an additional assignment.)
22. **EX** *Shopping for Upholstered Furniture*, Activity D, SAG. Students are asked to focus on one piece of furniture in a department or furniture store and evaluate it using the worksheet provided. (Students may refer to a piece of furniture seen in Item 21.)
23. **ER** Have students gather and read brochures on the construction of various types of mattresses. Students should

compare them in terms of support, comfort, durability, and price.

24. **RF** Have students examine the mattress on a sleeper sofa and determine the type of springs (if any) and mattress used. Have students discuss the advantages and disadvantages of owning a sleeper sofa.
25. **ER** Have students examine brochures, catalogs, and advertisements showing beds. Have students compare prices for beds with different types of springs and frames.

## Consumer Protection

26. **EX** Have students write to the Federal Trade Commission and the Consumer Product Safety Commission for information on laws to protect consumers purchasing furniture. You may assign some students to contact various furniture companies about their product standards and consumer practices.
27. **ER** *Furniture Advertisements*, Activity E, SAG. Students are asked to mount one advertisement that pictures and describes furniture. Then they are asked to analyze the ad and complete the statements.

## Chapter Review

28. **RF** Divide the class into small groups. Have each group write appropriate multiple-choice questions for one of the following topics: traditional furniture, contemporary and modern furniture, wood materials and methods of furniture construction, upholstered furniture, shopping for furniture, and consumer protection. Also ask each group to prepare a list of answers. Collect the "questions" lists and redistribute them. Have group members work jointly to answer their new list of questions. Distribute the appropriate answer sheet to each group so answers can be checked.

# Answer Key

## Text

### *To Review*, page 355

1. (List three:) Louis XIII, Louis XIV, Louis XV, Louis XVI, Empire, French Provincial, Jacobean, Queen Anne, Georgian, Regency, Victorian, Early American, Colonial, Federal, Duncan Phyfe, Shaker (Descriptions are student response. See pages 332-337 of the text.)
2. D
3. Case goods are pieces of furniture made primarily of wood, such as dressers, chests, tables, and desks. Upholstered pieces of furniture are covered in padding and fabric, such as chairs and sofas.
4. Antiques are at least 100 years old. Collectibles are less than 100 years old, but become antiques if kept for 100 years.
5. false
6. (List four:) mortise-and-tenon, double-dowel, dovetail, tongue-and-groove, butt, corner
7. *Solid wood* means the entire piece is made from the same wood. *Genuine wood* means the face veneer wood differs from the wood used in the core.
8. D
9. Flat springs offer firm support at lower cost. Coil springs are softer, more comfortable, and more costly.
10. The Federal Trade Commission (FTC) monitors the truthfulness of advertising. The Consumer Product Safety Commission (CPSC) monitors product safety.

# Student Activity Guide

## *Furniture Styles,* Activity A

### French

| Letter | Style Name |
|---|---|
| A | Louis XIV |
| D | Louis XIII |
| G | Art Nouveau |
| I | Louis XV |
| N | Empire |
| P | Louis XVI |

### English

| Letter | Style Name |
|---|---|
| C | Regency |
| F | Chippendale |
| K | Jacobean |
| M | Hepplewhite |
| O | Queen Anne |
| R | Victorian |

### American

| Letter | Style Name |
|---|---|
| B | Eames |
| E | Saarinen |
| H | Windsor |
| J | Colonial |
| L | Early American Wainscot |
| Q | Duncan Phyfe |

1. R
2. K
3. A
4. Q
5. N
6. P
7. D
8. F
9. J
10. G
11. H
12. O
13. E
14. I
15. C
16. B
17. M
18. L

## *Wood Joints,* Activity C

A. corner block
B. dovetail
C. tongue-and-groove
D. butt
E. double-dowel
F. mortise-and-tenon
1. C
2. D
3. E
4. C
5. A
6. D
7. F
8. B
9. B
10. F
11. A
12. E

# Teacher's Resources

## Chapter 15 Test

1. C
2. B
3. A
4. A
5. C
6. A
7. B
8. B
9. B
10. C
11. A
12. B
13. B
14. A
15. B
16. F
17. F
18. T
19. T
20. F
21. F
22. T
23. F
24. T
25. F
26. D
27. C
28. D
29. D
30. B
31. B
32. D
33. B
34. C
35. A

36. Antique furniture is at least 100 years old. Collectibles are less than 100 years but could become antiques. Reproductions are copies of antique originals.
37. (List three. See Figure 15-23 of the text.)
38. (List three:) Government agencies monitor products' consumer safety; highly flammable fabrics are not permitted for home furnishings; labels give fibers' use and care instructions; individual manufacturers exceed government requirements and industry standards and provide guarantees.

Reproducible Master 15-1

# Wood Furniture Joints

**Name** _____ **Date** _____ **Period** _____

Examine three different pieces of wood furniture to determine the types of joints used. Record your findings below.

| Type of Furniture | Type of Joints Used | Sketches of Joints | Quality of Furniture Based on Types of Joints |
|---|---|---|---|
| 1. | | | |
| 2. | | | |
| 3. | | | |

# Upholstered Furniture Construction

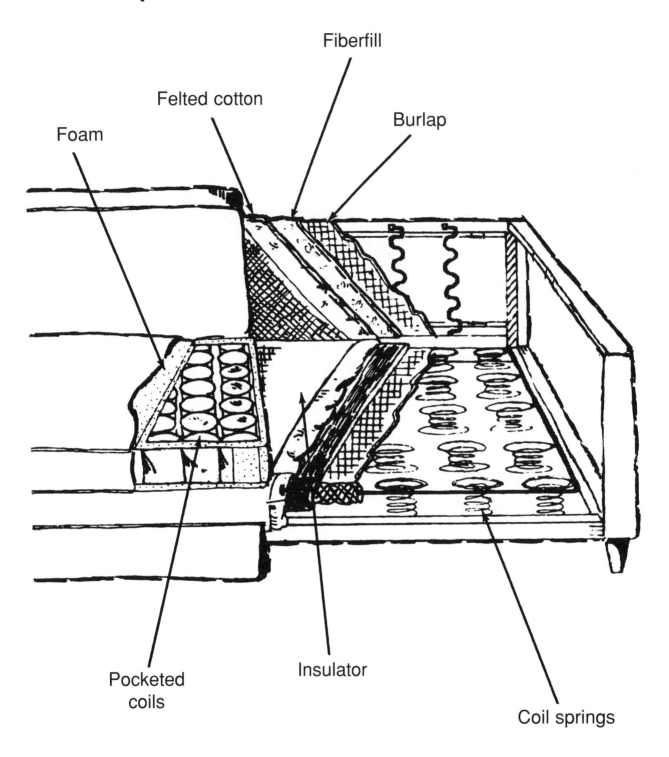

Reproducible Test Master

# Furniture Styles and Construction

Name _____

Date _____ Period _____ Score _____

**Chapter 15 Test**

❏ Matching: Match the following terms and furniture styles. (Terms are used more than once.)

_____ 1. Art Nouveau.
_____ 2. Chippendale.
_____ 3. Colonial.
_____ 4. Duncan Phyfe.
_____ 5. Empire.
_____ 6. Federal.
_____ 7. Georgian.
_____ 8. Hepplewhite.
_____ 9. Jacobean.
_____ 10. Louis XIV.
_____ 11. Organic.
_____ 12. Queen Anne.
_____ 13. Regency.
_____ 14. Shaker.
_____ 15. Victorian.

A. American
B. English
C. French

❏ True/False: Circle *T* if the statement is true or *F* if the statement is false.

T  F  16. The Queen Anne furniture style originated in France.
T  F  17. Early American furniture was made by machine and featured excessive ornamentation.
T  F  18. Contemporary furniture styles are the very latest designs.
T  F  19. Reproductions are copies of antique originals.
T  F  20. Solid wood furniture is less expensive than veneered wood furniture.
T  F  21. Butt joints are the strongest wood joints.
T  F  22. Plastic furniture is usually less expensive than wood furniture.
T  F  23. Most upholstery fabrics are knitted.
T  F  24. Upholstery tailoring can be checked by examining a cushion.
T  F  25. The Consumer Product Safety Commission monitors furniture advertising.

(Continued)

Multiple Choice: Choose the best answer and write the corresponding letter in the blank.

_____ 26. _____ is *not* a Traditional furniture style from England.
  A. Jacobean
  B. Hepplewhite
  C. Regency
  D. Shaker

_____ 27. A designer of modern furniture is _____.
  A. Adams Brothers
  B. Duncan Phyfe
  C. Frank Lloyd Wright
  D. Hepplewhite

_____ 28. A hardwood is _____.
  A. cedar
  B. pine
  C. spruce
  D. walnut

_____ 29. A softwood is _____.
  A. maple
  B. oak
  C. pecan
  D. redwood

_____ 30. Drawers of high-quality furniture have _____.
  A. double-dowel joints
  B. dovetail joints
  C. mortise-and-tenon joints
  D. tongue-and-groove joints

_____ 31. _____ keep the sides of furniture from pulling apart.
  A. Butt joints
  B. Corner blocks
  C. Double-dowel joints
  D. Tongue-and-groove joints

_____ 32. A sign of good upholstery tailoring is _____.
  A. securely fastened buttons and trims
  B. well-placed fabric design
  C. skirts lined and hanging straight
  D. All of the above.

_____ 33. The most important consideration when choosing furniture for sleeping is the _____.
  A. amount of padding
  B. comfort
  C. number of springs
  D. size of springs

(Continued)

_____ 34. _____ springs are the least expensive type of springs.
   A. Box
   B. Coil
   C. Flat
   D. Set

_____ 35. A furniture design that is *not* considered a Twenty-First Century style is _____.
   A. Art Deco
   B. Contemporary
   C. Country
   D. Eclectic

❑ Essay Questions: Provide complete responses to the following questions or statements.

36. How do antiques, collectibles, and reproductions in furniture differ?

37. List three questions to ask when buying upholstered furniture.

38. Describe three ways consumers are protected when buying furniture.

# CHAPTER 16
# Arranging and Selecting Furniture

## Objectives
After studying this chapter, students will be able to

- describe how to use a scale floor plan to arrange furniture.
- list factors to consider when arranging furniture.
- explain the steps to follow when selecting furniture.
- compare places to shop for furniture.
- determine ways to stretch their furniture dollars.

## Bulletin Boards

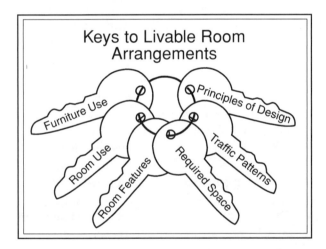

Title: *Keys to Livable Room Arrangements*

Cut out colorful shapes of keys and place them on the board as shown. Write one of the following guidelines on each key: *Furniture Use, Room Use, Room Features, Required Space, Traffic Patterns,* and *Principles of Design*.

Title: *Do Bargains Improve the Quality of Life?*

Have students find or draw cartoons depicting a funny situation that can occur as a result of getting a "bargain" for the home. Place the cartoons on the bulletin board under the title. Discuss with students how buying an item of furniture may seem a bargain, but may become a disappointment.

## Teaching Materials
**Text**, pages 358-378
  *To Know*
  *To Review*
  *In Your Community*
  *To Think About*
  *Using Technology*
**Student Activity Guide**
  A. *Arranging Furniture in a Bedroom*
  B. *Arranging the Social Area*
  C. *Deciding Where to Shop for Furniture*
  D. *Bargain Brochure*
  E. *Comparing Information Sources for Buying Furniture*
  F. *Test Your Knowledge*
**Teacher's Resources**
  *Graph Paper and Templates,* transparency/reproducible master 16-1
  *Evaluating Furniture Arrangements,* color transparency CT-21
  *Furniture Arrangement,* reproducible master 16-2
  Chapter 16 Test

## Introductory Activities
1. Have students brainstorm factors they think they will consider when selecting and arranging furniture for their first homes.
2. Have students find and discuss the glossary and/or dictionary definitions of key terms listed in the *To Know* section of the text. Have them add these to their card files.

# Strategies to Reteach, Reinforce, Enrich, and Extend Text Concepts

## Arranging Furniture

3. **RF** *Graph Paper and Templates,* transparency master 16-1, TR. Use this master as a transparency, along with the furniture templates, to introduce the concept of using a floor plan drawn to scale to arrange furniture. Draw a floor plan on the transparency using an overhead projector pen. Cut out various pieces of furniture from the template and arrange on the floor plan. Discuss traffic patterns for each arrangement. (Make several transparencies using this master and repeat the activity for several different rooms.)

4. **ER** Have students work in small groups to make a list of guidelines for furniture arrangement. Students should include furniture use, space requirements, room features, traffic flow, and the principles of design. Have the groups compare lists and make a master list for students to use.

5. **ER** *Arranging Furniture in a Bedroom,* Activity A, SAG. Students are asked to select furniture from the furniture templates and design a bedroom for a teen using the graph paper provided. They are then asked to evaluate their arrangements on the forms provided. (Have students save the templates for later use.)

6. **ER** *Graph Paper and Templates,* reproducible master 16-1, TR. Make a photocopy of this master for each student. Have each student use the graph paper to draw the floor plan and walls of his or her bedroom or another room in the home. Following Figure 16-4 in the text, have students fold up the walls and cut out windows and doors. Have them use the furniture templates to experiment with room arrangements.

7. **ER** *Arranging the Social Area,* Activity B, SAG. Students are asked to select furniture from the templates and design a social area using the graph paper provided. They are then asked to write an evaluation of their floor plans.

8. **ER** Have students look through magazines for various room arrangements. Evaluate the arrangements in terms of practicality and function. Have each student select a particular arrangement and discuss with the class if the room is poorly or well designed. Students should give reasons for their opinions.

9. **RF** *Evaluating Furniture Arrangements,* color transparency CT-21, TR. Have students evaluate the furniture arrangements shown and point out traffic patterns.

## Selecting Furniture

10. **RF** Have students make priority lists of furniture they think their rooms should have. Students can have their parents or roommates look at the lists and suggest how the priority order might be changed.

11. **ER** Have each student select a picture of a room arrangement and imagine the composition of the living units and their lifestyles. Students should explain their choices in a short report and attach the picture.

12. **EX** Have students determine the budget amount that could be allowed for furniture if the family income is $40,000 and one-third of it is used for housing expenses. (Review Chapter 5 if necessary.)

13. **ER** *Deciding Where to Shop for Furniture,* Activity C, SAG. Students are asked to compare four stores that sell furniture and report their findings on the worksheet.

14. **ER** Have students collect advertisements, brochures, and catalogs to compare costs of similar items of furniture. Have them determine if the items are on sale, and if so, the type of sale.

15. **EX** Have students search *Consumer Reports* or a similar publication for information concerning furniture. Have them report their findings to the class.

## Stretching Your Furniture Dollars

16. **RF** Have students discuss the terms *bargain, low cost, inexpensive,* and *cheap.* Ask them to check advertisements for terms that indicate price and quality.

17. **ER** *Bargain Brochure*, Activity D, SAG. Students are asked to design pamphlets explaining the advantages and pitfalls of purchasing items at discount.
18. **EX** *Comparing Information Sources for Buying Furniture*, Activity E, SAG. Students are asked to find examples of the furniture information sources and use the worksheet to compare their usefulness.
19. **ER** Have students find pictures and discuss ways of using furniture for dual purposes. Students should compare furniture designed for a single purpose with multipurpose furniture.
20. **EX** Have students compare prices on three similar pieces of furniture that are: unfinished and unassembled, finished and unassembled, and finished and assembled.
21. **EX** Arrange for students to work with the school librarian to develop a reference file containing information about shopping for home furnishings.
22. **RF** Have students discuss why furniture should be recycled. Have them list ways to recycle furniture in their homes. Have them discuss where they can recycle furniture and purchase recycled furniture.
23. **EX** Ask students to discuss the possible consequences of making the following purchases: two dining room chairs on sale because the line is being discontinued, a king-size canopy bed, a beanbag chair, and a sofa with a print fabric in the latest pattern and color. Have students recommend other purchases and discuss their consequences.
24. **RF** Have students list ways to renovate furniture and provide advantages and disadvantages of each.
25. **EX** Challenge students to provide the most functionally furnished apartment for the least amount of money. Students should divide into two or more teams and decide which furnishings they will need for their apartments. Then each student should shop for one or two of the items needed to find the best bargain. Students should bring in some form of documentation to show price, such as advertisements or statements from the person selling the furniture. Each group should then make a list of all the items they would use, along with the prices and the places to purchase them. Students should give a total for the cost of furnishing their apartments.
26. **ER** Have students find pictures of rooms decorated with an eclectic look. Students should discuss what styles are combined and what features help the styles go together.

# Chapter Review

27. **EX** *Furniture Arrangement*, reproducible master 16-2, TR. Using the furniture template provided, have students design a living area that includes dining for six people and a conversational grouping that seats at least six. Have them rearrange the furniture as needed to meet the guidelines. Students should gather pictures of the furniture to be used in the room. For each picture, they should list the following information: type of furniture, style, function, source, and care requirements. Students should indicate if the cost of furnishing the room is low, moderate, or high. Have them share their final arrangements with three classmates and evaluate one another's projects.
28. **RF** *Test Your Knowledge*, Activity F, SAG. Students are asked to write questions and answers for each of the topics listed. Have students test one another in small groups.

# Answer Key

## Text

### *To Review*, page 376

1. Moving furniture templates on paper or on the computer takes much less work than moving actual pieces of furniture.
2. (List three:) furniture use, furniture space requirements, room use, room features, traffic patterns
3. to clarify which purchases to buy first and which can wait
4. to help stay within budget and look for the best merchandise for the price
5. (List three:) retail stores, warehouse showrooms, catalogs, online Web sites, salvage stores, garage sales, auctions, flea markets (The advantage is a student response.)

6. A. You are expected to buy other items not on sale.
   B. You may have to wait for the sale.
   C. Delivery and service may not be available.
   D. The extent of damage may not be obvious, and you cannot buy matching items later.
7. (List five:) libraries, online, books, magazines, product-rating organizations, advertisements, labels, Better Business Bureau
8. (List five:) shopping for bargains, buying multipurpose furniture, buying unfinished and unassembled furniture, recycling furniture at home, buying recycled furniture, renovating furnishings, creating an eclectic look
9. (List two:) recycle, restore, renew
10. repair, refinish, reupholster
11. Furniture pieces of different styles and periods can be combined.

31. (Student response.)
32. (Student response.)
33. (List three:) books, magazines, labels, product ratings, advertisements, Better Business Bureau
34. repair, refinish, reupholster
35. furniture from different periods and countries mixed together

# Teacher's Resources

## Chapter 16 Test

| | | | | | |
|---|---|---|---|---|---|
| 1. | H | 11. | T | 21. | C |
| 2. | E | 12. | F | 22. | D |
| 3. | C | 13. | T | 23. | B |
| 4. | F | 14. | F | 24. | D |
| 5. | D | 15. | F | 25. | C |
| 6. | K | 16. | F | 26. | D |
| 7. | G | 17. | T | 27. | A |
| 8. | I | 18. | T | 28. | D |
| 9. | B | 19. | F | 29. | D |
| 10. | A | 20. | T | 30. | A |

Transparency/Reproducible Master 16-1

# Graph Paper and Templates

**Name** _____ **Date** _____ **Period** _____

Scale: ¼ inch = 1 foot

(Continued)

Transparency/Reproducible Master 16-1 (Continued)

# Graph Paper and Templates

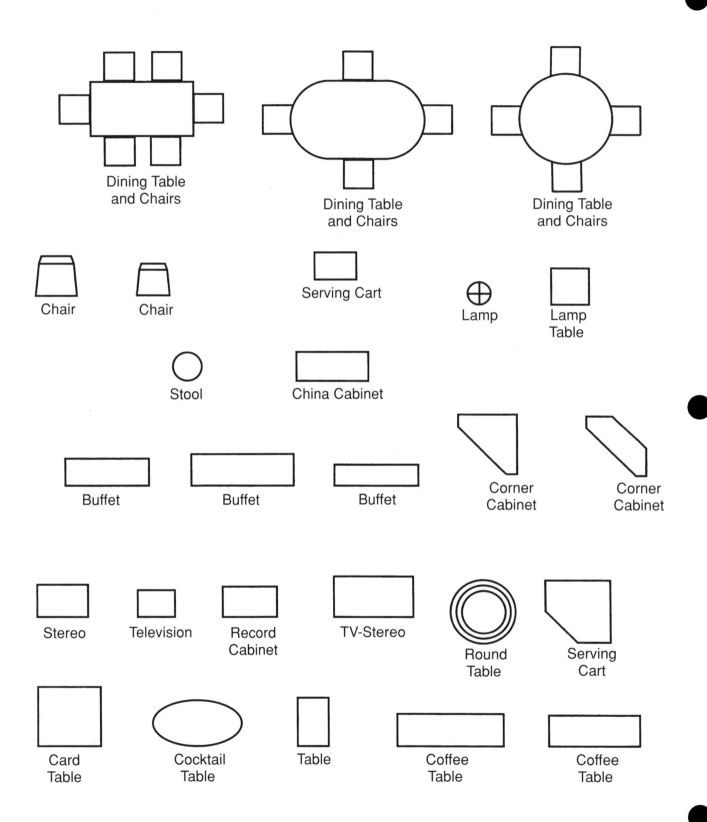

Transparency/Reproducible Master 16-1 (Continued)

# Graph Paper and Templates

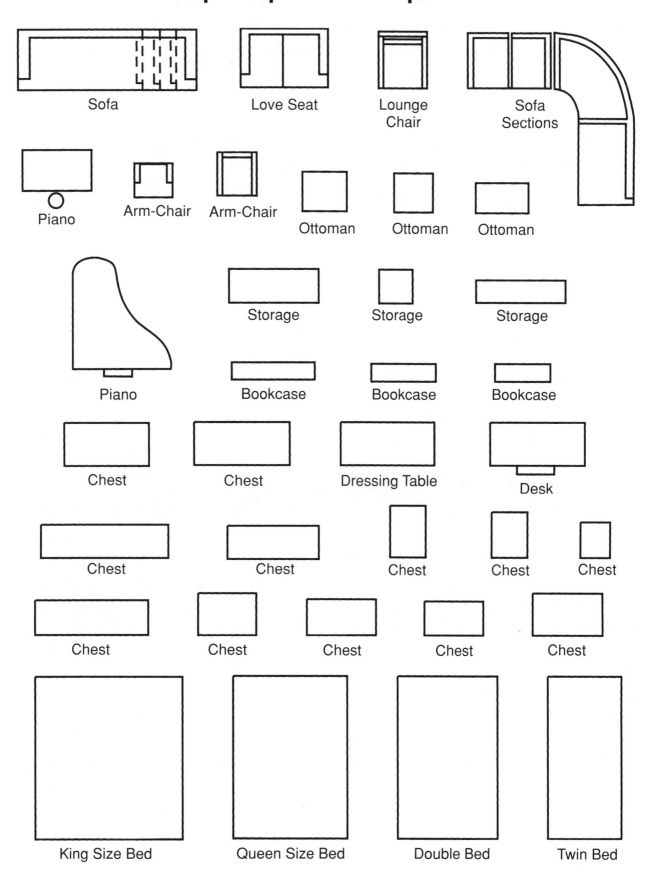

Chapter 16  Arranging and Selecting Furniture

Reproducible Master 16-2

# Furniture Arrangement

Name _____ Date _____ Period _____

Design a living area that includes dining for four to six people and a conversational grouping that seats at least six. Choose appropriate furniture pieces from the furniture template and mount them on the following plan. Indicate the traffic patterns and answer the question below.

Scale: 1/4 inch = 1 foot

Do you believe this area is functional? Explain. _____
_____
_____
_____
_____
_____
_____
_____
_____
_____

**244** *Chapter 16    Arranging and Selecting Furniture*

Reproducible Test Master

# Arranging and Selecting Furniture

Name _____

Date _____ Period _____ Score _____

## Chapter 16 Test

❏ Matching: Match the following terms and identifying phrases.

_____ 1. A store that offers the most services, such as custom orders.

_____ 2. A way to buy high-quality furniture at lower prices.

_____ 3. A furniture source that does not allow inspection before purchase.

_____ 4. Offered by stores that do not provide full service.

_____ 5. Moving or "going out of business" sale.

_____ 6. A store that provides quick service and savings, but few brands or styles of merchandise.

_____ 7. Sale to get people into the store to buy nonsale items.

_____ 8. Sale to make room for new items.

_____ 9. Purchases that stretch furniture dollars.

_____ 10. A means of recycling furniture.

A. auctions and garage sales
B. bargains
C. catalogs
D. closeout sales
E. discontinued items
F. discount prices
G. loss leader
H. retail store
I. seasonal sale
J. unassembled furniture
K. warehouse showroom

❏ True/False: Circle *T* if the statement is true or *F* if the statement is false.

T  F  11. A convenient scale for a floor plan and furniture templates is ¼ inch equals 1 foot.

T  F  12. A conversational grouping should *not* be less than 12 feet across.

T  F  13. When prioritizing furniture needs, a person ranks them in order of importance.

T  F  14. Seasonal sales are held to get people to come into a store and then buy items that are not on sale.

T  F  15. A good source of information about making purchases is the Greater Business Association.

T  F  16. A bargain is always the least expensive item.

T  F  17. One way to stretch furniture dollars is to buy multipurpose furniture.

T  F  18. Recycling furniture can be done in a person's own home.

T  F  19. Updating the upholstery fabric on a chair is an example of restoring the furniture piece.

T  F  20. The "eclectic look" is achieved by using furniture with designs from different periods and countries.

(Continued)

❑ Multiple Choice: Choose the best response. Write the letter in the space provided.

_____ 21. _____ are not factors to consider when planning furniture arrangement.
   A. Features of the room
   B. Traffic flow patterns
   C. Furniture accents
   D. Uses of the room

_____ 22. The main advantage of prioritizing your furniture needs is _____.
   A. accent pieces can be purchased
   B. good design will be chosen
   C. multipurpose furniture will be chosen
   D. a person knows which purchases can wait

_____ 23. When looking at the quality and prices of similar items sold in different places, a person is _____.
   A. buying at a discount house
   B. comparison shopping
   C. custom-ordering furniture
   D. visiting a warehouse showroom

_____ 24. A reduced price on patio furniture in August is an example of a _____ sale.
   A. damaged goods
   B. discontinued lines
   C. loss leader
   D. seasonal

_____ 25. A likely disadvantage of buying something at a discontinued line sale is _____.
   A. the items are damaged
   B. the items are inferior
   C. matching items may not be available later
   D. the service is inferior

_____ 26. Sources that will give information about the quality and reliability of furniture are _____.
   A. advertisements
   B. books and magazines
   C. labels
   D. All of the above.

_____ 27. Furniture purchased on sale may *not* be a bargain if _____.
   A. it does not fulfill the intended purpose
   B. it improves the quality of life
   C. it is not recycled
   D. the owner really wants it

_____ 28. Furniture that needs to be stained or painted when purchased is _____ furniture.
   A. multipurpose
   B. renovated
   C. unassembled
   D. unfinished

(Continued)

_____ 29. Furniture items that can serve more than one purpose include _____.
   A. flat-topped trunks
   B. plastic or wooden cubes
   C. sofa beds
   D. All of the above.

_____ 30. Recycling furniture means that it is _____.
   A. adapted to a new use
   B. not worth repairing
   C. purchased from a seasonal sale
   D. All of the above.

❑ Essay Questions: Provide complete responses to the following questions or statements.

31. Describe three pieces of furniture that would be wise selections for a first home. Justify your answer.

32. Explain one way to purchase low-priced furniture. Identify any possible drawbacks.

33. List three sources of information for selecting furniture.

34. List briefly the steps in restoring furniture.

35. What is the "eclectic look" in furniture?

# CHAPTER 17

# Addressing Windows, Lighting, and Accessories

## Objectives

After studying this chapter, students will be able to

- describe types of window treatments.
- explain the differences between incandescent and fluorescent lighting.
- plan residential lighting for visual comfort, safety, and beauty.
- distinguish between structural and nonstructural lighting.
- list guidelines for the use, placement, and care of accessories.

## Bulletin Boards

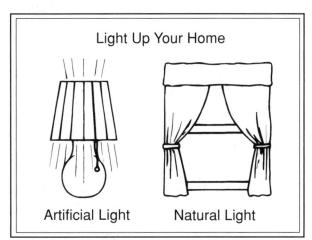

Title: *Light Up Your Home*

Make a lamp base and a large, pleated lampshade from construction paper and place on the board as shown. Add a knotted piece of cord for the pull cord. Place a piece of yellow tissue paper under the lamp to represent light. Make a large window from construction paper and place fabric over the window for curtains. Place the labels *Natural Light* and *Artificial Light* as shown.

Title: *Know Your Window Treatments*

Mount pictures of various types of windows and their treatments. Label each window treatment.

Title: *Accessorize for the Fun of It*

Have students contribute pictures of fun, economical accessories and mount these on the board. (Students may display homemade accessories.) Contributors should place note cards under their accessories, explaining how to make them.

## Teaching Materials

**Text**, pages 379-401
    *To Know*
    *To Review*
    *In Your Community*
    *To Think About*
    *Using Technology*

**Student Activity Guide**
    A. *Choosing Window Treatments*
    B. *Measuring for Window Treatments*
    C. *Lighting for Activities*
    D. *Lighting for Safety*
    E. *Structural and Nonstructural Lighting*
    F. *Accessories*

**Teacher's Resources**
    *Window Treatments*, color transparencies CT-22A and CT-22B
    *Reflecting and Absorbing Light*, reproducible master 17-1
    Chapter 17 Test

## Introductory Activities

1. Have students review window styles by reexamining *Window Styles* color transparencies CT-11A, CT-11B, and CT-11C

from Chapter 8. Discuss how windows affect the interior appearance of a room and which window styles are appropriate in various rooms. Introduce the concepts of window treatments and natural lighting. Discuss the need for artificial lighting.

2. Have students find and discuss the glossary and/or dictionary definitions of key terms listed in the *To Know* section of the text. Have them add these to their card files.

# Strategies to Reteach, Reinforce, Enrich, and Extend Text Concepts

## Window Treatments

3. **RF** *Window Treatments*, color transparencies CT-22A and CT-22B, TR. Use these transparencies to introduce various window treatments. Discuss the appropriateness of each treatment for the window style.
4. **RF** Have students find and mount pictures of window treatments for Bulletin Board II.
5. **RF** Have students label other types of window treatments appropriate for Bulletin Board II.
6. **ER** *Choosing Window Treatments*, Activity A, SAG. Students are asked to sketch treatments appropriate for the various window styles illustrated.
7. **EX** *Measuring for Window Treatments*, Activity B, SAG. Using the illustrations, students are asked to describe how to measure windows for draw draperies, curtains, and cafe curtains.
8. **EX** Have students identify and list the various types of window treatments used in their homes and/or school.
9. **RF** Have students discuss ways to reduce the transfer of heat through windows.

## Artificial Light

10. **EX** Have students give reasons why natural light varies, creating a need for artificial light.
11. **RF** Have students examine an object indoors with only artificial light. Then have them examine the same object in bright sunlight. Compare the appearance of the object under different lighting conditions.
12. **ER** Have students make charts comparing incandescent and fluorescent light. The charts should include shapes and sizes, typical wattage, type of light provided, advantages, and disadvantages.
13. **ER** Have students collect illustrations of incandescent and fluorescent lighting and explain where each is most beneficial.
14. **RF** Have students explain the meaning of the term *watts* in their own words. Have students explain how wattage differs in fluorescent and incandescent light.

## The Properties of Light

15. **EX** *Reflecting and Absorbing Light*, reproducible master 17-1, TR. Have students work in small groups to devise and conduct an experiment on how light is reflected and absorbed by various surfaces. Students should record their procedures and results on the worksheet provided.
16. **RF** Have students explain the relationship between watts, surfaces that reflect and absorb light, and foot-candles.
17. **RF** Have students explain the differences between direct and indirect light. Students should give examples of how to use direct and indirect light in homes.

## Functions of Lighting

18. **EX** *Lighting for Activities*, Activity C, SAG. Students are asked to name activities that might be carried out in the rooms listed. Students are to indicate the minimum recommended foot-candles for those activities. Then they are to mount pictures of lighting fixtures appropriate for each room.
19. **ER** Have students analyze a room or picture of a room to find sources of general and specific lighting. Discuss their observations.
20. **EX** Set up an experimental room for determining the kind of light that is best for various tasks. Let students try tasks with the following types of lighting: a lightbulb, a lightbulb with a diffuser, a lightbulb with a shade surrounding it, and a lightbulb with an opaque surface underneath

to reflect light up. Students should try such tasks as reading, talking, or sewing with the different types of light. Have students discuss their lighting preferences.
21. **ER** Have students analyze a home to determine whether lighting is adequate for safety. Discuss the results with the class.
22. **ER** *Lighting for Safety*, Activity D, SAG. On the floor plan provided, students are asked to indicate where light switches should be located for safety and identify statements that express good lighting plans.
23. **RF** Have students find and discuss pictures of rooms or homes where lighting is used for beauty.

## Structural and Nonstructural Lighting

24. **RF** Have students list and describe the types of structural lighting.
25. **ER** Have students evaluate two or three lamps according to the recommendations in the text. Have them determine which lamps they would purchase and why.
26. **ER** *Structural and Nonstructural Lighting*, Activity E, SAG. Students are asked to select, mount, and analyze two examples of nonstructural lighting and three examples of structural lighting.
27. **EX** Have students work in small groups to create a lighting dictionary. Students should look through the text glossary and other resources to find terms that refer to light or lighting. Have students rewrite the definitions in their own words and place them on index cards for alphabetizing. Students may illustrate the terms as appropriate.

## Choosing Accessories

28. **RF** Bring in a variety of accessories (or pictures of accessories) and have students identify them as functional or decorative. Students should explain their choices.
29. **ER** *Accessories*, Activity F, SAG. Students are asked to mount a picture on the worksheet showing accessories in a room and evaluate their use.
30. **EX** Have students develop ideas for accessories that are both decorative and functional. Students should explain in what settings the accessories would be appropriate.
31. **RF** Have students make a list of accessories and classify them as functional, decorative, or both.

## Chapter Review

32. **EX** Arrange a class visit to a lighting specialty store. Have store personnel discuss the features of lighting fixtures and effective ways of using the lighting. Have students prepare questions ahead of time.

## Answer Key

### Text

*To Review*, **page 399**

1. Draperies are pleated panels of fabric. Curtains are flat fabric panels.
2. because they can easily be opened and still provide privacy and sunlight control
3. Incandescent lights are cheaper to install than fluorescent lights, but more costly to use.
4. E-lamp, compact fluorescent bulb
5. reflected light, absorbed light, diffused light (Examples are student response.)
6. to provide a low level of light to see objects clearly and maneuver safely as well as to provide higher levels of light to do tasks
7. (List five:) valance, bracket, cornice, cove, soffit, and track lighting; recessed and surface-mounted downlights; wall washers; luminous ceilings
8. Decorative accessories simply add beauty, but functional accessories add beauty and usefulness.
9. to help tie the furnishings together

## Student Activity Guide

*Lighting for Safety*, **Activity D**

(Light switch locations are student response.)

(These statements should be checked: 1, 2, 3, 5, 8, 9, 12, 13, 14)

# Teacher's Resources

## Chapter 17 Test

1. G
2. F
3. A
4. E
5. D
6. B
7. E
8. F
9. G
10. C
11. T
12. F
13. F
14. F
15. T
16. T
17. T
18. F
19. F
20. T
21. B
22. B
23. C
24. C
25. C
26. B
27. D
28. A
29. B
30. D
31. (List five:) window style, size, and location; sun control; noise control; ventilation; privacy; insulation; purchase cost; maintenance cost; desired style
32. Dark colors and rough textures absorb light, but light colors and smooth or shiny textures reflect light.
33. (List two each. Student response.)

Reproducible Master 17-1

# Reflecting and Absorbing Light

Date _____ Period _____

**Group Members:**
_____
_____

Devise an experiment to find how light is reflected and absorbed by different surfaces. Be sure your procedure can be done several times with the same surface. This will allow you to compare results accurately. List the supplies you need and write the procedure you will use. Then record your results.

Supplies needed:
_____
_____
_____

Procedure:
_____
_____
_____
_____
_____
_____
_____
_____
_____

Results:

| Surface Color | Surface Texture | Light Absorbed | Light Reflected |
|---|---|---|---|
| | | | |
| | | | |
| | | | |
| | | | |
| | | | |
| | | | |

*Chapter 17  Addressing Windows, Lighting, and Accessories*

Reproducible Test Master

# Addressing Windows, Lighting, and Accessories

Name _____

Date _____ Period _____ Score _____

### Chapter 17 Test

❑ Matching: Match the following terms and definitions. The section is divided into two parts.

### Part 1

_____ 1. Are hinged sections.

_____ 2. Can be raised and lowered only.

_____ 3. Can be tilted to any degree.

_____ 4. Determines privacy of window treatments.

_____ 5. Open and close with a cord.

A. blinds
B. cafes
C. curtains
D. draw drapes
E. opaqueness
F. shades
G. shutters

### Part 2

_____ 6. Used in an E-lamp.

_____ 7. Part of a fluorescent tube.

_____ 8. Part of an incandescent bulb.

_____ 9. Amount of electricity a bulb uses.

_____ 10. Unit of measure for amount of light that reaches an object one foot away.

A. coil
B. electronic bulb
C. foot-candle
D. light meter
E. mercury vapor
F. tungsten filament
G. wattage

❑ True/False: Circle *T* if the statement is true or *F* if the statement is false.

T  F  11. Window treatments help control the amount of light in a room.

T  F  12. Curtains are pleated panels of fabric that can cover windows completely or be pulled to the sides.

T  F  13. Shades are appropriate for windows used for air circulation.

T  F  14. Fluorescent light is produced when an electric current passes through a filament wire.

T  F  15. Light is reflected by light colors and smooth, shiny surfaces.

T  F  16. Diffused light covers a large area and has no glare.

T  F  17. The majority of indirect light is reflected from walls and ceilings.

T  F  18. Bracket lighting fixtures are mounted over windows.

T  F  19. Cove lighting is directed upward and downward, giving both direct and indirect light.

T  F  20. Accessories placed near each other should have something in common.

(Continued)

❏ Multiple Choice: Choose the best response. Write the letter in the space provided.

_____ 21. The _____ is *not* part of a window.
   A. apron
   B. border
   C. sash
   D. sill

_____ 22. Flat fabric panels with a pocket hem at the top are called _____.
   A. cafes
   B. curtains
   C. double draw draperies
   D. draw draperies

_____ 23. Compared to incandescent bulbs, fluorescent tubes _____.
   A. are less expensive to install and replace
   B. give more light from smaller space
   C. last longer
   D. light up sooner

_____ 24. Light is reflected by _____.
   A. dark colors
   B. rough surfaces
   C. shiny surfaces
   D. All of the above.

_____ 25. Diffused means _____.
   A. direct
   B. rough
   C. scattered
   D. shiny

_____ 26. Direct light _____.
   A. provides soft light for a large area
   B. provides the most light possible to a specific area
   C. shines toward ceilings and walls
   D. All of the above.

_____ 27. Local lighting _____.
   A. can be called task lighting
   B. is needed when you read
   C. is used to supplement general lighting
   D. All of the above.

_____ 28. Structural lighting is _____.
   A. built-in
   B. easily moved
   C. high-level lighting
   D. low-level lighting

(Continued)

_____ 29. The type of structural lighting that begins near the ceiling and directs all light upward is called a _____.
   A. cornice
   B. cove
   C. valance
   D. wall bracket

_____ 30. A _____ is an accessory that provides *no* functional value.
   A. brass lamp
   B. crystal bud vase
   C. hand-embroidered pillow
   D. watercolor painting

❏ Essay Questions: Provide complete responses to the following questions or statements.

31. List five factors to consider when selecting window treatments.

32. Explain the effect of color and texture on lighting.

33. Name two examples of each of the following: decorative accessories, functional accessories, accessories that are both decorative and functional.

# CHAPTER 18
# Selecting Household Appliances

## Objectives

After studying this chapter, students will be able to

- list factors to consider when selecting household appliances.
- describe styles and features of various kitchen, laundry, and climate control appliances.
- choose household appliances to fit their needs.

## Bulletin Boards

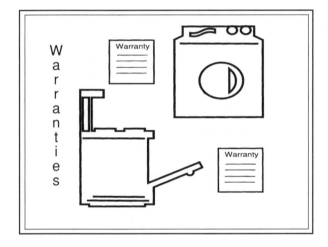

Title: *Warranties*

Draw pictures of various large appliances such as a refrigerator, range, washer, and dryer. Take copies of your appliance warranties and place each on the appropriate appliance illustration.

Title:

Have students find and clip pictures, descriptions, and articles of the latest appliances. Students may find pictures in current magazines or in sales brochures. Have the class discuss what new features, colors, and shapes are available. Students should determine three to four new appliance trends and select clippings to represent each. Have students label the trends on the board and mount the clippings.

## Teaching Materials

*Text*, pages 402-427
　*To Know*
　*To Review*
　*In Your Community*
　*To Think About*
　*Using Technology*
**Student Activity Guide**
　A. *Choosing Major Appliances*
　B. *Refrigerators*
　C. *Microwave Ovens*
　D. *Washers and Dryers*
　E. *Appliance Puzzler*
**Teacher's Resources**
　*Appliance Survey*, reproducible master 18-1
　*EnergyGuide*, color transparency CT-23
　*Analyzing Refrigerator EnergyGuides*, reproducible master 18-2
　Chapter 18 Test

## Introductory Activities

1. *Appliance Survey*, reproducible master 18-1, TR. Have each student survey a household to find out about the appliances in that home. Students should bring their surveys to class to tally and evaluate the results.
2. Have students find and discuss the glossary and/or dictionary definitions of key terms listed in the *To Know* section of the text. Have them add these to their card files.

## Strategies to Reteach, Reinforce, Enrich, and Extend Text Concepts

## Appliance Considerations

3. **RF** Have students list five factors to consider before purchasing any major appliance.
4. **RF** *EnergyGuide*, color transparency CT-23, TR. Use this transparency to

Chapter 18　*Selecting Household Appliances*　**257**

introduce the EnergyGuide labels. Have students identify and discuss the importance of the information shown on these labels.

5. **ER** *Analyzing Refrigerator EnergyGuides*, reproducible master 18-2, TR. Use the master to make worksheets for students to take to an appliance store. Ask them to find a refrigerator they like and explain why. Have them record all nine blocks of information from the EnergyGuide label. In class, have students compare one another's worksheets and discuss what they learned.

6. **ER** Have students bring in examples of warranties for the class to discuss. Explain full and limited warranties. Emphasize the important details of each warranty, such as how and when the warranty is activated, what it covers, and what it does not cover.

## Consumer Satisfaction

7. **RF** Have students look for appliance advertisements stating or implying that complete satisfaction is guaranteed. Have students bring copies to class from magazines and newspapers to discuss what the ads really say. Survey students to determine which ad has the most persuasive message.

8. **ER** *Choosing Major Appliances*, Activity A, SAG. Students are asked to create an appliance checklist, mount a picture of an appliance, and evaluate it according to the checklist.

## Choosing Kitchen Appliances

9. **RF** *Refrigerators*, Activity B, SAG. Students are asked to compare four models of refrigerators.

10. **EX** Have students write a newspaper article on choosing a refrigerator. Students should research recent magazine articles and pamphlets as well as the text. Information should be included on the latest styles and features.

11. **RF** Ask students to list advantages and disadvantages of the different types of freezers.

12. **RF** Have students evaluate a freezer using Figure 18-11 in the text.

13. **RF** Ask students to list the styles of ranges available and provide advantages and disadvantages of each.

14. **RF** Have students explain how a convection oven works.

15. **RF** Have students explain how food is heated in a microwave oven.

16. **ER** *Microwave Ovens*, Activity C, SAG. Students are asked to compare two models of microwave ovens.

17. **EX** Have students compare electric and gas ranges according to their purchase prices and installation costs.

18. **ER** Ask students to list the special features that may be found on ranges. Discuss the purposes and advantages of each.

19. **RF** Have students compare built-in and portable dishwashers and explain which model they would choose.

## Choosing Laundry Appliances

20. **ER** Have students write a one-page paper on energy-saving features of automatic washers.

21. **RF** Have students discuss what features they want in a clothes dryer. Students should also discuss what features they would be willing to do without.

22. **ER** *Washers and Dryers*, Activity D, SAG. Students are asked to obtain use and care manuals for washers and dryers and evaluate the appliances with the checklists provided.

## Choosing Climate Control Appliances

23. **RF** Have students explain the difference between a dehumidifier and a humidifier.

24. **RF** Have students research and write a paragraph on the significance of a *Btu* rating.

## Choosing Other Appliances

25. **ER** Have students discuss the size of water heaters needed for their living units. Have them identify the types of fuel used in their homes to heat water.

26. **EX** Invite representatives of the gas, electric, and appliance industries to class for a

panel discussion. Have them address innovations in major appliances that save effort, energy, and money.

27. **RF** Have students work together to make a chart about vacuum cleaners. The headings should include *Type, Uses, Advantages,* and *Disadvantages*.
28. **EX** Have students research whether it is more economical to buy appliances for a new house from the builder as part of a package deal or purchase them separately. Students should figure the cost of the major appliances that come with a newly built home and determine the amount of interest paid on them during the term of the mortgage. Students should also determine how long payments will be made on the appliances and whether their appliances are likely to last that long.
29. **RF** Have students discuss the types of personal computers they use and the new computer features they want.
30. **EX** Working in small groups, have students make a list of energy-saving features found on major appliances. Have students describe ways to save energy in the use of major appliances.
31. **RF** Have students list the small appliances in their homes. Which five do they use most often?
32. **RF** Have students list guidelines to follow for choosing and using small appliances. Ask students to identify small appliances in their homes that are rarely used.
33. **EX** Divide the class into small groups to develop a shopping checklist for purchasing the portable appliance of their choice. Have the groups report to the class.

## Chapter Review

34. **RF** *Appliance Puzzler*, Activity E, SAG. Students are asked to complete the statements about appliances by filling in the blanks.
35. **ER** Have students work in small groups to make a list of questions about the chapter. Have the groups exchange lists and answer the questions they received. Ask the groups that developed the questions to check answers.

# Answer Key
## Text
### *To Review*, page 426

1. A full warranty provides free repair or replacement of an item. With a limited warranty, a consumer may be charged for repairs.
2. chest freezer
3. cast iron, steel, or other magnetic materials because they resist the electric current that causes the production of heat
4. because heated air is constantly forced onto the surface of the food
5. As food absorbs microwaves, the molecules vibrate within the food, causing the friction that produces the heat.
6. true
7. a setting on top-loading washers that adjusts the water level to match the load size, the tilted tub of the horizontal-axis washer that limits the water level to just below the front-door opening
8. A dehumidifier removes moisture from the air, but a humidifier adds it.
9. to prevent heat from escaping and thus reduce energy costs
10. Air is filtered to the outside of the home.
11. (List three. Student response. See pages 423-424 of the text.)

## Student Activity Guide
### *Appliance Puzzler*, Activity E

1. EnergyGuide
2. Energy Star
3. full
4. limited
5. refrigerator
6. freezer
7. chest
8. upright
9. frostfree
10. range
11. induction
12. freestanding
13. slide-in
14. built-in
15. hood
16. self-cleaning
17. continuous-cleaning
18. convection
19. microwave
20. dishwasher
21. compactor
22. disposer
23. automatic washer
24. dryer
25. water heater
26. canister
27. software
28. portable

# Teacher's Resources

## Chapter 18 Test

1. F
2. A
3. D
4. H
5. E
6. T
7. F
8. T
9. F
10. T
11. F
12. T
13. F
14. F
15. T
16. C
17. A
18. D
19. A
20. C
21. D
22. D
23. B
24. A
25. D
26. (List five:) purchase price, energy cost, features, size, safety, quality
27. (Student response.)
28. advantages—save time, save energy, perform new functions, provide more convenience; disadvantages—are expensive, may not be used (Students may justify other answers.)
29. (List two of each:) input—keyboard, camera, video recorder, scanner; output—monitor, speakers, printer

Reproducible Master 18-1

# Appliance Survey

**Name** _____ **Date** _____ **Period** _____

Give the following survey to someone who uses appliances regularly. Ask him or her to complete the survey. Then bring it to class.

*Please complete the following survey by listing the 10 most used appliances in your home. For each, indicate how often it is used and check any categories that apply.*

| | Name of Appliance | How Often Used | Kitchen-Related | Laundry-Related | Climate Control | Other |
|---|---|---|---|---|---|---|
| 1. | | | | | | |
| 2. | | | | | | |
| 3. | | | | | | |
| 4. | | | | | | |
| 5. | | | | | | |
| 6. | | | | | | |
| 7. | | | | | | |
| 8. | | | | | | |
| 9. | | | | | | |
| 10. | | | | | | |

Chapter 18  *Selecting Household Appliances*

Reproducible Master 18-2

# Analyzing Refrigerator EnergyGuides

**Name** _____ **Date** _____ **Period** _____

In an appliance store, find a new refrigerator you like and explain why below. Study the refrigerator's label and record the information found in the numbered areas. Use the appropriate spaces.

Explain why you chose this refrigerator: _____

_____

_____

_____

_____

1. _____

2. _____

3. _____

4. _____

5. _____

6. _____

7. _____

8. _____

9. _____

262   Chapter 18   *Selecting Household Appliances*                Copyright Goodheart-Willcox Co., Inc.

Reproducible Test Master

# Selecting Household Appliances

Name _____

Date _____ Period _____ Score _____

## Chapter 18 Test

❑ Matching: Match the following terms and definitions.

_____ 1. Cooks food through friction produced by vibration of molecules.

_____ 2. Cooks food in a stream of heated air.

_____ 3. Gives instant infrared heat.

_____ 4. Burns spatters and spills away.

_____ 5. Uses a magnetic field to generate heat.

A. convection oven
B. conventional oven
C. glass or ceramic cooktop
D. halogen cartridge
E. induction cooktop
F. microwave oven
G. sealed burner
H. self-cleaning oven

❑ True/False: Circle T if the statement is true or F if the statement is false.

T  F  6. Safety-testing seals are attached to the electrical cords of portable appliances.

T  F  7. A person may be charged for repairs if his or her appliance has a full warranty.

T  F  8. The Association National Standards Institute (ANSI) help develop performance standards for appliances.

T  F  9. A one-door refrigerator does *not* keep ice cubes.

T  F  10. Chest freezers use less electricity than upright freezers.

T  F  11. Frostfree refrigerators and freezers are defrosted manually.

T  F  12. Induction cooktops heat food through a magnetic field.

T  F  13. A slide-in range can stand alone or be located between counters.

T  F  14. Convection ovens use more time and money to operate than conventional ovens.

T  F  15. A microwave oven does *not* brown food unless it has a special feature.

❑ Multiple Choice: Choose the best response. Write the letter in the space provided.

_____ 16. Most refrigerators made today are classified as _____.
  A. one-door refrigerators
  B. compact refrigerators
  C. two-door refrigerator-freezers
  D. None of the above.

_____ 17. In _____ ovens, food is baked and roasted in a stream of heated air.
  A. convection
  B. conventional
  C. conventional/microwave
  D. microwave

(Continued)

_____ 18. A hood is useful because it _____.
   A. dehumidifies the air
   B. humidifies the air
   C. cleans itself
   D. vents heat and odors

_____ 19. The basic steps that all washers have are _____.
   A. fill, wash, rinse, and spin
   B. permanent press, air fluff, delicate, and regular
   C. regular, permanent press, and delicate
   D. wash, rinse, and air fluff

_____ 20. You can purchase a clothes dryer that _____.
   A. has a water saver
   B. has time and load-size settings
   C. operates on either gas or electricity
   D. None of the above.

_____ 21. Considerations when choosing a water heater include _____.
   A. the size of your household
   B. the type of fuel in your house
   C. its energy rating
   D. All of the above.

_____ 22. A special feature on an appliance may control _____.
   A. temperature
   B. time of operation
   C. water use
   D. All of the above.

_____ 23. Deluxe models have _____.
   A. basic features only
   B. basic features plus special features
   C. special features only
   D. All of the above.

_____ 24. A central vacuum cleaner _____.
   A. is a built-in system
   B. has no attachments
   C. is awkward to use
   D. All of the above.

_____ 25. An example of a portable appliance is _____.
   A. an electric blanket
   B. a hair dryer
   C. a toaster
   D. All of the above.

❑ Essay Questions: Provide complete responses to the following questions or statements.

26. List five factors to consider before purchasing any major appliance.

27. Choose an appliance and list four questions to ask when evaluating it.

28. Give two advantages and two disadvantages of selecting an appliance with special features.

29. How are personal computers used in your home?

# PART 5
# A Safe and Attractive Environment

**Goal:** Students will explain the importance of keeping their homes safe and attractive through attention to landscaping and basic home maintenance.

## Bulletin Board

Title: *A Safe and Attractive Home*

Mount an illustration of an attractive home from a magazine. Attach ribbon or string from features of the house to circles labeled *S*, *A*, or *S&A*. These labels indicate whether the features provide safety, attractiveness, or both.

## Teaching Materials

**Text**
Chapters 19-21, pages 428-509
*To Know*
*To Review*
*In Your Community*
*To Think About*
*Using Technology*

**Teacher's Resources**
*A Safe and Attractive Environment*, transparency master V-A
*A Safe and Attractive Environment*, transparency master overlay V-B
*A Safe and Attractive Environment*, transparency master overlay V-C

## Introductory Activities

1. *A Safe and Attractive Environment*, transparency master V-A, TR. Use this transparency to contrast the concepts covered in Chapters 1-18 with those upcoming in Chapter 19. Explain how landscaping can make a home safer and more attractive.
2. *A Safe and Attractive Environment*, transparency master overlay V-B, TR. Superimpose this transparency on *A Safe and Attractive Environment*, transparency master V-A. Use the combined image to introduce the concepts in Chapter 20. Explain the importance of safety in the home.
3. *A Safe and Attractive Environment*, transparency master overlay V-C, TR. Superimpose this transparency on two others—*A Safe and Attractive Environment*, transparency master V-A and transparency master overlay V-B. Use the combined image to introduce the concepts in Chapter 21. Explain the importance of home maintenance in keeping the home safe and attractive.

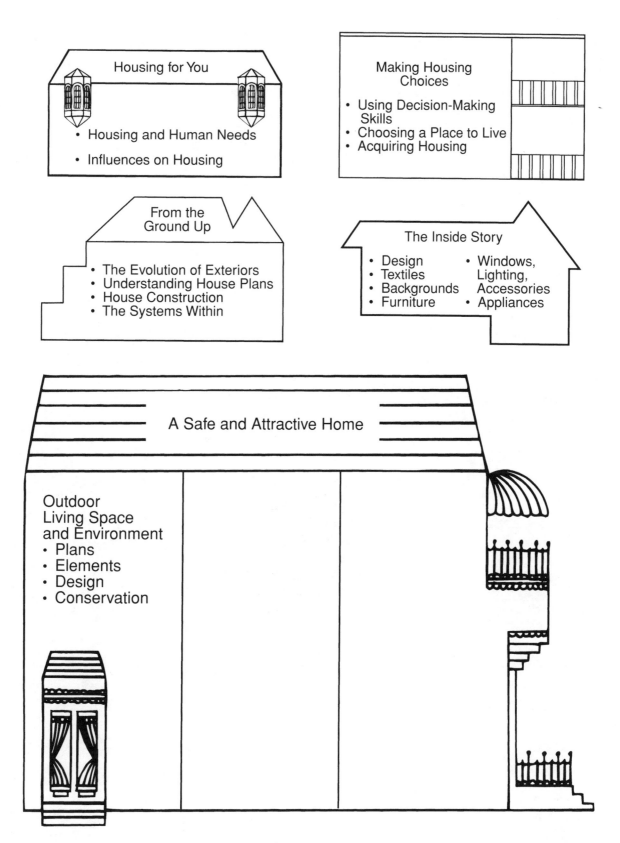

Transparency Master Overlay V-B

Keeping Your
Home Safe
and Secure
• A Safe Home
• A Secure Home
• Equipping for
  People with
  Disabilities

Transparency Master Overlay V-C

Maintaining
Your Home
- Clean Home
- Outdoor and
  Lawn Care
- Home Repairs
- Storage
- Redecorating
- Remodeling
- Resources

Part 5  *A Safe and Attractive Environment*  **269**

# CHAPTER 19
# The Outdoor Living Space and Environment

## Objectives

After studying this chapter, students will be able to

- identify the goals of landscaping.
- list natural and manufactured landscape elements.
- determine zones in a landscape site.
- select furnishings for outdoor living.
- list conservation measures for landscaping.
- design an outdoor living space.

## Bulletin Boards

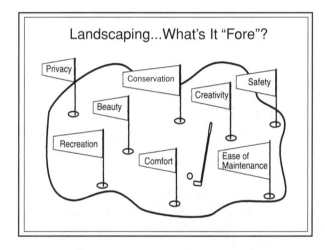

Title: *Landscaping…What's It "Fore"?*

Sketch a golf course on green paper and mount it on the board under the heading. Cut flag poles and flags from different colored paper and place on the holes in the course. Label each flag with one of the goals of landscaping as shown.

Title: *Landscape Elements*

Divide the board into two sections. Label the sections *Natural Landscape Elements* and *Manufactured Landscape Elements*. Have students mount appropriate illustrations in each section.

## Teaching Materials

**Text**, pages 430-455
  *To Know*
  *To Review*
  *In Your Community*
  *To Think About*
  *Using Technology*
**Student Activity Guide**
  A. *Landscape Elements*
  B. *Landscape Backgrounds*
  C. *Landscape Accents*
  D. *A Look at Outdoor Furnishings*
  E. *Designing a Landscape*
**Teacher's Resources**
  *Landscape Zones*, color transparency CT-24
  *Deciduous Trees*, transparency master 19-1
  Chapter 19 Test

## Introductory Activities

1. Discuss with students the term *landscape*. Ask them to define an attractive and functional landscape.
2. Have students find and discuss the glossary and/or dictionary definitions of key terms listed in the *To Know* section of the text. Have them add these to their card files.
3. Have students collect and mount pictures of different landscapes and discuss what they like about each. (Save pictures for Item 6.)

## Strategies to Reteach, Reinforce, Enrich, and Extend Text Concepts

### Planning the Landscape

4. **RF** Have students state the basic goal of landscaping and list questions to ask that

will help individuals clarify their respective landscaping goals.

## Landscape Elements

5. **RF** *Landscape Elements*, Activity A, SAG. Students are asked to mount a picture of a landscaped area and identify all natural and manufactured landscape elements.
6. **RF** Have students identify the natural and manufactured landscape elements in the pictures saved from Item 3.
7. **EX** In small groups, have students identify various landscape elements that could be added to the school grounds. Identify the goals for the landscaping of the school grounds and state how these elements would meet those goals.

## Designing the Outdoor Living Spaces

8. **RF** *Landscape Zones*, color transparency CT-24, TR. Use this transparency to introduce the concept of landscape zones. Point out the three landscape zones and discuss how they can be compared to rooms.
9. **RF** Have students recall the elements and principles of design and discuss how they can be applied to designing outdoor living spaces.
10. **ER** *Landscape Backgrounds*, Activity B, SAG. Students are asked to mount a picture of a landscaped area and answer the questions provided.
11. **ER** Have students study the various types of fences in Figure 19-10 and discuss where each type would be appropriate in landscapes. Have students discuss which types give the most and the least visual privacy and which are the best sound barriers.
12. **ER** *Landscape Accents*, Activity C, SAG. Students are asked to mount a picture of a landscaped site, identify the accents used, and list five suggestions to follow when choosing accents.
13. **EX** Have students describe a landscape feature and write a brief report about the household that would choose that feature.
14. **EX** Have students design a bulletin board for outdoor furnishings. Students are to find pictures of furnishings suitable for a landscape. Have students identify the furnishings as single or dual-purpose; and decorative, functional, or both.
15. **ER** *A Look at Outdoor Furnishings*, Activity D, SAG. Students are asked to find pictures of outdoor furnishings and provide the information requested.
16. **ER** Have students discuss reasons for outdoor lighting, list types of lights available, and give appropriate uses for each type.

## Landscaping for Conservation

17. **RT** Have students define the terms *conservation* and *xeriscaping* and discuss how they are related to landscaping.
18. **RF** *Deciduous Trees*, transparency master 19-1, TR. Use this transparency to discuss how landscape elements such as deciduous trees can be used to conserve energy.
19. **RF** Have students observe and report landscape conservation measures used in their community.
20. **ER** Arrange for someone from the county cooperative extension service office or a landscaping business to speak to the class about conservation of soil, water, and energy in landscapes.

## Completing a Scaled Plan

21. **RF** Have students make a list of factors to consider when making a landscape plan.
22. **EX** Have students work in small groups and draw to scale a site with a house on it. Have them make templates of natural and manufactured elements drawn to scale. Have them put *N* on the natural elements and *M* on the manufactured elements. Instruct them to use the templates to create a landscape. Have students identify the three zones and check the text to see if the information in the chapter has been followed. Have them list the goals of landscaping and indicate how each goal has been met. Have each group list ways their landscape includes conservation. Have two groups compare and evaluate each other's landscape.

## Chapter Review

23. **EX** *Designing a Landscape*, Activity E, SAG. Students are asked to make landscape designs, listing three goals they plan to achieve.
24. **ER** Have students walk or ride past 20 homes in your community and do the following:
    - List the natural and manufactured landscape elements observed.
    - Count and describe the enclosure structures found.
    - Notice the different methods of watering used.
    - Find the best example of a low-maintenance landscape.
    - Note the locations of deciduous and coniferous trees.
    - List the types of ground covers used.

## Answer Key

### Text

*To Review*, page 453

1. to create pleasing outdoor spaces for various activities
2. (List three:) soil, terrain, topography, trees, shrubs, flowers, ground covers, boulders, stones, wood, bark, water, sun, wind
3. A
4. (List five:) driveways, walkways, pathways, steps, walls, fences, patios, decks, lighting, outdoor furnishings
5. room
6. privacy, noise reduction, windbreak
7. (List three:) flower beds, planters, boulders, stones, sculptures, murals, mosaics, gazebos, water fountains, pools, birdfeeders, birdhouses
8. (List five:) comfort, convenience, durability, portability, storability, quality, design, maintenance
9. (List three:) increase safety, discourage intruders, add beauty, highlight outdoor features, enhance view from the house, illuminate outdoor work, illuminate leisure activities
10. creating landscapes to conserve water
11. deciduous
12. (List five:) property boundaries, the residence with location of windows and doors marked, other structures, orientation to sun and wind, driveway, sidewalk, above- and under-ground utilities, existing plant life, hardscape elements

## Teacher's Resources

### Chapter 19 Test

1. M
2. K
3. A
4. G
5. N
6. I
7. J
8. B
9. D
10. C
11. T
12. F
13. F
14. T
15. F
16. T
17. T
18. F
19. F
20. F
21. D
22. A
23. C
24. D
25. B
26. A
27. D
28. C
29. C
30. D

31. to create an environment that satisfies the needs and values of all members of the household
32. A landscape design is like designing a room because there is a floor with floor coverings such as grass; walls that enclose the space are formed by enclosure structures, shrubs, etc.; and a ceiling that may be the sky or a canopy formed by tree branches.
33. (List five:) comfort, convenience, durability, portability, storability, quality construction, design, maintenance
34. (Student response. See pages 446-449 of the text.)

## Deciduous Trees

- Give shade in the summer

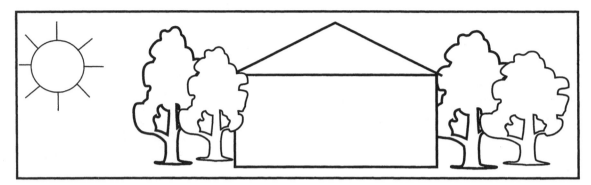

- Allow for sun in the winter

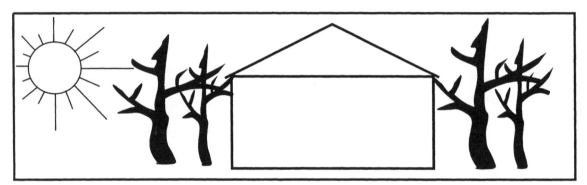

- Act as wind barriers

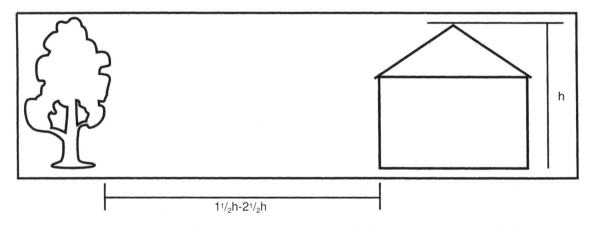

A tree should be at a distance $1\frac{1}{2}$ to $2\frac{1}{2}$ times the height of the house it protects to deflect wind over the roof.

Reproducible Test Master

# The Outdoor Living Space and Environment

Name _____

Date _____ Period _____ Score _____

**Chapter 19 Test**

❑ Matching: Match the following terms and examples.

_____ 1. Contour of the land.

_____ 2. Flowers that come up every year.

_____ 3. Flowers that last only a year.

_____ 4. Grass and low vines.

_____ 5. Plants grouped according to need for water.

_____ 6. Built structures and surfaces.

_____ 7. Trees, boulders, sun.

_____ 8. Trees that have no leaves during the winter.

_____ 9. Trees that are green during the winter.

_____ 10. Walls and fences.

A. annuals
B. deciduous
C. enclosure elements
D. coniferous
E. floodlight
F. general lighting
G. ground cover
H. landscape zones
I. manufactured elements
J. natural elements
K. perennials
L. spotlight
M. topography
N. xeriscape

❑ True/False: Circle *T* if the statement is true or *F* if the statement is false.

T  F  11. The outdoor living space should permit positive development of each member of the household.

T  F  12. The basic goal of landscaping is to provide ease of maintenance.

T  F  13. Natural elements of landscaping are those found in the behavioral environment.

T  F  14. Coniferous trees and shrubs remain green year round.

T  F  15. Freestanding walls have soil against one side.

T  F  16. Flowers are an example of a landscape accent.

T  F  17. Low-growing plants are examples of ground covers.

T  F  18. The service zone is for recreation and relaxation.

T  F  19. Landscaping cannot conserve water, soil, or energy.

T  F  20. Xeriscaping involves grouping plants according to color.

(Continued)

❏ Multiple Choice: Choose the best response. Write the letter in the space provided.

_____ 21. Natural landscape elements include _____.
- A. boulders and stones
- B. ground covers
- C. shrubs and trees
- D. All of the above.

_____ 22. The most common ground cover is _____.
- A. grass
- B. loose aggregate
- C. low-growing vines
- D. perennials

_____ 23. When planning for use of outdoor living areas, consider orientation to _____.
- A. boulders and stones
- B. manufactured elements
- C. water, wind, and sun
- D. All of the above.

_____ 24. Manufactured landscape elements include _____.
- A. enclosure elements
- B. hard surfaces
- C. structures
- D. All of the above.

_____ 25. The canopy created by spreading tree branches helps form the _____ of the outdoor room.
- A. accents
- B. ceiling
- C. floor
- D. walls

_____ 26. _____ land is the easiest and least expensive to landscape.
- A. Level
- B. Natural
- C. Rocky
- D. None of the above.

_____ 27. Light directed upward into plants and other landscape features is known as _____ lighting.
- A. down
- B. general
- C. spot
- D. under

_____ 28. The most effective watering method is _____.
- A. daily soil saturation
- B. portable sprinklers
- C. trickle or drip irrigation
- D. watering at night

(Continued)

_____ 29. The three landscape zones are _____.
   A. alley, street, and yard
   B. front, side, and service
   C. public, service, and private
   D. residence, utilities, and yard

_____ 30. When designing your landscape, it is best to _____.
   A. arrange the furnishings
   B. start with a map
   C. consider the different zones
   D. All of the above.

❑ Essay Questions: Provide complete responses to the following questions or statements.

31. Why is it important to identify your goals when landscaping?

32. Compare landscaping to designing a room.

33. List five features to consider when choosing outdoor furnishings.

34. Give three examples of landscaping for conservation.

# CHAPTER 20
# Keeping Your Home Safe and Secure

## Objectives

After studying this chapter, students will be able to

- list the types and causes of the most frequent home accidents.
- describe ways to keep the air in their homes clean.
- explain how to make their homes safe and secure.
- determine changes that can make the home safe and secure for those with special needs.

## Bulletin Boards

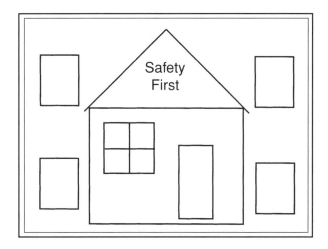

Title: *Safety First*

Place a silhouette of a house on the board as shown. Have students bring in pictures, articles, and brochures on ways to make a home safe and secure.

Title: *Know Your Locks*

Find or draw pictures of various types of locks used in homes, such as spring-latch, deadbolt, rim, jimmy-proof rim, flush-bolt, and cane-bolt locks. Secure a string or ribbon from each lock to its identifying type. Indicate the characteristics of each type.

## Teaching Materials

**Text**, pages 456-480
*To Know*
*To Review*
*In Your Community*
*To Think About*
*Using Technology*

**Student Activity Guide**
A. *Causes of Accidents and Safety Measures*
B. *Clean Air Puzzle*
C. *Protecting Your Home from Fire*
D. *A Plan for Fire Emergencies*
E. *Home Security Inspection Checklist*

**Teacher's Resources**
*Sources of Indoor Air Pollution*, transparency master 20-1
*Smoke Detector Placement*, color transparency CT-25
*Home Security*, reproducible master 20-2
Chapter 20 Test

## Introductory Activities

1. Have students discuss why home accidents occur so often and how they can be prevented.
2. Discuss what is meant by clean air in the home and what might cause pollutants.
3. Have students explain their concept of a safe and secure home. Ask them if additional measures are needed to provide a safe and secure home for people with special needs.
4. Have students find and discuss the glossary and/or dictionary definitions of key terms listed in the *To Know* section of the text. Have them add these to their card files.

# Strategies to Reteach, Reinforce, Enrich, and Extend Text Concepts

## A Safe Home

5. **ER** *Causes of Accidents and Safety Measures*, Activity A, SAG. Students are asked to list five types of home accidents, their probable causes, and prevention measures.
6. **RF** Have each student research and report on one safety measure to use in the home.
7. **EX** Have students work in small groups to develop a brochure on "Keeping Children Safe in Your Home." Have students take copies home.
8. **ER** *Sources of Indoor Air Pollution*, transparency master 20-1, TR. Use this transparency to introduce to students the concept of indoor pollution and possible pollutants. Discuss ways to combat indoor air pollution.
9. **RF** *Clean Air Puzzle*, Activity B, SAG. Students are asked to solve the word puzzle by filling in the blanks in the statements provided.
10. **RF** Have students discuss the noise levels of appliances listed in Figure 20-12 in the text. Ask students which noises particularly bother them.
11. **ER** Have students keep a log of sounds they hear during a 24-hour period and mark *N* by those they consider noise. Have them identify three annoying noises and give suggestions for reducing them. Have students form small groups to compare their lists and determine if there is agreement on which sounds are noise.

## A Secure Home

12. **RF** Have students give three examples of ways to make a home secure.
13. **RF** Have students view a video on home fire safety. Discuss how fires in the home are started and can be prevented. For additional resources, contact the National Association of Homebuilders in Washington, DC by phoning 202-822-0200.
14. **RF** *Smoke Detector Placement*, color transparency CT-25, TR. Use this transparency to discuss with students the placement of smoke detectors.
15. **ER** *Protecting Your Home from Fire*, Activity C, SAG. Students are asked to compare two types of smoke detectors and record their findings.
16. **EX** *A Plan for Fire Emergencies*, Activity D, SAG. Students are asked to draw a floor plan of their respective homes, mark fire escape routes, and provide details of their fire safety plans.
17. **ER** Have students make cartoon drawings of ways to make a home look "lived in" when the occupants are away. Mount the drawings on a poster and display at school where others can view them.
18. **EX** *Home Security*, reproducible master 20-2, TR. Invite a police officer to class to explain how to protect homes from burglars. Based on the information provided, have students write an article with general tips and precautions.
19. **ER** Have students examine the locks and other security devices at the school.
20. **EX** Have the class visit a home, check for security measures, and discuss what features to add to make the home more secure.
21. **ER** *Home Security Inspection Checklist*, Activity E, SAG. Students are asked to conduct a home security inspection following the checklist and identify any necessary changes.

## Equipping a Home for People with Disabilities

22. **ER** Have students list ways to equip homes for people with physical disabilities using information in the text.
23. **EX** Divide the class into four groups and "assign" each group a different physical disability. Have the students tour a home to check for ways the home is equipped for people with disabilities. In class, have students discuss what features could be added to make the home more secure for people with disabilities.

## Chapter Review

24. **EX** Have students form groups and create skits on one of the following topics:

home safety, home security, and equipping homes for people with disabilities. Have students act out the skits for community groups and other classes. (If a video camera is available, the skits could be taped and copies could be given to community groups and local libraries.)

# Answer Key

## Text

### To Review, pages 478-479

1. (List three:) falls, burns, electrical shock, poisonings, fires (Causes and precautions are student response.)
2. elderly, children
3. (List three:) death, brain damage, headaches, dizziness, nausea, lung cancer, allergies, tiredness
4. decibel (dB)
5. Noise is unwanted sound. Sound is the impression received by the sense of hearing.
6. (List three:) laundry and cleaning aids, medicines, cosmetics, garden and workshop chemicals, some houseplants
7. smoke detectors, fire extinguishers, escape plan
8. (List five. See page 471 of the text.)
9. (List two:) Don't let strangers in. Use the phone for help. Know where to find important phone numbers. Provide no information to caller.
10. deadbolt
11. (List two:) carbon monoxide detector, smoke detector, home security system
12. drivers license
13. everyone
14. (List three. See page 474 of the text.)
15. (List five. See pages 476-477 of the text.)

## Student Activity Guide

*Clean Air Puzzle*, Activity B

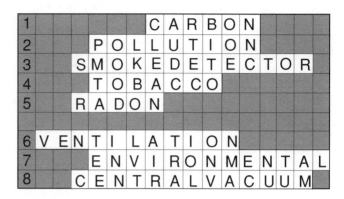

## Teacher's Resources

### Chapter 20 Test

1. A
2. M
3. E
4. J
5. B
6. G
7. K
8. F
9. T
10. F
11. F
12. F
13. F
14. T
15. T
16. F
17. T
18. F
19. B
20. A
21. C
22. D
23. B
24. D
25. D
26. B
27. D

28. children: because they are more curious; the elderly: because they have limited vision and mobility
29. (List three:) supervise children; follow local codes on installing a surrounding fence; keep phone and emergency numbers handy; learn cardiopulmonary resuscitation (CPR) procedures
30. (List four:) fuels, insulating materials, tobacco smoke, radon, personal and household products, asbestos, stagnant water (Suggestions are student response.)
31. (List four. See Figure 20-5 of the text.)
32. (List three. See Figure 20-6 of the text.)

Transparency Master 20-1

# Sources of Indoor Air Pollution

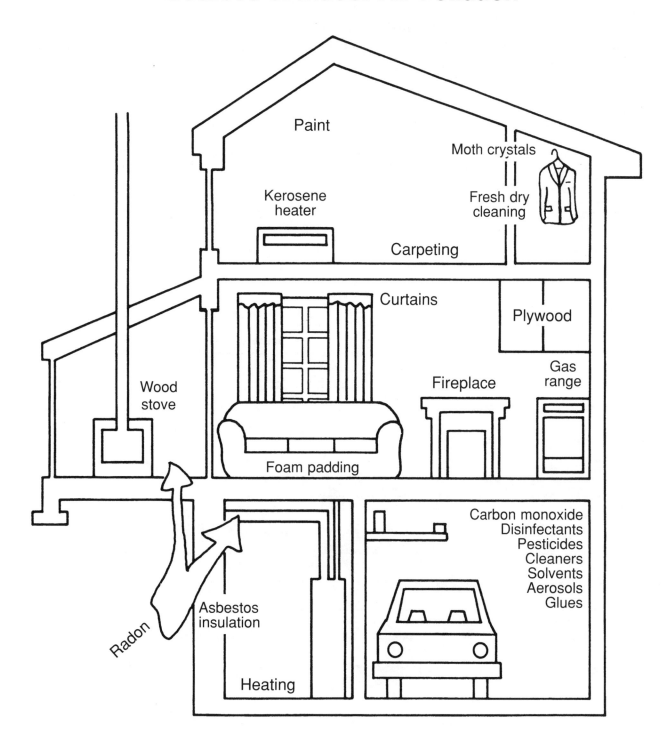

Reproducible Master 20-2

# Home Security

**Name** _____ **Date** _____ **Period** _____

In the space below, write an article with tips and precautions for protecting a home from burglars. Use the guest speaker's comments as the basis of your article.

_____
_____
_____
_____
_____
_____
_____
_____
_____
_____
_____
_____
_____
_____
_____
_____
_____
_____
_____
_____
_____
_____
_____
_____
_____
_____
_____
_____
_____

Reproducible Test Master

# Keeping Your Home Safe and Secure

Name _____

Date _____ Period _____ Score _____

### Chapter 20 Test

❑ Matching: Match the following terms and identifying phrases.

_____ 1. Triggers a loud noise when an intruder is sensed.
_____ 2. Allows an exchange of stale air for fresh air.
_____ 3. Burns easily.
_____ 4. Gives warning of fire.
_____ 5. Measure of sound.
_____ 6. Unwanted sound.
_____ 7. Poisonous.
_____ 8. Resists burning.

A. alarm system
B. decibel
C. fire escape plan
D. fire extinguisher
E. flammable
F. inflammable
G. noise
H. radioactive waves
I. radon
J. smoke detector
K. toxic
L. universal design
M. ventilation

❑ True/False: Circle *T* if the statement is true or *F* if the statement is false.

T F 9. More injuries take place in the home than anywhere else.

T F 10. The National Safety Council reports the kitchen is the most dangerous room in the house.

T F 11. The most common type of home accident is fire.

T F 12. Lowering the temperature of hot water to 170°F will prevent scalding burns.

T F 13. Covering or knotting a power cord can prevent accidents.

T F 14. Houses that are airtight to save energy have increased pollution levels.

T F 15. Radon, a natural radioactive gas found in the earth, is a pollutant.

T F 16. Household cleaning methods are all safe.

T F 17. Noise is unwanted sound.

T F 18. Smoke detectors are expensive and difficult to install.

❑ Multiple Choice: Choose the best response. Write the letter in the space provided.

_____ 19. The room of the home where fires and falls occur most often is the _____.
A. bathroom
B. bedroom
C. kitchen
D. living room

(Continued)

Reproducible Test Master

_____ 20. The following advice is *not* recommended: _____.
   A. For safety, run electrical cords under rugs to prevent tripping.
   B. Avoid mixing electricity and water since it can cause fatal accidents.
   C. A fresh battery should be installed once a year in a smoke detector.
   D. Grasp the plug to disconnect its electrical cord safely.

_____ 21. Most fatal poisoning accidents are caused by _____.
   A. improper disposal of toxic materials
   B. not reading labels
   C. swallowing common household products
   D. using laundry and cleaning aids

_____ 22. Prevention measures that safeguard children include _____.
   A. installing gates, bars, and railings
   B. keeping children away from open windows, porches, and stairways
   C. using night lights
   D. All of the above.

_____ 23. The most dangerous of all indoor pollutants is _____.
   A. asbestos
   B. carbon monoxide
   C. radon
   D. tobacco smoke

_____ 24. Cleaner inside air can be achieved through _____.
   A. changing/cleaning filters on the heating/ventilating system frequently
   B. proper house cleaning
   C. reducing air ventilation
   D. All of the above.

_____ 25. Exterior doors should _____.
   A. be solid core or of sturdy metal
   B. have a peephole
   C. have double cylinder locks
   D. All of the above.

_____ 26. Marking valuables with an identification number _____.
   A. is costly
   B. makes stolen items easier to trace
   C. prevents theft
   D. All of the above.

_____ 27. To make homes more accessible for people with vision limitations, _____.
   A. use highly visible colors
   B. place furniture away from traffic lanes
   C. prominently mark changes in floor and countertop levels
   D. All of the above.

(Continued)

❑ Essay Questions: Provide complete responses to the following questions or statements.

28. Which two groups are the victims of most home accidents? Why?
29. List three precautions for pool safety.
30. List four sources of indoor air pollution and give suggestions for eliminating them.
31. List four precautions to follow when using hazardous materials.
32. List three hazardous household chemicals and safe alternatives for them.

# CHAPTER 21
# Maintaining Your Home

## Objectives

After studying this chapter, students will be able to

- select the cleaning tools, products, and schedule needed to maintain their homes.
- summarize how to properly maintain the landscape.
- explain how to use basic tools for common home repairs.
- list ways to improve storage and organize space.
- assess their redecorating choices.
- identify the pros and cons of remodeling.
- list resources for home maintenance.

## Bulletin Boards

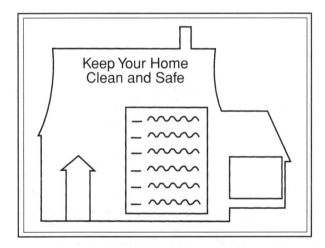

Title: *Keep Your Home Clean and Safe*

Place a silhouette of a house on the board as shown. Enlarge Figure 21-5 in the text. (You may want to use separate sheets for each of the four categories.) Arrange the list into a flipchart and secure it to the center of the house. Discuss each section of the chart with students.

Title: *Redecorating with Few $$*

Display inexpensive items that can be used to redecorate a room. Include the prices of the items. Encourage students to describe their own ideas on small cards and mount them to the board.

## Teaching Materials

**Text**, pages 481-509
    *To Know*
    *To Review*
    *In Your Community*
    *To Think About*
    *Using Technology*

**Student Activity Guide**
    A. *Cleaning Tasks*
    B. *Repair Work*
    C. *Meeting Your Storage Needs*
    D. *Redecorating*

**Teacher's Resources**
    *Comparing Cleaning Products*, reproducible master 21-1
    *Planning for Redecorating*, reproducible master 21-2
    *Guest Speaker*, reproducible master 21-3
    *Basic Home Repairs*, color transparency CT-26
    Chapter 21 Test

## Introductory Activities

1. Use humorous examples to make students aware that everyone has clutter. Emphasize that maintaining a home involves eliminating clutter. A possible resource is *Clutter's Last Stand*, a book by Don Aslett.
2. Discuss cleaning and maintenance of the home. Ask students to describe the appearance of a poorly cleaned and maintained home. Ask how the level of cleanliness and repair might affect a person's attitude or

feelings. Discuss how different standards of cleanliness in a home might cause friction between members of the household.
3. Have students find and discuss the glossary and/or dictionary definitions of key terms listed in the *To Know* section of the text. Have them add these to their card files.

# Strategies to Reteach, Reinforce, Enrich, and Extend Text Concepts

## Keeping the Home Clean and Well Maintained

4. **RF** In groups, have students list cleaning tools they believe are essential to keeping the home clean. Have them compare their lists with the items recommend in the text. Have students revise their lists as needed. From the groups' lists, make a master list for the class.
5. **ER** Gather a variety of cleaning products for students to examine. Have them read labels and discuss how each product should be used. Students should identify which products have just one purpose and which have several.
6. **EX** *Comparing Cleaning Products*, reproducible master 21-1, TR. Have students work in groups to devise an experiment that tests various cleaning products. Students should record their procedures and results on the worksheet.
7. **RF** *Cleaning Tasks*, Activity A, SAG. Students are asked to review the list provided and identify each cleaning activity as daily, weekly, monthly, semi-annually, annually, or never done.
8. **EX** Have students develop cleaning schedules appropriate for their homes. Have them separate indoor and outdoor tasks and recommend the appropriate tools, products, and methods.
9. **EX** Have students develop a brochure with helpful cleaning hints. The brochure should include lists of cleaning tools, products, and methods. Highlight products that are nontoxic, environmentally sound, and inexpensive. The brochure should include a sample cleaning schedule. Make the brochure available to students in other classes.

## Outdoor and Lawn Care

10. **ER** In pairs, have students choose a lawn or garden tool and evaluate two different brands of their chosen tool in terms of price, features, and durability. Students should write a report on their findings and bring in pictures to discuss with the class.
11. **RF** As a class, devise a lawn care maintenance schedule. Model the list of tasks after Figure 21-5, identifying separate categories for daily, weekly, monthly, and semiannual tasks.

## Making Common Home Repairs

12. **RF** Use Figure 21-13 in the text to introduce basic household tools needed for maintenance and repair. Discuss with students the purpose of each tool.
13. **ER** *Repair Work*, Activity B, SAG. Students are asked to itemize the cost of assembling a home repair kit and answer related questions.
14. **ER** Provide samples of various screws, nails, and home repair tools, or visit a local hardware store to view them. Discuss their different uses with students.
15. **ER** Have the school maintenance supervisor show the class a service entrance panel. Point out and discuss the difference between a circuit breaker and a fuse. Have the maintenance person demonstrate or explain the proper way to replace a fuse and reset a breaker.
16. **RF** Have students list home repairs that can easily be done versus those that should be left to a professional.
17. **EX** Divide the class into small groups. Have students in each group repair an electrical power cord plug.
18. **EX** Have students read a chapter from a how-to book and write a short report on one of the repair procedures presented in the chapter. Have students who choose the same topic compare reports and make one comprehensive report to share with the class.

## Meeting Storage Needs

19. **RF** Have students list storage needs for whole-house use versus individual needs.
20. **RF** Have students list types of built-in storage components and furniture.
21. **EX** Have students devise an evaluation form to gauge storage ideas in magazine articles and advertisements. (Students may use library resources.)
22. **ER** Have each student examine a room and make suggestions for adding or improving existing storage space.
23. **ER** Have students price various products that are available for organizing storage space. Have them report price, materials, ease of use, durability, and other important factors.
24. **EX** Arrange a class visit to a store or design studio that features storage components. Have someone in the store discuss different ways storage components can be arranged and used.
25. **ER** *Meeting Your Storage Needs*, Activity C, SAG. Students are asked to analyze a storage problem in their homes and recommend improvements.
26. **RF** Have students list ways to save space. Have them compare their lists to the ideas provided in the text.

## Redecorating

27. **RF** Have students discuss possible consequences of not planning before redecorating. Students should focus on two likely results: dissatisfaction and unexpected costs.
28. **EX** *Planning for Redecorating*, reproducible master 21-2, TR. Have students use the worksheets to develop a redecorating plan. Assign students a realistic spending range to use in planning.
29. **ER** Have students call businesses and stores that offer decorating services. Students should ask what types of services are provided, whether an interior designer provides them, and what costs are involved.
30. **RF** Discuss inexpensive ways to decorate walls.
31. **ER** Have students look at pictures of rooms that are 10 years old. Have students brainstorm ways to update the rooms' appearances while changing less than half the items in the rooms.
32. **ER** *Redecorating*, Activity D, SAG. Students are asked to mount a photo of a room on the worksheet and list changes they would make with a $500 budget versus a $1,500 budget.

## Remodeling

33. **RF** Discuss the difference between redecorating and remodeling. Have students decide which requires more planning, time, and money.
34. **RF** Have students study Figure 21-28 to discuss which remodeling projects are likely to increase a home's value and improve the quality of life for the residents.
35. **RF** Have students discuss the questions that should be asked before choosing a contractor. Discuss the possible consequences of having a contractor begin the job before getting answers to these questions.
36. **EX** Have students gather a variety of articles, brochures, and pamphlets about remodeling. Have students sort and file the information into appropriate categories. When the file is complete, have students advertise its availability. If possible, arrange to keep the file in the school library.
37. **ER** Have students research and write a short report about an energy-saving product or feature that can be added while remodeling.
38. **ER** Have students find pictures of houses that feature open floor plans and/or entertainment centers. Have students list the ways in which the quality of life for each household is affected by these remodeling changes.

## Resources for Home Care

39. **RF** Have students list the resources they used to do the activities in this chapter. Have them list additional resources to use when maintaining and improving a home.
40. **ER** *Guest Speaker*, reproducible master 21-3, TR. Have students use the worksheet to record the comments of a local remodeling contractor who is invited to class. Ask the guest speaker to discuss his or her work as well as key remodeling trends.

# Chapter Review

41. **RF** *Basic Home Repairs*, color transparency CT-26, TR. Use this transparency to review procedures for making basic home repairs. Working in groups, have students choose items from the illustration and explain how they are used.
42. **RF** Have a class tournament to review concepts in the chapter. Divide the class into two teams. Have each team develop 30 questions about the chapter to ask the other team. Review the questions before playing and add any questions you feel are needed.

# Answer Key

## Text

### To Review, page 507

1. false
2. glass cleaner, grease-cutting liquid, mild abrasive powder
3. (List two:) organizes a person's time, shows when each cleaning task needs to be done, divides tasks among members of the household
4. prevents the development of a healthy root system
5. true
6. (List five:) unclogging drains, fixing leaking faucets, installing fasteners, changing fuses, replacing wall switches, repairing power cord plugs
7. (List five. See Figure 21-13 of the text.)
8. (List two:) with a chemical drain cleaner, with a plumbing plunger, with a flexible spring cable, with the combined action of a plunger and a cable
9. Finish nails have a small head and can be driven below the surface with a nail set. Box nails have large flat heads and are used for rough work.
10. an undesirable current path that allows the electrical current to bypass the load of the circuit
11. plugs, cartridges
12. false
13. true
14. (List three. Student response. See pages 503-505 of the text.)
15. (List three:) cleaning services, outdoor maintenance services, interior designers, decorators, remodeling contractors, home improvement centers, local classes, publications, videotapes, TV programs, Internet sites

## Teacher's Resources

### Chapter 21 Test

1. A
2. F
3. D
4. B
5. C
6. T
7. F
8. F
9. F
10. T
11. T
12. F
13. F
14. T
15. F
16. C
17. A
18. D
19. D
20. A
21. B
22. D
23. B
24. B
25. D
26. long-nose pliers
27. pipe wrench
28. standard screwdriver
29. adjustable wrench
30. crosscut saw
31. (List 10. See Figure 21-5 of the text.)
32. (Student response. See pages 495-499 of the text.)
33. Redecorating is changing the decorating scheme, and remodeling is changing the structure.
34. (List three. See pages 500-502 of the text. Students may justify additional answers.)

Reproducible Master 21-1

# Comparing Cleaning Products

**Name** _____ **Date** _____ **Period** _____

**Group Members:**

_____

_____

Devise an experiment to test various cleaning products for their ability to do a specific cleaning task. State the task, list the needed supplies, and write the procedure you will use. Then record your results.

**Cleaning task:**

_____

**Supplies needed:**

_____

_____

_____

**Procedure:**

_____

_____

_____

_____

_____

_____

| Product | Results |
|---------|---------|
|         |         |
|         |         |
|         |         |
|         |         |

Chapter 21   *Maintaining Your Home*

Reproducible Master 21-2

# Planning for Redecorating

Name _____ Date _____ Period _____

Develop a redecorating plan for the room of your choice. You may choose a room in your home, someone else's home, or a magazine. Mount or sketch a picture of the room below and provide the information requested. Your budget for this project is $_____.

[          Space for mounted or sketched picture of the room          ]

List in order of preference the items you will keep. Summarize their use in the plan.

| | **Priority** | **Use in Plan** |
|---|---|---|
| 1. | | |
| 2. | | |
| 3. | | |
| 4. | | |
| 5. | | |
| 6. | | |
| 7. | | |
| 8. | | |
| 9. | | |
| 10. | | |

(Continued)

Reproducible Master 21-2 (Continued)

## Redecorating Plan

Sketch your plan below. Describe colors and other design features that cannot be illustrated on paper.

## Information for Shopping

Room dimensions_____

Sizes of windows and doors_____

_____

Colors/patterns used (Attach samples.)

(Continued)

Reproducible Master 21-2 (Continued)

## Items to Purchase

Attach pictures or sketches.

| Item | Size | Color | Where to Purchase | Cost |
|------|------|-------|-------------------|------|
| _____ | _____ | _____ | _____ | _____ |
| _____ | _____ | _____ | _____ | _____ |
| _____ | _____ | _____ | _____ | _____ |
| _____ | _____ | _____ | _____ | _____ |
| _____ | _____ | _____ | _____ | _____ |
| _____ | _____ | _____ | _____ | _____ |
| _____ | _____ | _____ | _____ | _____ |
| _____ | _____ | _____ | _____ | _____ |
| _____ | _____ | _____ | _____ | _____ |
| _____ | _____ | _____ | _____ | _____ |
| _____ | _____ | _____ | _____ | _____ |
| _____ | _____ | _____ | _____ | _____ |
| _____ | _____ | _____ | _____ | _____ |
| _____ | _____ | _____ | _____ | _____ |
| _____ | _____ | _____ | _____ | _____ |
| _____ | _____ | _____ | _____ | _____ |
| _____ | _____ | _____ | _____ | _____ |
| _____ | _____ | _____ | _____ | _____ |

Total Cost: _____

Reproducible Master 21-3

# Guest Speaker

Name _____ Date _____ Period _____

Use this form to record information provided by a remodeling contractor.

Name of contractor: _____

Most frequent types of projects: _____

Remodeling trends in this area:

_____
_____
_____
_____
_____
_____
_____
_____

Types of remodeling projects that help a home conserve energy:

_____
_____
_____
_____
_____
_____

Average costs of remodeling projects:

Adding a bathroom _____  Adding a bedroom _____

Remodeling a kitchen _____  Adding a fireplace _____

Adding a sunroom _____  Replacing the roof _____

Other important facts:

_____
_____
_____
_____

Chapter 21   Maintaining Your Home

Reproducible Test Master

# Maintaining Your Home

Name _____

Date _____ Period _____ Score _____

### Chapter 21 Test

❑ Matching: Select the correct tool for each task.

_____ 1. For use with nuts of different sizes.

_____ 2. To clear blocked drains.

_____ 3. To cut metal.

_____ 4. To hold pipe.

_____ 5. To detect electric current.

A. adjustable wrench
B. channel lock pliers
C. electrical tester
D. hacksaw
E. Phillips screwdriver
F. plumbing plunger
G. side-cutting pliers

❑ True/False: Circle *T* if the statement is true or *F* if the statement is false.

T F 6. Maintaining a home involves keeping it clean and safe.

T F 7. The best way to remove soil stuck to the floor is with a broom.

T F 8. Cleaning closets weekly is recommended.

T F 9. Household cleaning products are safe chemicals.

T F 10. A cleaning schedule helps a person organize his or her time.

T F 11. A lawn requires regular care during the growing season.

T F 12. Grass grows best if cut very close to the ground.

T F 13. A brick exterior requires no maintenance.

T F 14. A flexible-spring cable can be used to remove a stoppage in some drain clogs.

T F 15. A short circuit should *not* be repaired before a breaker is reset or a fuse is replaced.

❑ Multiple Choice: Choose the best response. Write the letter in the space provided.

_____ 16. A _____ is *not* usually used to remove loose dirt.
  A. broom
  B. dust mop
  C. wet sponge
  D. vacuum cleaner

_____ 17. The organization of time and people for cleaning the home is called a cleaning _____.
  A. schedule
  B. service
  C. supply
  D. task

(Continued)

_____ 18. Yard maintenance requires _____.
   A. thorough watering
   B. seasonal scheduling
   C. special tools
   D. All of the above.

_____ 19. A clogged drain can be cleared by _____.
   A. chemical cleaners
   B. a closet auger
   C. a plumbing plunger
   D. All of the above.

_____ 20. A circuit breaker _____.
   A. automatically interrupts an electrical current under abnormal conditions
   B. has a clear window with a metal strip across it
   C. screws in the entrance panel like a lightbulb
   D. None of the above.

_____ 21. To secure heavy objects to the wall, it is important to place the fastener in a _____.
   A. joist
   B. stud
   C. toggle bolt
   D. All of the above.

_____ 22. The best way to install a wood screw is to _____.
   A. drill a hole in a hard surface
   B. drill a pilot hole
   C. use a screwdriver that matches the screw
   D. All of the above.

_____ 23. An item that is *not* considered a space saver is _____.
   A. a sofa bed
   B. a refrigerator
   C. a drop-leaf table
   D. upper and lower twin beds

_____ 24. When considering a remodeling project, the best advice is _____.
   A. get a loan
   B. do your homework first
   C. work with a contractor in the neighborhood
   D. None of the above.

_____ 25. Good resources for home care, maintenance, and improvement are _____.
   A. house cleaning and yard services
   B. home improvement centers
   C. TV programs and Internet sites
   D. All of the above.

(Continued)

Identification: Name the tools shown below.

_____ 26.

_____ 27.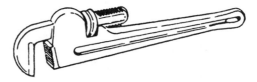

_____ 28.

_____ 29.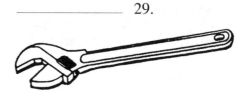

_____ 30.

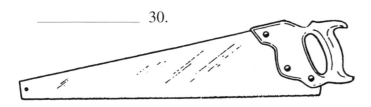

❏ Essay Questions: Provide complete responses to the following questions or statements.
31. List 10 cleaning tasks that should be done at least once a week.
32. Describe how to repair one of the following: clogged drain, blown electrical fuse, broken wall switch, or damaged power cord plug.
33. Explain the difference between redecorating and remodeling.
34. List three ways to extend storage space.

PART 6

# Progress in Housing

**Goal:** Students will find ways to promote progress in housing through knowledge of and involvement in housing issues.

## Bulletin Board

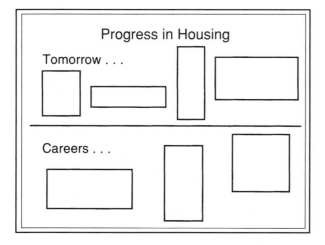

**Title:** *Progress in Housing*

Divide the board in half horizontally. Label the sections *Tomorrow* and *Careers*. Place articles on recent developments in housing, energy conservation, and environmental concerns related to housing in the top section and place information about careers in housing below. Encourage students to bring other articles to add to the board.

## Teaching Materials

**Text**
Chapters 22-24, pages 510-590
*To Know*
*To Review*
*In Your Community*
*To Think About*
*Using Technology*

**Teacher's Resources**
*Progress in Housing*, transparency master VI-A
*Progress in Housing*, transparency master overlay VI-B
*Progress in Housing*, transparency master overlay VI-C

## Introductory Activities

1. *Progress in Housing*, transparency master VI-A, TR. Use this transparency to contrast the concepts covered in Chapters 1-21 with those upcoming in Chapter 22. (This transparency is also used in Items 3 and 4.)
2. Have students discuss the ways housing has progressed since early America. Have them discuss how today's housing meets the needs and satisfaction of households.
3. *Progress in Housing*, transparency master overlay VI-B, TR. Superimpose this transparency on *Progress in Housing* transparency master VI-A. Use the combined image to introduce the concepts in Chapter 23. Ask students what steps they plan to take to prepare for career success. (This transparency is also used in Item 4.)
4. *Progress in Housing*, transparency master overlay VI-C, TR. Superimpose this overlay on two others—*Progress in Housing*, transparency master VI-A and transparency master overlay VI-B. Use the combined image to introduce concepts in Chapter 24. Discuss with students the jobs and careers that are related to housing.

Part 6   Progress in Housing   **301**

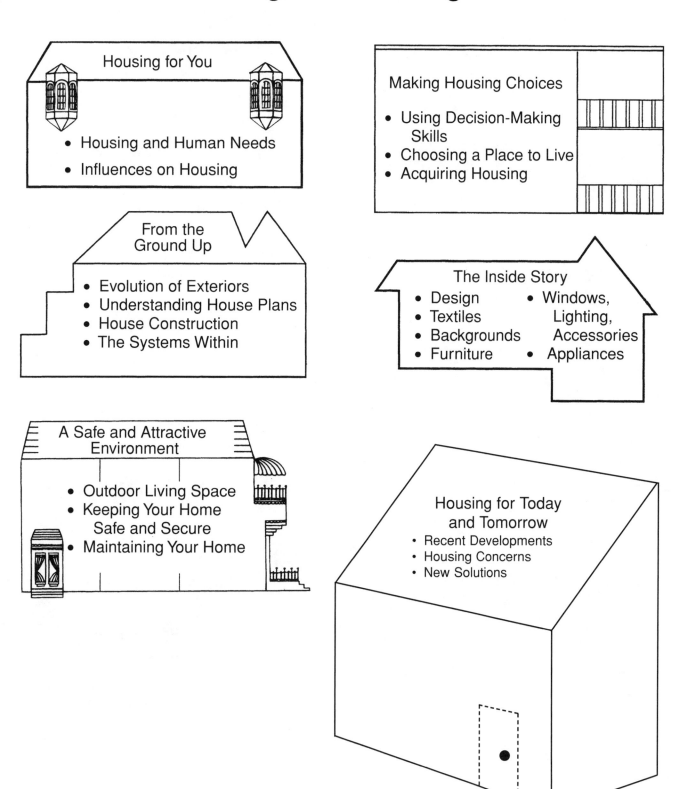

Transparency Master Overlay VI-B

Preparing for
Career Success
- Career Clusters
- Career Opportunities
- Career Levels

Transparency Master Overlay VI-C

Careers in Housing
- Career Goals
- Finding and Keeping a Job
- Careers and Lifestyle

Part 6  *Progress in Housing*

# CHAPTER 22
# Housing for Today and Tomorrow

## Objectives

After studying this chapter, students will be able to

- explain the impact of technology on housing.
- identify ways to provide and conserve energy.
- summarize the importance of a clean environment.
- describe ways to maintain a clean environment.
- determine new housing solutions.

## Bulletin Boards

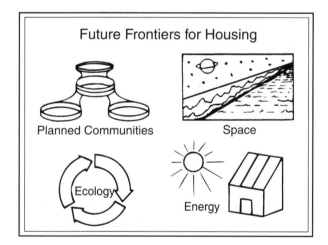

Title: *Future Frontiers for Housing*

Draw or mount pictures to represent high-tech advances in housing designs and materials as well as new ideas for the future. Label them accordingly.

Title: *Energy Update*

Place the title at the top of the board in type that simulates a newspaper's front page. Arrange article clippings of current energy issues and illustrations to create the appearance of a newspaper page.

## Teaching Materials

Text, pages 512-538
*To Know*
*To Review*
*In Your Community*
*To Think About*
*Using Technology*

**Student Activity Guide**
A. *Solar Energy*
B. *Pollution*
C. *Planning a Community*
D. *Future Housing*
E. *Housing: Today and Tomorrow*

**Teacher's Resources**
The SMART HOUSE, transparency/reproducible master 22-1
*Nuclear Energy Around the World*, color transparency CT-27
*Pollution and the Environment*, color transparency CT-28
*The Next-Generation Universal Home*, reproducible master 22-2
Chapter 22 Test

## Introductory Activities

1. Have students write a science fiction story describing housing of the future. Have volunteers share their stories with the class. Choose one or two stories and have students draw pictures of how future housing may look.
2. Have students find and discuss the glossary and/or dictionary definitions of key terms listed in the *To Know* section of the text. Have them add these to their card files.

# Strategies to Reteach, Reinforce, Enrich, and Extend Text Concepts

## Recent Developments in Housing

3. **ER** *The SMART HOUSE*, transparency/reproducible master 22-1, TR. Distribute copies of the legend to the class and use the transparency to have a class discussion about the SMART HOUSE. (The legend is also used in Item 4.)
4. **ER** Use the legend of *The SMART HOUSE*, transparency/reproducible master 22-1, for students to compare to Figure 22-2 in the text.
5. **EX** Have students research the use of computers in various areas of housing and write reports on their findings. Suggested topics include: interior or exterior design, improvement of efficiency, security, and house matching by real estate agents.
6. **ER** Have students check housing magazines for advertisements and articles about new housing materials and new uses for older materials. Have students discuss the advantages and possible disadvantages of the products found and work together to make a collage of their examples.
7. **EX** Arrange a class visit to an architectural firm for a demonstration of how computer equipment is used in designing a house.

## Housing Concerns

8. **RF** Have students discuss the kinds and sources of energy that are used in their homes. Have them discuss which energy sources are likely to be the least and most expensive and the least and most polluting.
9. **RF** Have students define *renewable resources* and discuss how energy is conserved when renewable resources are used in housing.
10. **ER** *Nuclear Energy Around the World*, color transparency CT-27, TR. Use this transparency to lead a discussion on nuclear energy. Ask students what concerns they have regarding using nuclear energy as a power source. Ask them why they think the United States uses so little nuclear energy.
11. **ER** *Solar Energy*, Activity A, SAG. Students are asked to learn more about solar energy by contacting a firm in the area that provides solar systems for housing in the community.
12. **EX** Have students develop a presentation on solar energy that includes a model showing how active and passive solar energy systems work, current figures on cost effectiveness, and a handout listing solar heating system installers. Arrange to have students give their presentation to a science class or videotape the presentation to show at a local home improvement center. Make the handout available when the videotape is presented.
13. **EX** Have students research an energy source other than solar and write a report on their findings. The report should include the following information about the energy source: how it is converted into usable energy, what current research is in progress, and what the potential use is. Have students include a bibliography of the references they use.
14. **EX** Have students develop a checklist for evaluating a home's energy conservation features.
15. **RT** Have students discuss the term *ecology*.
16. **RF** *Pollution and the Environment*, color transparency CT-28, TR. Use this transparency to introduce the various types of pollution in the environment. Have students discuss forms of pollution represented on the transparency that especially concern them.
17. **ER** *Pollution*, Activity B, SAG. Students are asked to investigate pollution problems in the community and report their findings. (Students can work in groups on this project.)
18. **EX** Have students review the hierarchy of preferred waste handling options developed by the Environmental Protection Agency, shown in Figure 22-15 in the text. Have students identify the options available in the community. Give examples of how households can help with waste management.

19. **RF** Have students give examples of materials that can be recycled. Have them list the recycling opportunities they have in their community.
20. **ER** Have students brainstorm the recycled materials that may be adapted to build or remodel houses.
21. **EX** Invite a member of an organization concerned with environmental control to discuss ways that students can become involved with environmental matters affecting housing.
22. **EX** Have students write a brief report about what is being done in their community to reduce various types of pollution. (The report is used in Item 23.)
23. **EX** Have students refer to their reports from Item 22 to choose a project to initiate. Students should obtain the approval of the necessary public officials before starting. Have some students contact local media to let them know what is being done and why.

## Innovative Solutions in Housing

24. **ER** *The Next-Generation Universal Home*, reproducible master 22-2, TR. Distribute copies to students to discuss additional housing modifications proposed by advocates of universal design. Ask students if they have observed any of the listed housing features in floor plans studied during this course or model homes visited. Can they envision the need for additional design modifications in future homes that would promote universal design?
25. **ER** Have students evaluate and discuss the ten criteria used in designing a planned community listed in Figure 22-25 in the text. Have students work in small groups to develop their own criteria for planning a city.
26. **ER** Have students discuss how living in "new urbanism" housing might feel.
27. **RF** Have students discuss cluster housing and identify any examples in their community.
28. **EX** As a class or in small groups, have students develop a planned city and build a model of it. If possible, display the model(s) in a public area of the school.
29. **ER** *Planning a Community*, Activity C, SAG. Students are asked to plan and describe a community for 25,000 people.
30. **ER** Have the class debate whether countries should develop communities in outer space.
31. **RF** Have students give advantages and disadvantages of building a community underground.
32. **ER** Have students order brochures that contain plans for earth-sheltered and other types of nonconventional housing. Students should evaluate the plans in terms of comfort, style, beauty, energy efficiency, security, and practicality.
33. **ER** Arrange to visit one or more nonconventional houses. Have someone available to describe the features of the houses and answer students' questions.
34. **ER** Have students find and discuss magazine or newspaper articles about new developments for housing in outer space and on or under water.
35. **ER** *Future Housing*, Activity D, SAG. Students are asked to list current housing trends (involving people, environment, building materials, and technology) and predict the possible effects of these trends on future housing.

## Chapter Review

36. **ER** Have students discuss the consequences of building structures to last 500 years. Students should discuss possible alternatives for reducing waste in housing.
37. **RF** *Housing: Today and Tomorrow*, Activity E, SAG. Students are asked to complete the statements by filling in the blanks.

## Answer Key

### Text

*To Review*, pages 536-537

1. SMART HOUSE features a home automation system based on computer technology that controls the house's subsystems.
2. (List four:) thermal comfort, indoor air quality, accessibility, waste reduction, use of recycled materials, water conservation
3. coal, nuclear power, hydroelectric power, natural gas, petroleum

4. (List one of each:) advantages: no polluting dust, no polluting gas, abundant energy disadvantages: radioactive waste, challenges of disposing the waste, possible release of radioactivity
5. Hydroelectric energy is generated from running water in rivers and dams. Geothermal energy is heat carried by hot streams or rock heated by the intensely hot center of the earth.
6. With the use of generators, air motion is converted to electrical current.
7. (List five. See Figure 22-12 of the text.)
8. ecology
9. source reduction, recycling and reuse, incineration with resource recovery, incineration without resource recovery, landfill
10. (List four. See Figure 22-17 of the text.)
11. Planned communities are carefully designed communities that meet the residents' current and future housing needs.

## Student Activity Guide

### *Housing: Today and Tomorrow,* Activity E

1. computer
2. renewable
3. nuclear
4. hydroelectric
5. active
6. Geothermal
7. ecology
8. landfills
9. lead
10. visual
11. source reduction
12. planned
13. cluster
14. Biosphere 2
15. universal design
16. new urbanism

## Teacher's Resources

### Chapter 22 Test

1. H
2. A
3. E
4. G
5. B
6. I
7. F
8. T
9. T
10. F
11. F
12. T
13. T
14. F
15. T
16. T
17. B
18. B
19. D
20. C
21. B
22. D
23. D
24. A
25. D
26. A

27. (List two of each:) renewable—sun, wind, water, geothermal energy; nonrenewable—oil, coal, natural gas
28. to show builders how universal design features can be incorporated in the houses they build and educate the general public about the housing features to expect in new homes
29. (List 10. Student response. See pages 526-532 of the text.)
30. It uses recycled steel instead of wood, a limited resource.

Transparency Master 22-1

# The SMART HOUSE

Reproducible Master 22-1

**Legend**

1. The SMART HOUSE provides important safety features for every member of the household. A chip in each SMART HOUSE device identifies what is being plugged into any outlet in the house as well as the specific amount of current needed for its operation. Only after this identification is made can the device receive current. A baby sticking a finger into a SMART HOUSE outlet would not be harmed because its finger is not an "authorized" device.
2. The SMART HOUSE can be instructed not to provide power to an electric guitar plugged into a bathroom outlet. Even if such an instruction were not given, a teenager trying to play an electric guitar in the shower would be protected, because if there is any deviation from the level of power that the system has been instructed to receive, power will shut off automatically. Likewise, a lamp with a frayed cord would not operate, and anyone sticking a knife into a toaster would not be harmed.
3. Stereo speakers can be plugged into any outlet in the house without running additional wiring. As illustrated, the stereo receiver in the living room can provide music to speakers in the bedroom as well as to speakers in the basement at the same time.
4. Any SMART HOUSE device can operate in any outlet. A person in the basement can unplug the stereo speaker and plug a telephone into the same outlet to make a call.
5. The SMART HOUSE can be instructed to turn off lights automatically when a person leaves a room and turn them on when the person re-enters. Similar instructions can be given to regulate the temperature in unused rooms.
6. A video display in a central location can alert people when the refrigerator door has been left open, when oven or stove burners have been left on, when the front door is unlocked, and so on.
7. Sensors placed throughout the house can activate an alarm when an intruder enters. The SMART HOUSE is so highly sophisticated that a dog walking through the house at night or a household member going to the kitchen for a midnight snack would not trip the alarm.
8. Sensors can also detect smoke or fire in the attic or any other part of the house. These same sensors can be used to regulate the heating and cooling.
9. The entire system can be controlled remotely from any distance simply by telephoning instructions to it. For instance, before leaving work a SMART HOUSE owner could instruct the oven to start cooking dinner. A working parent could also prevent small children alone in the house from using potentially unsafe appliances and power tools.
10. All SMART HOUSE devices can be given instructions from a control panel that can be placed anywhere in the house. A control panel next to a bed can be used to instruct a stereo system to wake you up, your coffeemaker to start operating, and the heat to be raised half an hour before you awaken.

Reproducible Master 22-2

# The Next-Generation Universal Home

Name _____ Date _____ Period _____

## In All Homes*

- **Reinforced walls**—to permit the installation of grab bars beyond the bathroom.
- **Another first-floor bedroom**—to accommodate someone assisting a sick or dependent person using the first-floor master bedroom. Can also be used for guests or a home office.
- **Compartmentalized bathrooms**—to allow dual use while maintaining users' privacy (perhaps with two entrances).
- **Bathing spaces**—to allow more than one method of use, such as standing, sitting, or reclining.
- **Adjustable heights**—for countertops, shelves, and toilet seats.

## In Two-Story Homes*

- **Stairways that permit installation of a chair or platform lift**—should be wider than normal, without turns, and with sufficient open space at top and bottom.
- **Storage closets that can be converted to an elevator**—require closets with removable floors that are centrally located in the same place on both levels. Eliminating the flooring exposes a "shaft" that permits the installation of an elevator without remodeling.

*Note: Two-story homes will continue to be built because of savings in construction costs. The recommended modifications will allow everyone access to the second floor.

## Additional Ways to Promote Universal Design

_____

_____

_____

_____

_____

_____

_____

*Source: North Carolina State University, The Center for Universal Design

Reproducible Test Master

# Housing for Today and Tomorrow

Name _____

Date _____ Period _____ Score _____

### Chapter 22 Test

❑ Matching: Match the following terms and housing concepts.

_____ 1. A housing conversion to a seagoing condominium.

_____ 2. Houses living beings and their environment.

_____ 3. Incorporates the latest computer technology.

_____ 4. Incorporates many features used in sustainable housing.

_____ 5. Example of a planned "new town" community.

_____ 6. Cosponsored by the American Association of Retired Persons (AARP).

A. Biosphere 2
B. Columbia, Maryland
C. Cousteau
D. Riverside, California
E. SMART HOUSE
F. Soleri
G. Southface Energy and Environmental Resource Center
H. SS United States
I. Universal Design Home of the Future

❑ True/False: Circle *T* if the statement is true or *F* if the statement is false.

T  F  7. Houses built using high technology waste energy.

T  F  8. Sunlight can be converted into electricity.

T  F  9. Nuclear energy does *not* pollute the air with gases or dust.

T  F  10. Hydroelectric power is generated by the wind.

T  F  11. Geothermal energy is stored just below ground level.

T  F  12. Solid waste can be recycled to provide heat and electrical power for homes.

T  F  13. Poisonous waste materials that damage the environment and cause illness are called hazardous wastes.

T  F  14. The most preferred waste handling option is landfills.

T  F  15. Columbia, Maryland, is an example of a planned community.

T  F  16. New urbanism focuses on houses where people both live and work.

❑ Multiple Choice: Choose the best answer and write the corresponding letter in the blank.

_____ 17. Fuel begins as _____.
   A. electricity
   B. solar energy
   C. water
   D. wind

(Continued)

_____ 18. Geothermal energy comes from _____.
   A. garbage
   B. steam
   C. the sun
   D. wind

_____ 19. _____ affects a home's energy efficiency.
   A. The orientation of the house
   B. Thermal resistance
   C. The number of windows
   D. All of the above.

_____ 20. Visual pollution _____.
   A. exists indoors only
   B. harms your eyes
   C. includes debris and signboards
   D. All of the above.

_____ 21. The least preferred option of handling waste is _____.
   A. incineration
   B. landfills
   C. recycle and reuse
   D. source reduction

_____ 22. Examples of items made from recycled materials that are used in housing include _____.
   A. home insulation
   B. roofing felt
   C. fences and decks
   D. All of the above.

_____ 23. When designing planned communities, _____ are considered.
   A. lifestyles of the residents
   B. recreational facilities
   C. the many uses of public resources
   D. All of the above.

_____ 24. Satellite communities are villages that are _____.
   A. built around an urban downtown
   B. located in space
   C. small and isolated
   D. All of the above.

_____ 25. It is true that cluster housing _____.
   A. provides good use of space
   B. creates high-density housing
   C. saves space for gardens and parks
   D. All of the above.

(Continued)

Reproducible Test Master

_____  26.  The concept of housing in outer space is promoted by _____.
           A.  Biosphere 2
           B.  National Association of Home Builders
           C.  new urbanism
           D.  James Rouse

❏ Essay Questions: Provide complete responses to the following questions or statements.

27. List two renewable and two nonrenewable energy sources.

28. Describe the purpose of the Universal Design Home of the Future.

29. List 10 universal design features.

30. Explain why a house with a steel frame is considered a "green building."

CHAPTER 23

# Careers in Housing

## Objectives

After studying this chapter, students will be able to

- explain how to learn about careers related to housing.
- describe several careers within the housing field, including those held by entrepreneurs.
- list ways that computers are used to help professionals make housing decisions.
- determine the significance of a career ladder and lifelong learning to a successful housing career.

## Bulletin Boards

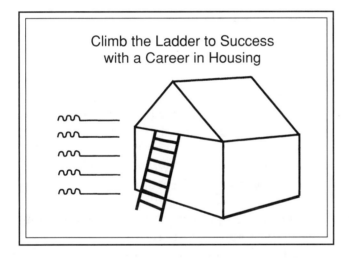

Title: *Climb the Ladder to Success with a Career in Housing*

Cut shapes of a large house and ladder from construction paper. Place them on the board as shown. Place a job title next to each rung of the ladder to form a career ladder.

Title: *Career Spotlight*

Draw a spotlight at a top corner of the board. Have students write articles about people they have interviewed in housing-related careers. Place some of the articles on the board.

## Teaching Materials

**Text**, pages 539-564
  *To Know*
  *To Review*
  *In Your Community*
  *To Think About*
  *Using Technology*
**Student Activity Guide**
  A. *Career Cluster*
  B. *Job Description*
  C. *Planning, Engineering, and Design Careers*
  D. *Housing Careers Challenge*
**Teacher's Resources**
  *Career Clusters in Housing*, reproducible master 23-1
  *Starting a Business*, transparency master 23-2
  *Focus on Your Ideal Job*, color transparency CT-29
  *Career Ladder for Housing and Interior Design*, color transparency CT-30
  Chapter 23 Test

## Introductory Activities

1. Have students study the classified ads in the local paper to determine which jobs are related to housing.
2. Have students look up and discuss the glossary and/or dictionary definitions of unfamiliar words plus the key terms listed in the *To Know* section of their textbooks. Have them add these to their card files.

## Strategies to Reteach, Reinforce, Enrich, and Extend Text Concepts

### Who Provides Housing?

3. **ER** Have students discuss how career clusters can help identify future satisfying careers.
4. **EX** Have each student use the *Occupational Outlook Handbook,* the *Guide for*

*Occupational Exploration,* or the Occupational Information Network to look up a different housing-related career. Students should investigate job duties and responsibilities; education, training, and experience; personal traits; workplace; employer; earnings; employment outlook; rewards; and related careers. Have students write brief reports on their findings.

5. **ER** *Career Cluster,* Activity A, SAG. Students are asked to research a housing career area and design a career cluster.

# Career Opportunities in Housing

6. **RF** *Career Clusters in Housing,* reproducible master 23-1, TR. Have students list specific careers that belong in each category shown on the handout. Then have them describe the personal traits of people who are likely to succeed in each career. Have students indicate the clusters that appeal to them.
7. **ER** Have students write a newspaper want ad based on one of the job descriptions in the text.
8. **ER** Have students develop a chart of various housing-related jobs and their descriptions.
9. **ER** Invite a member of AIA, NSPE, ASID, or another housing-related professional organization to speak to the class. Have the speaker discuss how membership in a professional organization can benefit a person's career.
10. **ER** *Job Description,* Activity B, SAG. Students are asked to research a specific job by using the publications or resources suggested in the text.
11. **RF** *Planning, Engineering, and Design Careers,* Activity C, SAG. Students are asked to match several job descriptions with job titles and attach two want ads.
12. **EX** Have each student research a different entrepreneur in housing and write a report on his or her findings. Students should focus on the personal qualifications that help the entrepreneur in his or her business.
13. **RT** *Starting a Business,* transparency master 23-2, TR. Use the transparency to introduce students to some of the major tasks a would-be entrepreneur would have to handle before opening a new business.
14. **EX** Have students host a career carnival. The carnival may consist of booths, a series of speakers, or a combination. Students should invite representatives from trade schools, community colleges, and universities. (Students should be sure that school representatives will focus on preparation for housing-related careers.) Have students print flyers inviting other classes to attend.

# Effect of Technology on Housing Careers

15. **RF** Have students explain the use of computers to housing professionals involved in design and management functions.
16. **ER** Invite a building contractor to class to discuss how technology has changed his or her job. Ask for examples of how cellular phones, pagers, and computers have affected the construction industry.

# Career Levels

17. **RF** Have students describe professional-, mid-, and entry-level positions.
18. **ER** Have students interview someone in a midlevel position. Students should find out how someone in that position relates to people working in the other two career levels.
19. **EX** Have students work in groups to develop career lattices for different areas of housing. Ask each student to choose the one lattice that lists jobs they can see themselves holding in the future.
20. **ER** Invite several people with successful careers in housing to speak to the class about their advancement through various career ladders.
21. **ER** *Focus on Your Ideal Job,* color transparency CT-29, TR. Use the transparency to have students discuss the many work- and employer-related factors that make one job very different from another of the same job title.
22. **ER** *Career Ladder for Housing and Interior Design,* color transparency CT-30, TR. Use the transparency to show students the various levels of training needed for

careers in housing and interior design. Have students choose specific occupations related to housing and determine where their positions are on the career ladder.

## Chapter Review

23. **EX** Have students learn about volunteer opportunities related to housing in their community. (Habitat for Humanity is a possibility.) Have students determine if the positions lead to a career ladder or lattice. Have them write a job description and list of personal qualifications for one of the volunteer positions.
24. **RF** *Housing Careers Challenge*, Activity D, SAG. Students are asked to complete statements about careers in housing by filling in the blanks.

## Answer Key

### Text

*To Review*, page 562

1. false
2. cluster
3. (List three:) school counselors, teachers, family members, friends, libraries, Internet, U.S. Department of Labor sources (*Occupational Outlook Handbook, Guide for Occupational Exploration*, and the Occupational Information Network)
4. (List five:) job duties and areas of responsibility; required education, training, and experience; important personal traits; usual work environment; leading employers; minimum, average, and peak earnings; employment outlook; job rewards (if any); related careers
5. (List four:) planning, engineering, design, construction, sales, service, entrepreneurship, education, government
6. four
7. false
8. false
9. (List five:) excellent communications skills, strong self-motivation to do the best work possible, enthusiasm for the product or service, nonstop desire to promote the business and look for future work, understanding of the legal and financial aspects of running a business, ability to recognize when to seek advice from experts, supervisory skills (if employees are hired)
10. management
11. midlevel
12. A career ladder includes opportunities within the field, while opportunities outside the field may appear in a career lattice.
13. It helps the person stay up-to-date in his or her field of expertise.

### Student Activity Guide

*Planning, Engineering, and Design Careers*, Activity C

1. D
2. B
3. G
4. E
5. A
6. C
7. H
8. F

(Job ads are student response.)

*Housing Careers Challenge*, Activity D

1. career
2. occupation
3. career cluster
4. bachelor's
5. master's
6. Architects
7. Professional Engineers
8. Interior Designers
9. trade
10. apprenticeship
11. unskilled labor
12. semiskilled labor
13. skilled labor
14. entrepreneurs
15. cooperative education
16. lifelong learning

### Teacher's Resources

#### Chapter 23 Test

1. K
2. H
3. D
4. J
5. F
6. C
7. B
8. A
9. E
10. I
11. T
12. T
13. F
14. F
15. T
16. T
17. F
18. T
19. T
20. F
21. D
22. D
23. A
24. B
25. B
26. D
27. B
28. D
29. C
30. A

31. (Describe two:) The *Occupational Outlook Handbook* describes the major U.S. jobs and their working conditions, requirements, average salaries, and future outlook. The *Guide for Occupational Exploration* clusters jobs according to key worker traits. The Occupational Information Network provides tools for exploring careers, examining job trends, and assessing personal abilities and interests.
32. (List four:) excellent communications skills, strong self-motivation to do the best work possible every time, enthusiasm for the unique product or service, a nonstop desire to promote the business and look for opportunities for future work, understanding of the legal and financial aspects of running a business, ability to recognize when to seek advice from competent experts, supervisory skills (if employees are hired)
33. (Student response. See pages 555-558 of the text.)
34. (Student response.)

Reproducible Master 23-1

# Career Clusters in Housing

**Name** _____ **Date** _____ **Period** _____

Brainstorm careers that belong in each category. Describe personal traits of people who are likely to succeed in these careers.

| Planning, Engineering, and Design | |
|---|---|
| Careers | Personal Traits |
|  |  |
| **Construction** | |
| Careers | Personal Traits |
|  |  |
| **Sales and Service** | |
| Careers | Personal Traits |
|  |  |
| **Allied Housing Fields** | |
| Careers | Personal Traits |
|  |  |

Chapter 23  *Careers in Housing*

## Starting a Business

- Determine what type of business you would like to start.
- Identify who your customers will be.
- Evaluate your potential competition.
- Choose a name and location for your business.
- Prepare a budget.
- Obtain required permits and licenses.
- Obtain needed financing.
- Rent or purchase building facilities, equipment, and supplies.
- Hire and train employees.
- Plan a publicity/advertising strategy.

Reproducible Test Master

# Careers in Housing

Name _____

Date _____ Period _____ Score _____

**Chapter 23 Test**

❏ Matching: Match the following careers and job descriptions.

_____ 1. Directs how land will be used in a community for growth or revitalization.

_____ 2. Is concerned with the design of equipment for plumbing and heating.

_____ 3. Plans the electrical service needed for a household by calculating total lighting and equipment needs.

_____ 4. Locates the corners and boundaries of tracts of land.

_____ 5. Plans the placement of natural and manufactured landscape elements around buildings.

_____ 6. Prepares detailed drawings used by a builder.

_____ 7. Focuses on residential air quality problems that involve excess moisture.

_____ 8. Constructs the wooden framework of buildings and installs windows, doors, and cabinets.

_____ 9. Studies architectural drawings and determines how much a proposed project will cost to build in terms of materials, labor, and other expenses.

_____ 10. Installs pipe systems that carry water, steam, natural gas, and other liquids and gases.

A. carpenter
B. certified industrial hygienist
C. drafter
D. electrical engineer
E. estimator
F. landscape architect
G. mason
H. mechanical engineer
I. plumber
J. surveyor
K. urban planner

❏ True/False: Circle *T* if the statement is true or *F* if the statement is false.

T  F  11. Occupations or jobs that are closely related make a career cluster.

T  F  12. Personality traits that are in conflict with the requirements of a job can interfere with career success.

T  F  13. Declining career areas offer potential employees the greatest number of job choices.

T  F  14. A master's degree is a college degree that usually requires four years of study.

T  F  15. Training beyond high school is required for interior designers.

T  F  16. An apprenticeship involves learning a trade under the direction and guidance of an expert worker.

(Continued)

Reproducible Test Master

T  F  17. Educators of housing and design often deal with building codes, housing standards, and zoning.

T  F  18. Architects use computers to produce plans showing front and side elevations and section views of proposed structures.

T  F  19. People who help carry out decisions made by others are called support personnel.

T  F  20. Once employees have received proper training, they have the knowledge and skills needed to remain successful in their chosen fields until they retire.

❑ Multiple Choice: Choose the best response. Write the letter in the space provided.

_____ 21. Paid employment that involves handling one or more tasks is a _____.
   A. career
   B. career web
   C. job
   D. occupation

_____ 22. Career information can be obtained from _____.
   A. school counselors
   B. *Occupational Outlook Handbook*
   C. teachers
   D. All of the above.

_____ 23. Components of a complete job description include all the following *except* _____.
   A. currently available job openings
   B. employment outlook
   C. important personal traits
   D. usual work environment

_____ 24. Which of the following construction tradespeople is responsible for a building's footings, foundation walls, and patios?
   A. Floor-covering installer.
   B. Mason.
   C. Plasterer.
   D. The responsibility is shared equally among all the tradespeople who work on a project.

_____ 25. Workers who fill entry-level jobs that require no previous knowledge or experience are called _____.
   A. multiskilled labor
   B. unskilled labor
   C. semiskilled labor
   D. skilled labor

_____ 26. Which field of housing careers includes real estate agents?
   A. Allied fields.
   B. Construction.
   C. Planning, engineering, and design.
   D. Sales and service.

(Continued)

_____ 27. Workers who start and run their own businesses are called _____.
   A. apprentices
   B. entrepreneurs
   C. professionals
   D. tradespeople

_____ 28. Professional-level positions _____.
   A. are held by apprentices
   B. are held by support personnel
   C. offer on-the-job training
   D. include architects and interior designers

_____ 29. Programs that offer opportunities to work part-time and attend classes part-time are called _____.
   A. apprenticeships
   B. career lattices
   C. cooperative education
   D. lifelong learning

_____ 30. When jobs in a career cluster are ordered according to the qualifications they require, they form _____.
   A. a career ladder
   B. a line of authority
   C. a professional pyramid
   D. levels of training

❑ Essay Questions: Provide complete responses to the following questions or statements.

31. Describe two career information resources available from the U.S. Department of Labor.

32. What are four skills and personal qualities needed by successful entrepreneurs?

33. Explain how computers might be used by three types of housing professionals.

34. Identify an entry-level housing position along with midlevel and professional level positions that would be on the same career ladder.

# CHAPTER 24
# Preparing for Career Success

## Objectives

After studying this chapter, students will be able to

- set career goals and make a career plan.
- know the steps to take to find jobs in their career fields.
- identify the skills, attitudes, and behaviors important for maintaining a job and attaining career success.
- describe the relationships between careers and personal and family life.

## Bulletin Boards

Title: *Picture Your Career*

Cut pictures of workers in various housing-related careers from magazines and mount them under the title on the board. Place different shapes and colors of borders around them to simulate a wall display of portraits.

Title: *Top Ten Qualities of Good Employees*

Under the title, mount a large sheet of colored paper and print the following 10 terms on it: *Punctual, Dependable, Self-Motivated, Upbeat Attitude, Good Communicator, Ethical, Team-Oriented, Negotiator, Potential Leader,* and *Safety Conscious*. Make large checkmarks in front of each term.

## Teaching Materials

**Text**, pages 565-590
  *To Know*
  *To Review*
  *In Your Community*
  *To Think About*
  *Using Technology*
**Student Activity Guide**
  A. *Taking a Look at Your Career Interests*
  B. *The Job Search*
  C. *Leadership as a Job Qualification*
  D. *The Impact of Work on Family*
**Teacher's Resources**
  *Chart Your Course to a Career in Housing*, color transparency CT-31
  *Interview Skills*, reproducible master 24-1
  *Leadership Practice*, reproducible master 24-2
  Chapter 24 Test

## Introductory Activities

1. *Chart Your Course to a Career in Housing* color transparency, CT-31, TR. Introduce the high school courses related to housing. Students are to list those your school offers. Students who have taken some of the courses should discuss how each course could help someone in a housing career.
2. Have students name occupations related to housing careers based on what they recall from Chapter 23. Write the occupations on the board as students name them. One by one, read through the list and ask students to raise their hands to each career that interests them.

Chapter 24   *Preparing for Career Success*   327

# Strategies to Reteach, Reinforce, Enrich, and Extend Text Concepts

## Setting Career Goals

3. **RF** *Taking a Look at Your Career Interests,* Activity A, SAG. Students answer questions about factors that relate to their career interests and, based on their answers, identify appealing careers.
4. **ER** If students have not been given a formal aptitude test recently, have the school counselor administer the test to the class. Ask students to identify five housing careers for which their test results indicate they are suited.
5. **EX** Have students write a poem, jingle, or rap that emphasizes the five steps of the goal-setting process. Invite volunteers to perform or recite their creations.
6. **EX** Ask students to make an informal career plan for a career goal to which most students can relate, such as a police officer or computer technician. Have students work independently to design a realistic career plan, listing short-term and long-term goals. Hold a class discussion to highlight how different individuals can pursue the same career in different ways.

## Finding a Job

7. **ER** Have students interview five employed people they know to learn how they acquired their jobs. Ask students to share their findings with the class, keeping the identity of the individuals confidential.
8. **RF** Bring to class examples of attractive resume formats for students to examine. Check your school's guidance counselor for samples. Have students prepare personal resumes.
9. **EX** Lead students in an exercise to acquaint them with how to "market their skills," which simply is the process of highlighting their strengths and accomplishments. For example, instead of having a resume say "took food orders," point out the importance of restating the action with more expressive language. Some possible restatements are "explained menu items to customers" or "served restaurant patrons and responded quickly to requests." Emphasize that all information in a resume must be accurate, never an untruthful exaggeration. Divide the class into small groups to brainstorm interesting ways to express four accomplishments usually stated in plain terms in resumes:
    - worked as a salesclerk
    - delivered newspapers
    - stocked inventory
    - worked as a babysitter
10. **RF** Ask students to explore U.S. Department of Labor resources for job seekers on its Web site (doleta.gov) and provide a full report on what it contains. Direct students to search the *jobseekers* section.
11. **RF** Have students write a sample letter of application to an employer in their career field.
12. **ER** Invite a representative from a local company who has hiring responsibilities to speak to the class about what qualities he or she seeks in a job candidate. Ask the guest to discuss ways to favorably impress a future employer during the job application process.
13. **RF** Have students prepare written answers to the interview questions in Figure 24-9 of the text. Direct students to write answers based on their respective career goals. (Inform students that their answers will remain confidential unless they want to volunteer a comment or question. Encourage students who have difficulty with this activity to talk with a guidance counselor.)
14. **EX** *Interview Skills,* reproducible master 24-1, TR. Make handouts for students to use in preparing for a job interview. Invite several employers in various aspects of housing to class to conduct the mock interviews and evaluate student performance.
15. **ER** *The Job Search,* Activity B, SAG. Students interview adults about their job search experiences and record their responses.

## Maintaining the Job

16. **RF** Have students brainstorm general qualities needed for success in any career. Students should determine qualities they

have already perfected as well as qualities they must acquire or perfect.

17. **EX** Have students figure out how much time an employee wastes if he arrives five minutes late, leaves 5 minutes early, and extends his lunch 10 minutes longer each day. Assume the individual works a 40-hour workweek. If the employee makes $10 per hour, what is the value of the company time wasted by the employee?

18. **EX** Divide the class into small groups to decide which job candidate to hire: a pleasant person who makes some mistakes but is eager to do a good job versus an angry person who knows the job completely and can do it very well. Ask the groups to share their decisions and rationale with the class.

19. **RF** Have students name examples of annoying nonverbal behavior that workers should avoid, such as humming, whistling, and loudly chewing gum. Ask students what they would do if they supervised a department in which one of their employees displayed behavior that annoyed or upset other department members.

20. **RF** Ask students to write *To Be Effective in the Workplace* at the top of a sheet of paper and fold it in half vertically. Then, have students write *Teammates Need:* and *Leaders Need:* at the top of the two columns. Ask students to list all the qualities that come to mind for each category.

21. **RF** Have students describe workplace behaviors that are not ethical. Ask what they would do when confronted with such behaviors in the workplace. Would they report them or simply keep quiet? Are there instances when certain behaviors are so serious they must be reported?

22. **EX** Ask students to write two versions of a case study in which teamwork is used to accomplish a goal. Have them describe the positive results of team cooperation versus the negative results of team conflict.

23. **EX** *Leadership as a Job Qualification,* Activity C, SAG. Students are to explain how they would handle given situations if they were the leaders.

24. **EX** *Leadership Practice,* reproducible master 24-2, TR. Divide the class into groups of three or four students with a leader and an antagonist. Cut worksheet strips apart, fold them, place the strips in a container, and have each group randomly select one. Each group discusses ways to solve its problem and members agree on a course of action. After most groups have finished, have students discuss their feelings about their group's leadership. The exercise is repeated with new leaders, antagonists, and strips.

25. **RF** Have students list factors that contribute to a safe working environment. Write the suggestions on the board and ask students to select the five most important and the five least important factors. (This is a trick question because every safety factor merits top priority. "Unimportant" safety factors do not exist.)

26. **ER** Ask students to research the high cost of accidents in the workplace and cite their sources. (Expect to get many different responses based on how the source measured accident costs and when the estimate was made.)

27. **RF** Have students work in small groups to create a list of actions that departing employees should not take when they leave a job. Ask group spokespeople to share their lists with the class.

## Careers and Lifestyle

28. **RF** *The Impact of Work on Family,* Activity D, SAG. Students read case studies about people who work in the housing industry and answer related questions.

29. **ER** Have students interview a person who has changed jobs within the last two years. Students should ask how the job change affected such lifestyle factors as spending habits, location, friendships, and leisure time. Students should write an article based on the interview.

30. **EX** Ask the class to develop a list of work situations that may cause stress or dissatisfaction. For each situation, students should discuss possible effects on personal and family life. Students should also discuss possible ways of resolving the stressful situations.

31. **EX** Have students work in groups of four to develop a plan for meeting the family responsibilities of a dual-career family

with two teenagers. Ask students to role-play the key parts of their plan to demonstrate how various responsibilities will be met.
32. **ER** Invite several adults to participate in a discussion on balancing career with personal and family life. Panelists should include a single person, a couple with one employed spouse, and a dual-career couple. Students should prepare questions in advance.

# Chapter Review

33. **EX** Have students create a career plan for their respective career fields by doing the following:
    - Indicate the courses necessary to take in high school to qualify for entry into the education/training program required for entry into their chosen career fields.
    - Describe the postsecondary education/training program to pursue.
    - List at least five examples of accomplishments to make in the following categories to provide experiences to cite in their resumes: part-time jobs, volunteer work, community activities, hobbies, and special school projects.
34. **RF** Ask students to list the steps they plan to take to find jobs in their respective career fields. Have students provide a brief written description of each step.

# Answer Key

## Text

### *To Review*, page 588

1. false
2. Identify a goal. Create a plan. Identify your resources. Take action. Evaluate results.
3. short
4. a person's education, work experience, and other qualifications for work
5. false
6. open
7. (List five:) Research the employer and the job. Be prepared to answer questions. List the questions you want answered. List the materials you plan to take. Decide what to wear. Practice the interview. Know where to go for the interview.
8. initiative
9. ethical
10. conflict
11. Occupational Safety and Health Administration
12. (List three:) income, spending habits, location of residence, friends, leisure activities
13. true

## Teacher's Resources

### Chapter 24 Test

1. D
2. G
3. B
4. A
5. E
6. I
7. K
8. J
9. C
10. H
11. F
12. F
13. T
14. F
15. T
16. T
17. F
18. F
19. T
20. T
21. T
22. F
23. T
24. F
25. T
26. D
27. C
28. B
29. C
30. A

31. (List five:) school placement office, the Internet, family, friends, newspaper want ads, job fairs, professional journals, professional organizations
32. (List four:) physical surroundings, work schedule, income and benefits, job obligations, advancement potential
33. (Student response.)

Reproducible Master 24-1

# Interview Skills

**Name** _____ **Date** _____ **Period** _____

Use this form to prepare for a mock interview with a guest employer involved in the housing field. Record any helpful information provided by the guest.

Guest employer: _____

Description of job opening: _____
_____
_____

Your qualifications: _____

**Education:**
_____
_____

**Honors and activities:**
_____
_____

**Work experience:**
_____
_____

**Other important skills:**
_____
_____

Helpful interview information provided by guest:
_____
_____
_____
_____
_____
_____
_____

Reproducible Master 24-2

# Leadership Practice

| | |
|---|---|
| 1. | Your group has the task of painting the classroom, using up to three colors of paint. Decide what color(s) to choose and how to best use them. |
| 2. | Your group has the task of converting a room the size of a classroom into a student lounge. Decide how you would furnish the room to make it usable for as many students as possible. |
| 3. | Your group has been chosen to paint a mural in the most-traveled school hallway. Choose a theme for the mural. |
| 4. | Your group will select a speaker in a housing-related field for school career day. Decide who that speaker should be or which area of housing the speaker should represent. |
| 5. | Your group will decide where to take the class on a housing-related field trip within the community. Choose an interesting place to visit. |
| 6. | The school is building a house to be used for receptions and overnight guests of the school. The school board wants your group's recommendation on the most appropriate exterior style for the house. |
| 7. | Your class will be given a lab room to use for housing projects. Decide how to furnish it to make the room as functional as possible. |
| 8. | Your group will choose three main reasons as the focus of a school brochure for incoming freshmen explaining why they should take a housing decisions course. |

Reproducible Test Master

# Preparing for Career Success

Name _____

Date _____ Period _____ Score _____

**Chapter 24 Test**

❑ Matching: Match the following terms and identifying phrases.

_____ 1. An aim or target a person tries to achieve.

_____ 2. Someone with greater experience and knowledge who guides a person in his or her career.

_____ 3. A natural talent.

_____ 4. A skill a person develops with practice.

_____ 5. An arrangement with an educational institution whereby a student is supervised while working with a more experienced jobholder.

_____ 6. The exchange of information or services among individuals or groups.

_____ 7. A brief outline of a person's education, work experience, and other qualifications for work.

_____ 8. An individual who will provide important information about a person to a prospective employer.

_____ 9. Actions that conform to accepted standards of fairness and good conduct.

_____ 10. The process of agreeing to an issue that requires all parties to give and take.

A. ability
B. aptitude
C. ethical behavior
D. goal
E. internship
F. leadership
G. mentor
H. negotiation
I. networking
J. reference
K. resume

❑ True/False: Circle *T* if the statement is true or *F* if the statement is false.

T  F  11. Most teens know exactly what careers they want.

T  F  12. A person who is interested in people may enjoy a job designing landscaping plans.

T  F  13. Long-term goals usually require six months or longer to achieve.

T  F  14. A family member makes a good reference.

T  F  15. The letter of application is often the first contact you have with a potential employer.

T  F  16. Writing "negotiable" for salary on a job application form means you are willing to consider offers.

T  F  17. You should avoid asking questions at a job interview.

T  F  18. A thank-you letter can be sent to an interviewer up to one week after the interview.

(Continued)

T  F  19. Poor communications in the workplace can result in lost time and lost customers.

T  F  20. The development of good communication skills is an ongoing process.

T  F  21. Some disagreements in the workplace can lead to productive change.

T  F  22. Self-motivation is the ability to guide others to achieve goals.

T  F  23. Showing off in the workplace is careless behavior that can lead to accidents.

T  F  24. When leaving a job, a two-day notice to the employer is acceptable.

T  F  25. On-site child care is an example of a benefit that helps dual-career families.

❑ Multiple Choice: Choose the best response. Write the letter in the space provided.

_____ 26. Observing a person in the workplace to learn more about his or her job is known as _____.
   A. an internship
   B. negotiation
   C. networking
   D. shadowing

_____ 27. Which is the first step in the goal-setting process?
   A. Create a plan.
   B. Evaluate results.
   C. Identify a goal.
   D. Identify available resources.

_____ 28. A job portfolio _____.
   A. is prepared by your references
   B. includes examples of work and achievements
   C. should follow the standard form of business letters
   D. should be e-mailed to interviewers

_____ 29. Which is an example of nonverbal communication?
   A. Writing.
   B. Speaking.
   C. Body language.
   D. Listening.

_____ 30. Which of the following is true about teams in the workplace?
   A. Teams complete work faster than an individual working alone.
   B. Teams reach decisions faster than an individual working alone.
   C. Team members are comfortable with one another right from the start.
   D. Teamwork in the workplace is unnecessary.

❑ Essay Questions: Provide complete responses to the following questions or statements.

31. List five examples of sources for job leads.

32. List four work factors a person should explore when considering a job offer or comparing two or more jobs.

33. Explain the relationship between careers and personal and family life.

- 
- 
-